The Oldie

Annual 2020
Introduction

By *Harry Mount*, Editor, The Oldie

If a Martian asked me what Britain was really like over the last century, I'd give him a copy of this *Oldie* annual.

While newspapers deal with the ephemeral, the trashy and the here-today-gone-tomorrow celeb, *The Oldie* is devoted to the eternally interesting. Because the pieces in this annual – edited by planet-brained Liz Anderson – weren't chosen to go with a long-forgotten news event, they never stale.

Where else but in *The Oldie* could you read Patricia Highsmith, mistress of noir fiction, on Greta Garbo, queen of the silver screen? What a beguiling tale Highsmith draws out of her Manhattan meeting with Garbo – a snatched, wordless encounter on the south-east corner of Fifth Avenue and 57th Street.

If the news does intervene, it is intercepted and interpreted by a great mind like Auberon Waugh's. Here, in a piece written 24 years before the 2016 European referendum, Bron completely nails down the world view that led to that referendum's result.

In an increasingly humourless world of no-platforming and trigger warnings, *The Oldie* is wonderfully free of earnest, dictatorial articles; and full of joyfully rude, I-couldn't-care-less-about-offending-you articles.

Just read Dame Edna Everage on visiting Melbourne Cemetery 'to buff up my late husband's obelisk', after a visit to the Hong Kong home of Ednacare, her multi-million-dollar beauty conglomerate. Products include Granny Cranny Cream – 'extra soothing and packaged in finger-friendly suppositories'.

One of the many great joys of editing *The Oldie* is having such a well-informed readership. It means you don't have to explain to readers who, say, the sublime Geoffrey Palmer is (read his brilliant interview in these pages); or, indeed, who the actor and playwright are in what Palmer says would have been his

'If you begin to feel unwell, start or stop taking aspirin'

favourite part: 'Kenneth More's role in Terence Rattigan's *The Deep Blue Sea*'.

Again and again, my predecessors in *The Oldie* editor's chair – the hallowed Richard Ingrams and the late, much-missed Alexander Chancellor – effortlessly pulled of the hardest thing in editing: getting the perfect person to write about the perfect subject. Here is Craig Brown, the funniest writer alive, on Ken Dodd, the funniest if recently dead performer. When Craig saw him at the Ipswich Regent, Doddy opened the show 'by observing that, though Ipswich isn't twinned with anywhere, it has a suicide pact with Grimsby'.

And here is Germaine Greer on a subject she hadn't been associated with until Richard Ingrams alighted on it – her love and deep knowledge of nature. It isn't just the famous who appear here. *The Oldie* has always drawn deeply on a broad range of journalists – the lion's share of their articles chosen by our much-missed Deputy Editor, Jeremy Lewis (a gifted writer, whose memoir is reviewed here).

And it's only by having such a wide range of writers that there's such an eclectic lot of subjects covered here. No other magazine in the world would have an article on 'What was a Rechabite tent?', written by Alan Thomas. No other magazine would have a review of the best Cambridge church floors to sleep on, as filed by *The Oldie*'s Gentleman of the Road, Wilfred De'Ath.

And no other magazine is quite as irreverent because it isn't in hock to the great and the good. Here is Elisabeth Luard, *The Oldie*'s chief chef, on being lunged at by a groping Claus von Bülow. Thank God, she says, for her whaleboned Hartnell dress and the paperback kept in her knickers so that she could read in the loo at parties and avoid the debs delights she was supposed to be dancing with.

Any decent Martian would be enthralled by this annual. I hope you are, too.

Published by The Oldie magazine, Moray House, 23/31 Great Titchfield Street, London W1W 7PA www.theoldie.co.uk
Copyright © 2019 Oldie Publications Ltd. Printed by Wyndeham Roche Ltd
The Oldie would like to thank all the writers, illustrators and cartoonists whose work is reproduced in these pages
Editor: Liz Anderson **Design:** Lawrence Bogle **Cover:** Willie Rushton

Contents

63

18

82

89

104

116

News from Stump Cross

Germaine Greer begins a love-hate relationship with her new house

I regret to admit that when I asked the assistant manager of my very grand bank if he would lend me the rest of the money needed to buy The Mills, I babbled on rather about the undoubted value of the property. 'In the M11 corridor, you know. Only 25 minutes from the M25. The railway line has just been electrified. Stansted is only 25 minutes away and we are not in the flight path. The house isn't worth much, but it does have three acres of land, which if released for development...'

'I don't understand,' said the assistant manager, patiently, slightly too patiently, I thought. 'Do you want this property as a home or as an investment?'

'Can't it be both?' I asked brightly. The assistant manager looked at me reflectively and smiled a wintry smile. 'Perhaps,' he said. So young and so wise.

What I hadn't told him was that I did not really like the house. Its long flint wall ran flush with the verge of the kind of country road that commercial travellers and courier vans take at 90 miles an hour. The remains of smashed hares, pheasants, rabbits, pigeons, blackbirds and foxes are left to rot there because there is no space between the speeding vehicles for the crows to do their work. The few remaining hedgerows are hung with fluttering magnetic tape, plastic bags and the wrappings from chocolate bars. In the lay-bys stand caravans where failed small businessmen and their wives cook up fast food for the drivers of the lorries pulled up higgledy-piggledy on the verges.

This is not at all a picturesque part of the world. Even if the M11 had not been flung over it and light stanchions and power lines did not disfigure it, Stump Cross would not be a picturesque place. Because it is always windy here and most of the soil is poor, free-draining or shallow, there are few noble trees and no great parks in sight. Instead we have the travellers' camp and the sewage farm. The crossroads might have looked more handsome when King Charles II and his brother rode through on their way from Whitehall to Newmarket, but not much.

The fields were always open champlain; no great oaks were laid low here to create pasture or farmland. Here are no fells or dales or dells, just the steady roll of farmland and over it the booming sky. In the rubble and flint, so few trees grew to any size that the crossroads where the Newmarket road and the Cambridge road diverged was called, sufficiently, Stump Cross. And I suppose, as often as not, the rotting body of a malefactor hanged from one of the Stump's dead branches turned and turned in the wind, forcing the courtiers to lift their pouncet-boxes to their noses.

The house used to be a row of workmen's houses, built without damp courses from the flints that children picked off the fields. My little lane used to run past two windmills, storehouses and

stables, to another little cluster of hovels (one up, one down). The mills were disabled at the turn of the century, but the buildings were not demolished until after the war, when the owners of the estate simply bulldozed them. The rubble, the clay pipes, the lemonade bottles, the broken earthenware and blue-and-white china, the flooring pammets and the pantiles, the foundations and the cellars are all still there. The best soil is where the workers' earth-closets and hen-houses were. The row of cottages nearest the road was left standing; a series of extensions built out of Cambridge white bricks turned it into something they called Mill Farm House, but the water bill is still addressed to The Mills and that, out of deference to the vanished owners of the pipes and the

willow pattern china, is what I call it.

The hovels the house is made of were tiny. The fireplaces on the ground floor will hold a single coal. The staircases to the sleeping rooms above must have been no more than ladders. The washing of people, dishes and clothes was done in the cobbled yard, with rain water pumped up from underground tanks. Where the kitchen is now, there seems to have been a killing floor, so I guess the miller's wife kept a pig or two.

Now the little houses have become a single house with not a single handsome room. Too many rooms open out of other rooms, with no connecting passages. The front door opens against the newel post of the stair, so visitors have to be herded like sheep through a dip to get in at all.

Before I bought it I visited the house at night. If the hideous orange light from the roundabout turned night into monochrome day, I absolutely did not want it. I drove quietly down the little lane. Too bad, the orange light was everywhere. No deal. The house agent rang me; I had come to the place three times. Wouldn't I buy it? It was too expensive, I said. How much would I pay? I suggested a lower price. He upped it a bit. Having made the mistake of beginning to negotiate, I found myself agreeing. Ah well, I thought, when the right house comes along I can get rid of it again. Off I went to the bank.

There is a school of thought, to which many North London landlords adhere, that holds that the first rule of investment in property is to spend no money beyond the initial purchase price, even for routine maintenance. My new house had eight rotten windows, outhouses and a stable that would soon be roofless, and a ramshackle garage too small for my car. I resolved to ignore them all.

Though the garden was a mess, it would have to stay that way. I reckoned without the trees. I was responsible for six of the most important trees for miles, three full-grown beeches of great majesty, their crowns top-heavy, a half-dead cedar, a thirsty horse-chestnut and a soaring *Robinia pseudacacia*. There were as well 12 sycamores that had been pollarded and were now shapeless, six apple trees and a Victoria plum that had not been pruned in five years, and a seedling walnut tree with 11 trunks. As soon as their leaves fell, the tree surgeons came in, lopping dead branches, thinning

crowns, removing dead wood. The spending had begun; the bridging loan began to expand with frightening speed.

In the meantime I had noticed the thing one never notices in London, the sky. My house, which stands on the summit of a long gradual swell of land, so that all around the skyline is slightly below the eyeline, can boast one of the biggest skies in England. Today, a wild west wind with a tang of harsh metal has sliced the scum off the goose pond and sucked the dimness out of the sky.

This is not at all a picturesque part of the world

Above it the cloud wrack moves inexorably south, purple chased out by peach glow and powder blue crowded in their turn by gloomy fields of indigo. Where the sun finds a chink, spokes of white light wheel over the landscape until dark masses jostle them out only to bounce apart and let new shafts come stalking. I can see clear to the horizon across roll upon roll of amber fields stitched and scribbled by briar and hawthorn as dark as ink. Closer the plough still holds the warmth of suntan, except where it bleaches to chalk and where the winter wheat lies on it like a green veil. I cannot move from my workshop window, though there are dozens of letters to answer. I cannot bear to take my eyes away from the great sweep of the sky and the pigeons bodysurfing upon the tides of frigid air.

While I have been writing, the wind has dragged the great air-force blue cloud blanket away to the south-west to reveal a lofty, sunlit firmament of baby-blue rippled with rows of fluffy tufts and ridges of frozen cirrus. The heron has swung in over the trees, dangling his anglepoise legs. The geese stand to attention while he inspects their half-frozen pond. The sunlight has turned faintly rose. A pallid moon like a broken plate is sidling up the sky behind the rags of thinning cloud. The night will be very, very cold. I am so full of joy that I am almost afraid to move in case I spill some. The young man in the bank was (of course) right. An investment you could never bear to part with is no investment at all.

A curious and melancholy life

Jeremy Lewis recalls a sad, compelling masterpiece by a forgotten author

In 1953 Dom Aelred Watkin, the headmaster of Downside, sent an account of his grandmother's curious and melancholy life, written by her daughter, to Evelyn Waugh. Waugh wrote back to say that although he thought it unpublishable in its present form, it was a 'tale of haunting beauty and pathos', and he urged Fr Watkin to revise and improve his mother's version. Three years later they were in touch again on the subject of Maria Pasqua. Waugh felt that some of the story's magic had now been lost, though admitting that 'perhaps it is the novelist in me that wishes to defeat the historian . . . Perhaps I have played with the idea of Maria Pasqua so long in my mind that I have added inventions of my own.' To Nancy Mitford he wrote that 'it is a most moving story of Beauty in captivity, very sad and full of authentic, bizarre detail. Not a plot for you or me, but it could be made a great work of art by someone. Who?'

Dom Aelred's sister, Magdalen Goffin, inherited Helena Watkin's papers, including Waugh's helpful suggestions for the book's improvement, after their mother's death in 1972; and it was her version of Maria Pasqua, brief but highly potent, that landed on my desk one day in 1978. I was then working as an editor on the general (as opposed to the academic) side of Oxford University Press, and was so bowled over by the beauty of the writing and the sadness of the story that I persuaded my boss, the admirable Hugo Brunner, to take it on, despite the absence of footnotes, and despite touches more reminiscent of a novel or even an unhappy fairy story than a scholarly monograph. Of all the books I have worked on as a publisher's editor it is, perhaps, the one I love most: I'm amazed that so touching and terrible an account of the *lacrimae rerum* has been allowed to go out of print.

Maria Pasqua was born in the Abruzzi in 1856, the daughter of impoverished peasants. Because she was very beautiful,

Maria Pasqua: sold to a Baring

with great liquid eyes, she was soon supplementing the family income with work as a child model in Rome. When she was six she and her father made their way to Paris – and Maria left behind forever a country that would increasingly assume, in her eyes, all the attributes of Paradise Lost. In Paris she was painted and much admired by Academicians of

Shepheard was a just landowner but as a husband he was dour

the kind that were soon to be elbowed aside by the Impressionists, who did brisk business in the meantime selling their wares to the rich and the famous. Among these was the Comtesse de Noailles, who – pipped at the post by a Rothschild also in pursuit of a saccharine study of the beautiful Italian girl – went one further by buying the model herself from her father for the price of a vineyard.

'Madame' was, despite her name, an Englishwoman: as a Baring, she was also very rich. Childless and separated from her husband, she spent her days moving restlessly between Paris, the South of France and various English seaside resorts. Though formidable, she was also engagingly eccentric, with strong views about the health-giving properties of cows' breath – a cow would be tethered by each ground-floor window so as to infuse the room – and rose-tinted glass. She refused to travel if the wind was in the east or stay in a house with an oak tree nearby, wore a fur hat in bed and ate all her meals behind a specially constructed screen.

From a life of Bohemian poverty, Maria was translated into a very different world. She learned French and English, grew more beautiful than ever, and was eventually sent to school in England – where she encountered the 'black-coated figure' who was to shape, and to blight, the rest of her long life.

Philip Shepheard was a widower, 18 years older than Maria Pasqua, and as soon as he set eyes on her he determined to marry her. He was a just and conscientious landowner and country squire, but as a husband he was dour, economical with candles, and prone to hurrying his wife and children off to bed at nine each night. Locked away in a remote Norfolk farmhouse, Maria Pasqua spent the rest of her life pining for a world she had lost and waiting, resentfully, for *le vieux* to die so that she could revisit Italy once again; but by the time he eventually died, aged 94, she was an old woman herself, and it was too late.

'Can't you take a deep breath & invoke Virginia Woolf & Max Beerbohm and start again with the aim of creating a literary masterpiece?' Evelyn Waugh asked Fr Watkin. It's hard to imagine that Magdalen Goffin's account of Maria Pasqua's sad, compelling life would not have met with Waugh's approval. Nothing could be more pleasing than to see it in print again.

An orthodox voice

by *John Michell*

People are always asking: do you believe this, do you believe that, what do you believe then? Sometimes they get quite angry when I say that I have no beliefs whatsoever, and absolutely no opinions either, except occasionally for amusement.

The trouble began during the process of education when I lost my faith. At that time the dominant religion was Scientific Materialism, the most stupid, arbitrary, low-minded, detrimental faith that has ever been imposed on any society. Even at school it seemed dreary and incredible, and it became evident later on that its relevance to ordinary life and experience was about the same as the laws of cricket. Both materialists and cricketers are supposed to ignore everything that happens beyond the boundaries. A game of cricket only lasts for a while and people enjoy it, but Scientific Materialism tortures its victims through whole lifetimes.

This thing, Scientific Materialism, is a product of beliefs. Beliefs and opinions are its only basis. Take Darwin, for example. His theory, that we are descended through apes from slugs and sea anemones, has no proof attached to it. Nor has it been shown that any one species has ever transmuted into another. It is all, properly speaking, a myth. Darwinism in its time was found to be a useful myth, supporting progress, imperialism and racial superiority in the 19th century. These ideas are no longer so well regarded, but Darwin's myth survives intact in our modern education system.

Then, of course, comes the question: if you don't believe in Darwin's myth of evolution, how do you explain the origin of the species? All I know is what I can see, that life exists in a great variety of species, all producing their own kind, and those which have been discovered as millions-of-years-old fossils are exactly the same as they are today. That these fossils are really millions of years old is just something I have been told. I can't say I really believe it.

If you really do need a creation myth and a science of life – and these may indeed be social necessities – it seems best to choose a harmless version, one which does not lead to notions of master race and the survival of the fittest. See, for example, Rupert Sheldrake's account (*A New Science of Life* etc) of semi-Platonic form-fields They are, he says, scientifically demonstrable. Even so, can one actually believe in these things?

Can one actually believe in big bangs, black holes, quarks and superstrings?

Can one actually believe in big bangs, black holes, quarks, superstrings and the other phantasmagoria of modern cosmology? When you go into it you find that they are imaginings. They are dreamt up to plug the holes in someone's mathematics. Not only are they creatures of myth, but creatures of bad, ugly myths. The black hole is, of course, Kali, the swarthy, all-devouring goddess of the East. Do we really have to accept this gloomy image as literal, scientific reality?

The products of human minds are not fit objects for belief. I paraphrase Charles Fort, of whom much more another time. All explanation systems, he said, whether religious or scientific, are based on exclusions. They can only be maintained by ignoring the evidence which contradicts them. If you would like to relieve your mind of all cumbersome beliefs and theories, read the ever-amazing, icon-busting books which constitute the *Complete Works of Charles Fort*. And if you really believe that these are his complete works, you are mistaken. He also wrote a novel and some other stuff which no one now bothers to read.

TELEVISION
RICHARD
INGRAMS

TV Heaven on Channel Four, introduced by Frank Muir, has been one of the few recent bright spots in the viewing week. The idea is to select a year in the not too distant past and then show some of its telly highlights.

This has thrown up some excellent things like the very first episode of *Upstairs Downstairs.* However, one is sometimes left wondering what the low-lights must have been like if Frank's offerings are the highlights. Surely 1969, for example, could have produced something better than a sub-standard Galton & Simpson comedy and a completely forgotten detective series called *Randall & Hopkirk*.

One difficulty faced by *TV Heaven* has been the refusal of the BBC to co-operate in the venture. For this they have rightly received a great deal of stick from the critics. I find it hard to understand the BBC's attitude since, while refusing to co-operate with ITV, they are apparently quite happy to sell off all their finest old programmes like *Dad's Army* to Sky. Perhaps somebody in the hierarchy has realised that showing too many old programmes may have given viewers the wrong idea. Every time a series like *The Rise and Fall of Reginald Perrin* is put on (as it was recently) the old cry goes up – 'They don't make 'em like that any more.' And it is perfectly true.

In the old days the BBC would have been the obvious producers of a PG Wodehouse series starring Hugh Laurie and Stephen Fry as Wooster and Jeeves. As it is, Granada is responsible for the production of one of the most consistently funny series to be put on in the past ten years. It was probably a mistake to make each episode an hour long, as it meant dovetailing two separate stories into one. This did not always work. The series has been saved by the flawless performances of Fry and Laurie (Fry's parsonical manner being particularly felicitous), the witty scripts, which preserve the spirit of Wodehouse, and the enormous trouble taken to recreate the Drones Club. I remember especially one wonderful episode when the entire membership of the Drones blacked up as minstrels and sang *Lady of Spain* to their own banjo accompaniment.

Are you an oldie?
20 tell-tale signs

1 Can you work the video?

2 Do you not only talk to yourself but see nothing odd about it?

3 Do you know quite a lot of poems by heart?

4 Do you spend more than an average amount of time in stationery shops?

5 Do you refer to the wireless?

6 Did you know who Freddie Mercury was before he died? Do you still not know who he was?

7 Are you obsessively concerned about the size and shape of spoons?

8 Do you mend clothes rather than throw them away?

9 Do you write letters?

10 Do you still wind your watch up?

11 Are there at least 20 people in your address book who are dead?

12 Do you know what a pronoun is?

13 Do you know any prayers apart from the Lord's Prayer?

14 Do you save string?

15 Are you frightened of going to the Barbican?

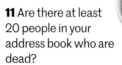

16 Have you ever been to a Japanese restaurant?

17 Can you waltz?

18 Do you go round turning lights off?

19 Do you clean your shoes with a brush and proper shoe polish?

20 Have you taken out a subscription for *The Oldie*?

If you answer yes to more than 15 questions and no to three, you can consider yourself an oldie

---

Dictionary for our time

Cab, taxi A mobile debating chamber.
Call, cheap-rate Description of a call made on someone else's telephone.
Campaign, military A series of recruitment ads for the armed forces.
Capable, highly Official description of any minister not up to his job.
Caravan A car-drawn home, always given pride of place at the front of any long, slow-moving procession of vehicles.
Carbonation Process that renders liquids drinkable to the young.
Carcinogenic Property of anything drunk, eaten, or inhaled that is pleasurable.
Card, greetings One of the great paintings of the world, reduced in size with 'Happy Birthday, Mum' written on the back.
Carefree 1. Drunk. 2. Sleeping around.
Carnivorous Morally outrageous dietary trait.
Celebration Word used solely in the titles of pointless books, as in 'Pips! A celebration of the Greenwich Time Signal'.

Centigrade The temperature abroad.
Cereal A traditional English breakfast for farm animals.
Chairperson Correct term for any man or woman in a wheelchair.
Changeable How TV meteorologists describe weather they cannot predict.
Chastity belt The area of land surrounding a nunnery.
Cheerless Newspaper term for a pensioner's Christmas.
Churchyard A place where teenagers can smoke undisturbed.
Classical music Highbrow jingles used in advertising.
Clear conscience Short memory.
Climate, current Euphemism for everything except the weather eg political situation, number of HIV cases etc.
Closing-time A challenge to lager drinkers.
Cloud-cuckoo land A fiercely-contested political constituency.
Colony Administrative area where the population can still get away with blaming another country for their problems.
Comedian Anyone the police think is trying to be smart.
Common Rare or threatened, as in common frog, common land, common decency, etc.
Controversial One-sided, irresponsible, or ill-researched.
Cooking, home M & S food microwaved at home.
Correspondence A series of complaining letters to dry-cleaners, the gas-board etc.
Creation An impractical designer costume.
Credit Debt.
Criminal, convicted A private security guard.
Crucified Losing six-nil in football.
Curry house Restaurant offering unlimited lager after-hours.
Mike Barfield

My life with Garbo

by *Patricia Highsmith*

I hasten to say that I never met Greta Garbo. But I came close to it several times in New York in the late 1940s and early 1950s, when I had a flat at First Avenue and 56th Street, in a building on the north-west corner, to be exact. Greta Garbo lived 'somewhere' in the East 50s, and three or four times a year I would glimpse her, striding along in dark clothes usually, head bent under a broad-brimmed hat that was usually black. Of course, I stopped and stared, if she was across the street or avenue, or even on the same pavement. Staring could not have bothered her, because she never looked round at anybody. Always she was in flat shoes, and usually a loose coat with collar turned up, as if to conceal more of her face than the hat did. Sometimes she carried a small sack, as if she had bought a sweater or a book, but not groceries. I never attempted to follow her, never saw her with anyone.

There was a time when I nearly met her in the sense of bumping into her. This was at the south-east corner of Fifth Avenue and 57th Street, which had a sharp and windowless angle, because of a big office building there, so that anyone coming round it at normal speed and encountering someone coming from the opposite direction would collide with that person, and this I nearly did one windy afternoon, jumping back just in time. It was Greta Garbo, all in black, with the famous hat on, too. How thrilled I was – though I hadn't touched her, or exchanged a glance, much less a smile. I remember turning and watching her clump off purposefully downtown on Fifth Avenue.

'Do you know I almost bumped into *Greta Garbo* this afternoon?' I remember telling someone that evening, smiling proudly.

'Did you? How? *Where*? ... What was she wearing? ... How tall is she?'

'A little taller than me.'

'Did her feet look so big?'

Not for her height. 'I came within inches! Sort of embarrassing,' I went on, pleased as Punch.

How easy it would have been to embroider, to say that we had a collision, that Greta Garbo rubbed her nose, laughed quickly, and said with a heavy Swedish accent, 'Ooo-ooh, my fault! Sor-ry!'

'Oh, no, *my* fault,' I would have insisted politely, and then we would have gone on our ways. This conversation would have been like a biblical episode in which a recently deceased person is *wished* to reappear, and so he or she does, and maybe even says a few words. The narrator knows he is stretching things, but after a few recountings comes

to believe it absolutely himself.

However, there was no doubt that Garbo did exist in what I called my neighbourhood. I saw her also – but rarely of course – when I drifted along Third Avenue and gazed into the cluttered windows of antique shops. One could buy a charming egg-cup from England or France, for instance, for a dollar. For 20 dollars I acquired a Victorian stereopticon plus at least 200 marvellous old photographs from the 1880s to about 1910 to go with it. If I saw Garbo on Third Avenue, I never saw her raptly gazing, as I did, but always hurrying along, looking at the pavement, only her nose visible under her hat,

perhaps a hand clasping the coat closer about her rather lanky figure. Still, it was a day when I could say to myself and others, 'Guess what, I saw Greta Garbo today!'

This was of course not the same as living with Garbo, merely to have a dwelling in her neighbourhood, as I had. Now however in a different sense (Garbo is dead, after all), I feel that I do live with her, because I have a delicately coloured drawing – watercolour, pen and ink, grey, yellow and sepia wash – from the Greta Garbo Collection, framed and hanging in my bedroom-workroom. This drawing was auctioned by Sotheby's in New York a couple of years ago, bought and sent to me by an acquaintance now living in the United States. He enclosed no comment on the drawing.

It is some nine-and-a-half inches wide and 12 inches high (or 24 by 30.5 centimetres), and shows a gentleman of the Louis XV period with long brown (sepia) wig, dark hat, long beige coat with buttons down the front, cane and slipper (only one is showing) with buckle and heel, about to get into his waiting carriage, the back half of which, with curtained window, is evidenced in the background. He is bidding adieu to, or being bidden adieu by, a most affectionate-looking figure in black wearing a brimmed black hat, who presses against him and rests a hand delicately upon the gentleman's left forearm. This erect figure in black has blondish straight hair of more than shoulder length, and the question which arises almost instantly on looking at this composition is, is the figure in black a young woman or man? The hand of the young person (younger than the gentleman who has two creases down his cheek, partly caused by his faint smile) looks feminine, but so do the hands of the older gentleman, whose right hand rests upon the head of his cane, and the left just above his left thigh, as if he is in doubt whether to take the hand of the figure in black. They gaze closely at each other, and with knowing smiles.

In the background, greyish rooftops silhouette themselves against the sky, there are two steeples, the higher bearing a cross. Between the carriage and the rooftops, a few trees are indicated in pale wash. The two figures are hidden from any viewer on the church side by the tall body of the carriage. Some words are written in pencil below this composition, on a paper mat on which the drawing itself has been pasted:

and when he went from London, he said he believed

he should never come to town more

The handwriting is quite legible and even simple.

Could Garbo have written those words herself, made them up or copied them from some favourite poem or story? Where did this drawing come from? Shall I make an effort to find out, or live with it as I do now (I've had it about two months), enjoying the wanderings of fancy?

That there is a sexual business between the two figures is in no doubt. The slender figure in black could be 20 or 18. The bewigged gentleman, elegantly slim though he is, is certainly 40. The pronouns in the pencilled statement are masculine. The real ambiguity is in the beautiful face of the blond figure, which except for a strong jaw appears female. The interesting question to me is, did Greta Garbo buy or acquire this drawing somehow, because the figure with the longish blond hair looked like herself?

I confess that is what I prefer to believe. The young blond-haired figure in black suggests to me the Garbo I saw so many times in Manhattan. The mouth certainly, close-lipped and slightly smiling, resembles Garbo's. A curve of black trousers suggests a feminine hip, though this could be caused by a tight belt. The height of the two appears the same; the blond-haired figure looms slightly taller, because the older man is about to take a big step (with the aid of a walking stick) to a cement slab of some kind which will put him on a level to enter his carriage.

If one stands back from the drawing, the figure in black dominates the composition. Because of the pavement rise at the knee level of this figure, and the grey-stockinged lower left leg of the older gentleman, the dark trousers are partly obscured at ankle level, suggesting that the younger man has unusually long feet – but only from a distance. This is an intimate picture, however, asking for close examination.

Did a contemporary of Garbo – an artist friend or acquaintance – create this little picture for her as a spoof, a private joke? This is probably exactly what she would have liked and preferred. Something the public would never know about, private laughter, delight, pleasure. A thing of beauty, really, to glance at every day or every other day, as she entered her bedroom, for instance.

Towards the upper left corner of the drawing, printed by hand, vertically, are the letters INGRE but with no final S, and the N is written backward, in sepia wash against the greyish wash of the sky. The letters are as faint as a watermark. Is the amateur or the art historian to pay attention to INGRE, try to determine provenance? Is it another joke between the artist and Greta Garbo?

And since it was rumoured about Garbo that she preferred women – easy

This is probably exactly what she would have liked... Something the public would never know about

to rumour as she never married – the composition in question could be a double joke. If the figure in black is female, the tableau becomes quite proper. Yet this supposition is made dubious by the pencilled statement below, with its masculine pronouns.

The mind wanders, or mine does, to Garbo films, her often unsmiling and rather cold face lifted like a ship's figurehead in a *Catherine the Great* poster, for instance. Garbo laughs – in *Ninotchka* – and the world heard it! One of the wonders of the 20th century. *Anna Karenina* demanded passion, duplicity, a burst of bliss, finally tragedy. Garbo made it – herself unique and untouchable somehow, even by the male lovers who embraced her.

I can never forget – and I can hear this too – Garbo's voice saying, 'I vant to be alone,' in a deep and earnest tone that meant to any hearer, Garbo speaks the truth. That statement may be the most certain thing anyone will ever be able to say about Garbo. Some of her contemporaries in Sweden may have known her well, fairly well, or only slightly. There was an altercation after her death about who inherited. The newspapers mentioned a nephew who was to have been the main inheritor, and I think he finally was.

One imagines Garbo living in Manhattan, seeing a very small circle of friends. When the telephone rang, it would have been one of this circle. She evidently preferred New York, with the anonymity afforded by its swarming eight million to the more sparsely populated Sweden and Stockholm. I hope she had Swedish salmon flown in sometimes, pressed between ice slabs with salt and sugar and the herb called *til*, plucked from the highest mountain slopes. One can only imagine her telephone bills. How nice to imagine Garbo laughing – and lifting her lidded eyes to the drawing I'm describing, gazing at the mysterious androgyne in black with his delicate hand pressing the gentleman's puffed silk sleeve with a light touch that implies the heaviest of passions.

Garbo laughs on the telephone! 'Come for some champagne and a supper tonight. I don't vant to be alone.'

Neither do the two in the drawing. And what have they been doing that afternoon, or the preceding night? The sky is rather clear, no indication of dusk. What time is it? Do lovers ever know? There is one thing definite about the words: they are a farewell, and a sad one, only mitigated by the tender smile on the lips of each.

Did Greta Garbo speculate in the same vein about these two?

'This is our last evening – shouldn't we make more of it?'

'Why? – You know I'll remember you forever – all my life – after I die –'

'You make me die a little now.'

'Your carriage – Dismiss that damned coachman!'

'Not so loud.'

No, quieter. Both faces show closed lips.

Did Garbo ever ask a friend – on seeing him or her gazing at the drawing, 'What do you think? Is the figure in black a boy or a gir-rl?'

It is possible that the reply would be, 'A girl — in disguise?'

This presents a new scenario: the

older gentleman (though married) is enamoured of a beautiful young woman in London, whom he has to meet secretly. Perhaps the gentleman has rented an apartment especially for this purpose, and the young woman has to come to the apartment, and departs, in male attire for safety's sake.

Or – the possibilities are many – the gentleman prefers his females in male attire, being in love with his own fantasies too.

Then we have, 'and when he went from London, he said he believed he should never come to town more', a statement made by the gentleman about himself, and the 'should' takes on prudence rather than being merely a subjunctive.

But there remains the height, the strong jaw of the figure in black to argue for its being a male form. Plus the clothing, of course.

Now the picture hangs in a corner of my room, over a low green-painted chest-of-drawers, and near a bookcase. The young man in black faces inward to the room. Soon I shall hang it in the living-room, where more people will see it. I long to hear the comments, even to remark the silences, the blank glances that have brought nothing to the viewer's brain. Some people are blind to any kind of pictures – not usually my friends, but then all sorts of people come to my house. My friends usually notice everything, and they love to comment.

'Garbo! – How interesting – that she owned it. Looks sort of like Garbo here, don't you think?'

I would like to think that Garbo could hear such remarks from another world, from on high or wherever she is, but since I don't believe in consciousness after death, I cannot indulge in that fantasy. I simply imagine, knowing I'm making it all up, that Garbo, having much liked this drawing, takes an interest now in what people say, and laughs at or troubles to consider an interpretation of *The Farewell at the Carriage* – my title.

Thank you, Greta Garbo, wherever you are. Thank you for your films, your style, your beauty. Thank you for managing to stay alone, for the most part, not easy for people in your profession. After me, your picture will be passed on into good hands; with my request, keep passing it on into good hands.

Robert Graves
by *John Mortimer*

I once met Robert Graves. He was old, I don't know how old, but eternally handsome, grey-haired and he sat like an emperor on a sofa beside me and said, 'Jesus Christ, of course, lived to the age of 80, when he went to China and discovered spaghetti.' Someone else, so far as I can remember it was Jo Grimond, was also on the sofa with us. Mr Graves had puzzled him. 'Which Gospel is it exactly,' he asked politely, 'in which we read that Jesus went to China and discovered spaghetti?' 'It's not in a Gospel,' Graves answered with imperious simplicity. 'It's a well-known fact of history.'

Later I said, 'We all remember what you did in the 1914 war, but what did you do in the last war?' 'I won the Battle of Anzio,' he told me. 'How did you manage that?' 'Well, I was cycling round the island of Jersey during the War and I met an officer in my old regiment, the Welsh Guards. I asked him what he was doing and he said, "We're off to fight the Eyeties." So I said, "I'll think of a plan by which you can beat the Eyeties." So I cycled round the island again and when I got back to him I said, "There's one thing that really scares an Eyetie and that is the cry of a woman in labour. So you want to go to Queen Charlotte's

> 'Jesus Christ, of course, lived to the age of 80, when he went to China and discovered spaghetti'

Hospital and record all the women in labour, then play their cries on gramophones to the Eyeties and they'll run a mile." Well, that's exactly what happened and so we won the Battle of Anzio. Records of women in labour were playing all along the beaches.'

I had adapted *I Claudius* and *Claudius the God* – two books to which I had long been devoted – for the stage, and the play was directed by Tony Richardson, in whose house I met Robert Graves. To ensure the play's success he had brought a fragment of meteorite which he held in his hand. 'How will you get it to bring us good notices and a long run?' I asked him. 'I shall simply say to it: "Magic stone, do your job!".' Perhaps it was the wrong formula, for the stone went off-duty on the first night and the play was a flop. But I shall always remember, with joy, discussing the well-known facts of history on a sofa with Robert Graves.

Rage

Auberon Waugh

Perhaps we should welcome the epidemic of head lice which is about to hit Britain, according to the *Observer*. Although parents of small children are also at risk, I have seldom heard of grandparents who caught lice from their grandchildren, and the nation's baldies can give the broadest of smiles. My only hesitation about the plague is that it may bring more power and self-importance to John Carey, the unattractive Merton Professor of English at Oxford, who is our greatest expert on head lice, writing about them from time to time in the Murdoch press.

It won't do the young any harm to scratch their heads a bit. This is less serious than the plague of hairy caterpillars which is afflicting sunbathers on the south coast with an appalling itch, causing many of them (according to the *Telegraph*) to shed their skins and leave them on the beaches. The young deserve a few setbacks, in any case. A survey conducted by Trustee Savings Bank reveals them in an even more nauseating light than usual, being chiefly concerned with tropical rainforests and cruelty to animals, wanting better education and health care, with two thirds of them saying they are willing to pay more taxes. What taxes have these snivelling little prigs ever paid? It will serve them right if the ghastly Merton Professor attends to their head lice in person.

At least nobody has yet claimed that either plague is to be blamed on the Common Market. I was irritated to see Christopher Booker's article in the last *Oldie*, listing some of the ludicrous bureaucratic regulations which can now be laid at the door of the European Community in Brussels. Nearly every bloody fool in the country over the age of 50 has some silly attitude to strike about Brussels, but the truth is that all these regulations and many worse ones — banning the sale of unpasteurised cheese, imposing a £1,000 fine for frightening a bat, prison for picking a wild flower, forbidding us to have lavatories in our kitchens — have been gushing out of our repulsive House of Commons, year after year, almost unnoticed. Did you know that publicans were expected to wash their hands after handling money, and are forbidden to smoke even in the public part of the bar? All these things now listed as Euro-absurdities were autochthonous horrors which are just beginning to be imposed.

The simple truth is that every country in Europe is full of bossy people wishing to regulate our lives, push buttons and see us jump. They are called politicians, for the most part, but they also flourish in the civil service, teaching professions and, increasingly, in voluntary pressure groups. There is virtually no opposition to them, because anyone wishing to oppose them would first have to join them. The only sane approach is to ignore them as much as possible. Has any reader ever heard of anyone using the back seatbelts installed by some half-baked edict, whether from Westminster or Brussels?

The real reason for dislike of the European Community among oldies goes much deeper. It has nothing to do with defending the British Way of Life — our ghastly pubs and horrible food, our rotten railways and unspeakable prisons — against foreign perversions. They are perfectly well protected, for the most part. It is far more a resentment of many aspects of the modern age — the undeserved prosperity of the masses, the horrible noises, smells and ugly buildings of a threadbare modern culture in which the brashest and most ignorant seem to be calling the tune.

There is a feeling that all this will get worse under a single European market with harmonised national institutions and no doubt it will — but not nearly so bad as it would be under the only alternative, which would have us trailing behind the United States, pathetically adopting all its least attractive characteristics in an abject attempt to ride into the modem world as a passenger on its back.

Nothing on earth is going to stop certain of the nation's less reflective oldies from striking poses about all the good things we are losing. Almost without exception, we were losing them in any case. Some five or six years ago, Southern Television made a film about the idyllic Sussex village of Amberley, showing the village shop with the shopkeeper sitting by the real fire with strings of beautiful, home-made sausages. Last month STV showed the film again, but vigilantes of the local 'thought police' (West Sussex Trading Standards Department) did not recognise the Roman numerals on the copyright date and descended on the shop to check on the illegal practices in the programme. In fact, the shop had changed hands and been brought into line with the new regulations, no longer selling home-made sausages or having a fire. At first the inspectors refused to believe the film was five or six years old, and then went potty, taking the shop to pieces in their anxiety to find some regulations it had contravened.

There is anxiety among many oldies that Brussels will accelerate the spreading influence of these malign functionaries, the arbiters and rulers of the modern age. I feel it will almost certainly slow the process down. There are rumours of a French ban on smoking in public places, but we may be sure it will be universally ignored. We are right to feel anxieties about the modern age, but these are best faced with the Europeans with whom we share a common historical memory, ancient grudges, resentments and guilts, a culture which has gone through imperialism, fascism, socialism and understands itself.

The Americans, by contrast, have virtually no collective history and have deliberately forgotten what little they had; they neither understand nor like what little they know of Europe. Putting ignorance at the helm has gone much further in America even than it has in this country, with our ludicrous emphasis on youth. The other major countries of Europe, by contrast, are still comparatively sane about many of these things.

Dignity and majesty

High-quality oldie films available on video, chosen by *Larry Adler*

Henry V (1944)

I have seen both *Henry*s. The 1944 film was produced and directed by Laurence Olivier who, of course, played the star part and received a special Academy Award for the triple feat. Laurence Olivier seems to live the part. By contrast, Kenneth Branagh, in the 1989 film, is less Henry V than Hank Sank. He plays the King as if expecting someone else to play the Ace.

Olivier's is a splendid and beautiful film. Too much time is spent, at the beginning, on interminable panoramic shots of Old London with the part of Old London played by what is obviously a miniature mock-up. Yet more time is spent establishing that it is set in the Globe theatre. It takes too long and I kept willing Olivier to get on with it, for God's sake.

The picture is nearly stolen by Renée Asherson as Catherine of Aragon. Her French is flawless and her English, in her adorable attempts at it, has just the right French accent. I wonder how many others could have done that difficult job so well? (Incidentally, I recently saw Renée Asherson in a television play, with no French accent this time. The years have subtracted nothing from her captivating charm.) George Robey is superb in his one scene as Falstaff, and Robert Newton munches on the scenery as Pistol.

The score is a vital part of this film, and William Walton is at his best. For the scenes involving Princess Catherine he uses one of the *Songs of the Auvergne*, and it works beautifully. Following the death of Falstaff, he has a theme so touching that I would like to find the music so that I could play it (that is my admittedly personal way of judging music).

The British archers firing at the French provides a chilling sound effect. You see and hear the arrows in flight and their hissing sound is unforgettable.

Olivier's best scenes are during the night before the battle as he anonymously visits the tents of his soldiers. The lighting is a work of true art. Sometimes Olivier's face is barely seen as he sits at a camp-fire but his presence

The 'dazzling' Audrey Hepburn in *Breakfast at Tiffany's*

always dominates. A credible King has dignity and majesty. Olivier had it and Branagh hadn't...

Breakfast at Tiffany's (1961)

The star of this film is a song, *Moon River*. Henry Mancini composes melodies in the old, grand style. It has the added pleasure of a Johnny Mercer lyric with that strange, unforgettable phrase, 'My huckleberry friend'. Now why 'huckleberry'? It's a wonderful word for a romantic lyric, but makes no particular sense. I think Johnny Mercer was a fan of Mark Twain, who wrote what many consider the great American classic novel, *Huckleberry Finn*. It scans too. The film opens with the theme played by a mouth-organist who isn't me (sob).

The characters are not very pleasant people. The dazzling Audrey Hepburn wants only to marry a rich man, any rich man, even the idiotically grinning oaf who is brought to her cocktail party. George Peppard is a writer, kept by the

> The film opens with the theme played by a mouth-organist who isn't me (sob)

rich and deeply unpleasant Patricia Neal. The worst characterisation is a nastily stereotyped Japanese. He's portrayed in an essence of hokum by Mickey Rooney, all protruding teeth and mangled English. Truman Capote, who wrote the original novel, seems determined not to forget Pearl Harbor. I doubt that this character would get by in any modern film or play. The surprise is that the script is by one of the best in the business, George Axelrod, and directed by Blake Edwards, another fine pro. I just don't get it. Perhaps the date, 1961, explains items such as the Rooney character.

Martin Balsam is excellent as a fast-talking Hollywood agent, every sentence punctuated by 'Ya know what I mean?' Buddy Ebsen gives the film its one moment of honest emotion. Once married to Holly Golightly (the Hepburn character), he comes to New York to reclaim her since, as it is revealed, Holly Golightly was born Lulu May Barnes. He is rejected by Holly... well, he just isn't rich... and she sees him off on a bus.

It is hard to care at all for these superficial characters. George Peppard and Audrey Hepburn not only breakfast at Tiffany's, they shoplift there as well. However, there is that glorious song running through the film. You'll be singing it coming *in*.

Travels with a superstar

Dame Edna Everage

Hello possums, I've been a bit of a lady of leisure lately, like a lot of *Oldie* readers no doubt! Caesar, my gorgeous old butler and personal gynaecologist, has been urging me to take the weight off my feet, so right now I've cancelled squillions of engagements and I'm about as busy as Neil Kinnock's social secretary.

Call me old-fashioned, but I relax best when I'm travelling, pampered by those little BA hostesses as I sit back watching *Silence of the Lambs 3*, or *Nightmare on Elm Street 12*, and sending my scrummy leftovers in an airsick bag back to my bridesmaid in Economy.

On this last trip, my first stop was Hong Kong, where I visited the merchandising nerve centre of Ednacare, my multi-million-dollar beauty conglomerate. Here I examined some of the new glamour products bearing my famous name, which will soon be available from Dame Edna boutiques in quality stores all over the planet.

There is my exciting fragrance 'Menopause', which may be sprayed into the usual nooks, or worn on the arm like a hormone replacement patch. Then there is my famous Cranny Cream, made from a secret formula containing wombat spleen jelly painlessly derived from the spleens of humanely culled wombats.

A big favourite with *Oldie* readers will be the new spin-offs from this popular product: 'Granny Cranny Cream' – extra soothing and packaged in finger-friendly suppositories.

Whilst in Honkers, I looked up one of my many financial advisors, David Tang, who whisked me up to the Hong Kong Club for a Chinese-style lunch. I still think it's funny eating a pricey meal made of the things our mothers used to throw away: cabbage stalks, pea pods, celery tops and – yuk – ducks' webs!

My attention wandered a little from my handsome host when I heard gales of tinted laughter from an adjoining table. Some Chinese businessmen were telling jokes, and this one – in English – shocked me to the core:

I was going to visit Melbourne Cemetery to buff up my late husband's obelisk

'Why do seagulls fly upside-down in Australia?'

The name of my homeland (I'm an Australian incidentally) really made me prick up my ears.

'I don't know,' cried the other Chinamen. 'Why do seagulls fly upside-down in Australia?'

When I heard the uncalled-for punch line I felt as though a cold hand had stolen into my breast and given my heart a little squeeze.

'Because there's nothing in Australia worth going to the toilet on!'

How those cruel and tasteless Chinamen hooted with laughter at this joke at the expense of my superlative homeland's ailing, beleaguered and embattled economy. And I'm sorry, readers, they did not employ the term 'going to the toilet' either, but something far less acceptable.

I was going back to Australia on the next leg of my trip to visit Melbourne Cemetery and buff up my late husband's obelisk. How tragic, I reflected, that

Australia's fiscal ills should be the butt of our saffron-hued neighbours. In the plane down to Sydney I tried to sleep, occasionally woken by Australian businessmen apologetically plucking at my sleeve and asking for small sums; sometimes only the price of a duty-free drink.

My trip Down Under coincided with a lot of hoo-haa by the so-called Republican Movement, a small band of Roman Catholic ratbags led by a publicity-crazed lawyer, who all want to cut our ties with the Queen and give Australia a green flag.

When I told my royal friend on the phone about this unsavoury element she rather took the wind out of my sails by saying, 'The sooner the better' – or words to that effect.

Although royalty are sick to death of visiting Australia only to get treated rudely by the public and groped by the Prime Minister, they are still firm favourites with the solid core of the Australian workforce – that is to say, Vietnamese taxi-drivers, Greek builders and Serbo-Croatian chemists and newsagents. To these old-fashioned Aussies, even Fergie is still a heroine.

Of course, we do have our own royalty in Australia, as the Queen never ceases to remind me, and I suppose if anyone other than my little friend from Windsor is going to have their head on the money, it might as well be me.

Now I'm in the States, all ready to give Hillary Clinton a little last-minute backstage grooming. Considering that, single-handed, I eased Barbara Bush out of polyester, Hillary should be a sartorial push-over.

Madonna's rather old-fashioned book is in all the shops here giving new hope to common young women with dark roots who don't mind how many times they are retouched. Outside one Beverly Hills bookshop today I saw the sign: MADONNA'S SEX, NOT RETURNABLE. What a spooky old world we live in!

A joyous heart always, *Edna*

THEATRE
BERYL
BAINBRIDGE

HG Wells was a reformer as well as a novelist who, when young, believed that the world could only get better. The First World War turned him into a cynic and made him morosely aware that things could only get worse.

I read his book, *The Invisible Man*, while at school and the plot is now somewhat hazy in my mind. I can't remember whether invisibility turned the hero into a monster or not. He certainly became one in Ken Hill's excellent and witty adaptation for the stage, now in production at the Vaudeville Theatre in the Strand.

The play is neatly enfolded inside a music-hall entertainment of the period, with a chorus-line cast, a master of ceremonies bawling out his lungs to introduce the action, scenery complete with woodland glades and a splendid use of a gauze front drop. Brian Murphy as Thomas Marvel (part tramp, part pantomime dame) is the narrator who links together the strange happenings which began and ended in a remote English village in 1904. Mr Murphy is a star, a great actor and comedian who, given good material, cannot strike a

false note. His performance is stunning, not least because he makes everything seem so easy. His sense of timing reminds one of that other superb thespian – alas, now rarely seen on the West End stage – Mr David Tomlinson.

Act one, scene three, the saloon bar of the village inn run by the busty and rumbustious Mrs Hall, excellently portrayed by Toni Palmer. Enter a grotesque stranger dressed in black clothes and white bandages wishing to rent accommodation and be left alone. People being what they are – nosy parkers – and the faceless man prone to disappearing and materialising at all hours of the day and night, not to

mention a burglary at the vicarage, another at the post office and the stabbing of a local bobby, it's perhaps not surprising that his desire to be treated like Greta Garbo should be thwarted.

Much has been written about the special effects created by the illusionist Paul Kieve, and it's all true. Desk drawers and curtains might just be opened and closed by remote control, but I watched with the eyes of a hawk when the Invisible Man unwound his bandages, and no, he didn't have a head. His arms moved, his knees jiggled and he harangued his tormentors throughout, but he definitely had nothing above the neck.

I can't praise this entertainment too highly. It has a zest and intelligence which raises it above the normal. I suppose a lot of this is down to HG Wells, but the cast are splendid, every single one of them, not least the Invisible Man himself, Michael Harbour. He appeared in the flesh for the first time in the last scene, and dead at that, but recovered in time for the curtain call.

I think I must be lucky in my choice of plays. Apart from *Henry IV, Part One*, and the unaccountably acclaimed revival of *An Inspector Calls*, I haven't seen a dud one yet.

Status of journalists

BLOG MARY KENNY, 2019

It would be surprising if things hadn't changed in over 50 years in journalism. But what intrigues me most is the alteration of status.

When I first became a journalist, back in the middle 1960s, it was not an entirely respectable trade. One of the ways you got into journalism was by hanging around a pub. My first excursion into hanging around a pub was, in retrospect, quite distinguished: the pub was 'Le Falstaff' in Montparnasse, where Peter Lennon used to drink with Sam Beckett (and talk about cricket). I knew Peter slightly, and was helped by another Irish pal, Joe Carroll, and that's how I started

worming my way into the newspaper trade.

And 'trade' is the operative word. The night editor of the *Manchester Guardian* (as it was then) told me, 'We don't want varsity men here. Give me rough, hard-working lads and lasses any time.'

In Fleet Street, when I got a full-time job, the bohemianism of the 'trade' was evident, and there were as many chancers, topers, bounders and rogues as there were genuinely conscientious and accomplished reporters. But I never heard the word 'ethics' mentioned.

The #MeToo generation of feminists might be appalled at some of the morals that prevailed. Fleet Street's ace female reporter, the late Anne Sharpley, advised me, upon embarking on a foreign assignment, 'Always sleep with the Reuters man, doll.' (That was to

ensure agency copy was endorsed by the copy from Reuters, the leading news agency.) If you had sex appeal – as Sharpley had – she regarded it as an asset to be advanced.

Then journalism grew *embourgeoisé*. The rough lads and lasses were replaced by the varsity guys and gals. I daresay it improved: more women meant more sobriety and, indeed, more ethics. Journalism became not only respectable but sought after. Perhaps television bestowed high status and now everyone wanted to be in 'the media'. Then the internet enabled nearly everyone to do so.

The 'trade' is taken much more seriously 50-plus years on. Yet puzzlingly (or perhaps not) there is less money available today, and the BBC, for example, often expects journalists to work for nothing. But heigh-ho – once upon a time the going was good!

THE DEATH FILES
BAMBER GASCOIGNE

My ideal way to go...
A few months ago my computer gave me a glimpse of an ideal way to go. I had more than three years' work in a database called Ency\Ency. But the screen declared: 'Ency\Ency does not exist'. Vanished. Snuffed out. Just like that. And painlessly, it seemed, from the point of view of the database – though not from mine. The human equivalent has to be a heart attack. I am told you can be pruning your roses and dead before you hit the ground. My equivalent of roses is hunched over the computer, so that must be the place as well as the method.

My life expectancy...
Ranges from five minutes to 35 years.

My last words...
Ideal way to go precludes.

My method of disposal...
I like the idea of books in a necrobibliotech. People's remains would be in book-shaped containers on shelves, with their names on the spine and a decent catalogue for researchers to find their way around.

My funeral arrangements...
The Humanist Association provides sympathetic 'ministers' who will conduct a dignified farewell based on some of the greatest passages in English literature.

My special effects...
Fewer than in life. No starters for 10.

Memorial service...
An event that all my friends go away from feeling much better than when they came. Only one condition: they must all wish I'd been there (frequently and aloud).

The other side...
I image D-Day + 1 as being like sleep, but without the pleasure of waking up and discovering there is time to go to sleep again.

My thoughts on life and death....
I believe life to be meaningless but utterly fascinating. Compared to the improbability of having won the original race, as the first spermatozoon to reach the egg of the month, the certainty of death is trivial.
Compiled by Richard Middleton

Off the cuff
Hardy Amies

I was recently staying in my company's flat in New York, which we have had for 20 years. The décor has become richer with our finances.

New York remains the same, but optimism rises over the wailing walls. We are only concerned with men's clothes. Business is terrible but Barney's has spent $30 million, it is said, on our new shop. And Ralph Lauren has done likewise, if marginally more modestly.

One of the joys of Manhattan is that everything is so near. There are cinemas within 10 minutes' walk. But there are also an awful lot of people, so it took us three hours to queue to get into the film *The Age of Innocence*. We did it in relays of three. It was fun. The film is splendid and all oldies should see it when it comes to London. It plays, as you all know, in the 1870s – which should bring back childhood memories for many of you.

I became an Edith Wharton fan several years ago, when I was able to visit Newport often. Here she lived, and it is the scene of much of the action in the film. A great deal of trouble has been gone to and much money spent on the film in order to create authenticity. But the story is one of great psychological subtlety, often perplexing in the film but vastly entertaining in the book. Wharton is superbly cynical and witty: 'Mr Welland was a mild and silent man, with no opinions but with many habits.'

May Welland is beautifully acted, but her rival Ellen Orlenska is less so. I fear the actress is miscast. She has no style. She is also made a blonde, which May is touchingly described as being. There is a terrible moment when she lets her hair down and it is revealed as a tumble of 'scrunch dried' permanent waving. More seriously disturbing are the cream silk ties the gentlemen wear with their evening tails. I can't believe there was no white piqué in New York in the 1870s.

These are dressmaker's quibbles.

Don't be put off. The book is well printed as a paperback.

Ever since its launch I have flown on Concorde. It was then an extravagance. Now the old man considers it a necessity. Six hours from door to door – you arrive an hour before you left. Its creation is a triumph for Britain. If we had supported a Concorde service to

***The Age of Innocence*: a splendid film**

Australia we would have less trouble with republicans.

I still get cross when I see the décor. The English style and taste in room decoration is famous, and admired and copied in the civilised world. But what do we do with Concorde, our great tourist and business showpiece? We decorate it in the most blatant American–German fashion possible! Leather is a tricky material. I happen to hate it because I am a wool man. But real leather in its natural colouring has an association with men's clubs and the saddle room.

All artificially coloured leather, with the exception of black and possibly red, is basically unattractive. Dyed grey it is remorselessly naff. You cannot hold a serious conversation with a man wearing grey leather shoes (suede is another but not very different story). Why not curtains (even chintz) of British make and design – and cushions, too? The interiors are upholstered, nothing is bleakly functional. They serve caviar, so why was not the châtelaine of Chatsworth consulted?

I do hope that a better job, more worthy of British taste, is done on the next fleet.

Sister Wendy Beckett

Interview by *Naim Attallah*

Although she regards herself as socially inadequate, and spends her days in silence, seclusion and prayer in a caravan, Sister Wendy, who was born in South Africa in 1930, has the gifts of a born communicator. Naim Attallah is but one of millions to fall prey to her charm.

Sister Wendy, your family was extremely devout. Do you think in that sense it could be said you 'inherited' your faith, rather than came to it by a more personal route?
I would qualify 'extremely devout'. We were not a family who had prayers in common, for example. It was just obvious to me that my parents' faith mattered a lot to them by what they were, as opposed to what they said, and I'm sure that's how most children receive their religion, as opposed to their faith. They get their politics through their family, their religion through their family, but faith comes completely from your own depths and your own personal contact with God, and it is faith which fills out the bare bones of the religion. Faith is the spirit; religion is the body. I inherited my Catholicism, but the faith was a gift to me, direct from God.

How do you define God? Who is God?
God is mystery... we can't possibly know. The point really about being a Christian is that we believe only one person ever was able to look deep into the mystery and turn round and say to us 'it's father...' Jesus saw that the infinite mystery was the father, it was total supportive love, and we live in the strength of that. But we can never make a definition of God or have an idea of God, because then it is something limited. We can't define what by its essence is so infinitely beyond the concepts of our mind.

Why exactly is chastity so important? What has chastity got to do with God? He has after all created our bodies which are designed to function in particular ways, including sexually. That must surely also be a gift from God.
I agree with you totally. God gave us these beautiful bodies, and He loves all parts of them. Anybody who feels that the vow of chastity involves pain and frustration should not take it, because God does not like us to suffer. He takes no pleasure out of people making themselves frustrated and unhappy. But we only have so much psychic energy, and for myself I know I could never have had a deep emotional relationship with anybody, let alone a sexual relationship – even on the emotional level I couldn't have done it. All my energies are utterly absorbed in loving God. This is not everyone's vocation; obviously most people's vocation is to come to God through loving somebody else. I don't compare myself to Jesus, but I'm sure He couldn't have had a sexual or emotional involvement at very great depth, because He was so totally taken up with His father.

Has chastity involved any degree of suffering for you?
No. I'm a totally fulfilled woman, and I don't miss a thing, but I recognise that it is not the normal way to God. The normal way is by receiving His gifts in gratitude and using them. But our vows are

'I was never taught repressively at a convent'

functional; they are meant actually to set you free for God. Obedience is to set you free from all the struggles of having a career and making your own decisions; poverty is to free you from all the hassles of earning and possessing; and chastity is to set you free from the psychic involvement with close friends and family. All your energies can then go out; if you're an active religious they go out to the world in service, if you're a contemplative religious they go out to the world in prayer.

Have you ever been criticised for doing what you do?
I may well be, but I don't know. People write saying how they love it, but the world may be full of people saying they think it's shameful. There was someone who wrote a letter after I was on the *Terry Wogan Show*, saying she was very 'disedified' by seeing me showing off on the programme and telling dear Cliff Richard that he was mistaken in his Christian views, and she said that she looked for more humility in a nun. I wrote back to her and said I was very sorry I had disedified her and would she please pray for me to become humble.

How aware were you of the political situation in South Africa while you were there? Was it possible for you to help in any way?
I was completely unaware. I only knew the servants in my parents' home. My grandmother was a great benefactress of the African schools, and I can remember her buying a great box of sweets when I was about nine and taking me with her to distribute them to the African children, and it never entered my head that this was all terribly wrong. It was only when I was an adult that it came as an awful shock to me to realise that in fact the only citizens of my country were white. It just shows that you can live in a situation that's crying out aloud to God for vengeance and never see it; rather like the American southerners who say all their black servants are so happy. It shocks me now to think that we were so fond of our servants and we did not see the injustice of it all. I pray a lot, and I get very upset about South Africa, and although I tremble for them at the moment, there's no doubt whatever that it's got to be lived through.

How did it come about that you entered an order in Sussex, such a long way from South Africa?
The nuns with whom I went to school in South Africa were an international order in America, on the Continent, in England, in Africa and in Japan, but their novitiate was in Sussex which I entered 47 years ago on 1st February. I keep that day with great joy.

When you are in your caravan,

do you talk to anybody?
No, I don't. I don't live with the other sisters. After morning prayers, the sister who looks after me brings me some coffee and sits down and tells me what's going on. Perhaps I'll say to her that I need a new pair of socks, or something like that, but I don't chat. As soon as Mass is over I take my basket of provisions and go back to the caravan and I stay there all day in complete silence.

But how is it possible to live in silence when you so obviously like people and enjoy talking?
This is going to sound very rude but I've never met anybody I'd rather talk to than be silent with God. That to me is the height of joy.

How did you reconcile your love for art, and its liberal expression, with the rather repressive teaching of the convent?
I was never taught repressively at a convent.

Would you dare in a convent, for example, to look at a painting of a nude and discuss pubic hair – as you have done in your books?
Yes, of course I would. I would expect all nuns to have reverence for the body God has given them. Anything else is narrow puritanism which has nothing to do with the faith. For some extraordinary reason this narrow puritanism seems to have taken over, but it's not Christian. Jesus speaks freely about excretion, for example, about faeces coming out, and He certainly didn't feel this wasn't quite nice. This fear of the body is a late development, and of course a lot of people have been taught it by the Irish, who have a real puritanical fear of the body. But I was lucky; I knew nothing of all this guilt that is supposed to cling to Catholicism. Guilt and sin were words never mentioned in my upbringing, and when I hear people talking like this I just feel very sad. If this is the way they think, they've got the wrong end of the stick, they never have been Catholics, because this is not the teaching of the Church. It is a version of it that is unfortunately favoured by people who like the tyranny of puritanism. God doesn't live in blacks and whites; God lives in the lovely fluid greys of the world, and he asks us never to accept black and white from above, but to

look into our own hearts and see what is true.

Is the urge to live an entirely solitary life a strength or a weakness, do you think? Christ after all seems to have been rather a gregarious person...
I'm positive it's a weakness. It's a life only for the very weak who cannot stand the normal strains of life, perhaps the almost neurotically weak, who also have such a strong passion for God that they can impose upon their life the austerity that the life demands.

Is there some connection between the contemplation of works of art and the spiritual life? Is it an avenue to God?
For me it is, absolutely, and I think this is potentially what it is for everybody. Whenever you look at real art you're looking at something that's challenging you to be more wholly human, to enter more deeply into truth; and whenever you touch truth, you touch God. God is truth.

But I thought God was indefinable...
He is indefinable, but wherever there is beauty and truth, there is God. Yes, I put that badly, you're quite right to have corrected me. Truth and beauty don't encompass God but their presence shows us the presence of God, just as light shows us the presence of the sun.

'God is asking me to do this now,' you said in an interview. How do you know it is God?
You only know what God is asking of you through the circumstances of your life. The context of your life tells you. The Good Samaritan knew that God was asking him to succour the man who had fallen among thieves because he actually met the man. If He hadn't met the man, God wouldn't have asked him; but that's the only way God does speak to people, through the actual context of their lives. Whom does God ask you to love? The people you know, the people you live with. So we only have to look at our lives to know what we're called upon to do.

You have expressed some ideas which do not at first sight seem compatible with the faith. In what sense, for example, can homosexuality not matter, given the views expressed in the Bible and in the tradition of the Church?
Let me give you a parallel: the Church condemned Galileo for saying that the earth went round the sun, and not vice versa. Only when everybody, the man in the street, understood, and it was common knowledge that the earth did indeed go round the sun, not the other way round, did the Church accept it. The fact that the Bible seemed to say the opposite was meant to be poetry. Now, I don't believe the Church is the glorious unspotted leader, marching ahead of humanity; that's not the Church Jesus left us. The Church is a poor wounded creature and it's moved at the pace of the slowest. When the man in the street understands the full meaning of love, then the Church will understand it, and a lot of the present prohibitions will just dissolve. But they haven't dissolved yet, and I don't think it helps people for somebody who's totally committed to the faith as I am to say the Church as yet hasn't fully understood. I'll say it to a friend, but I don't think it's wise to say it in public, because it doesn't help the Church.

There will be many who see the campaign for the ordination of women as just another feminist effort directed by women with no interest in religion. Do you see it as principally a theological or apolitical matter?
I don't know very much about the ins and

outs of it, but to me it's a completely theological matter, or perhaps I should say it's a matter of practical understanding of God's plans for His children, and in God's eyes gender is not very important. I don't think it's just a question of feminism. Men don't realise how terrible it's been for some women; the bright girl in the family who wasn't educated because her stupid brother had to get all the money; or the clever woman in a firm who could take responsibility easily and is overlooked because the men get it and make a mess of things. There is a lot of buried frustration and it'll take a long time for this to work itself out, but I think we'll see light at the end of the tunnel. Think how recently women weren't allowed to go to university, or to vote. We forget what enormous strides have been made to see women as fully human; there are more strides to be made still, but we are making progress.

You were reported as saying of sexual activity: 'There is not going to be a personal involvement, but I would cheer it on.' That seems a remarkably liberal view for a nun. What did you mean?
I don't remember saying it, but if I did say it, I would have meant that for me there is no sexual involvement and never has been and never will be because God is complete fulfilment, but I'm delighted that the world is full of people who appreciate God's good gift to them. Of course sex is something to cheer on. Why did God invent it if he didn't want it to be something of delight to people?

You speak of art as giving insight into mysteries. Can you elaborate on that? What sort of mysteries are involved here, and what is it to have 'insight' into a mystery?
Art works at a very profound level. It is almost by definition at the level of the mysterious. It is concerned with those things in us that are there but which we find it so hard to bring to the surface of our consciousness: the desire for goodness, the desire to be fully human, the desire for eternal life, the desire for happiness, the desire to make sense of suffering. A very great picture opens you up to a lot of these truths, perhaps not always consciously, but you're stirred at

'There is a beauty in ugliness, you know. Think of Rembrandt's old people, with gnarled features, but absolutely lit up with wisdom'

those depths, and if you have the kind of mind that wants to reflect upon what the experience has been, then you would have conscious insight into truths that perhaps you hadn't realised before you were faced with that great work of art. A work of art that leaves you untouched is not a great work of art, or you haven't opened yourself enough.

How do you think the idea of art as beauty correlates with paintings whose subject matter is ugly – of dead bodies, for example, or indeed of any picture in which the artist wishes to depict something ugly, like Goya's '3rd May 1808'.
There is a beauty in ugliness, you know. Think of Rembrandt's old people, with gnarled features, but absolutely lit up with wisdom. Goya was indeed painting something very ugly but he was showing the human spirit grappling with it – that's

the beauty. Beauty doesn't mean pretty; beauty means something of the spirit which can show itself in a misshapen form. Beauty is often horrible, terrifying, with nothing of the attractive or the gentle about it; but it is equally beautiful.

You admire the skill (which you say you yourself will never attain) of being able to use words so exactly that no one will misunderstand them. Would you agree that the language of faith is singularly imprecise, that it is impossible for one person to understand what another means by 'knowing God', for example.
Absolutely. I agree totally. Not only have you a language difficulty here, you have a moral difficulty in that we only know as much of God as we want to know. Psychologists say that if you're faced with an unbearable truth, you won't bear it, you'll just block it out. And I can understand this. In a way, the truth about God is unbearable because it is so enormously large, and it's easy to see that people may not want to hear it. With the real God you're completely out of control the minute you look at Him. So where there's a difficulty of language, there's a difficulty of desire. Oh yes, the language of religion is absolutely hopeless. Everybody has a different picture in mind, and some are horrible. That's why I say I love atheists, because they're people who've thrown out a false God. They were perfectly right to disown the kind of God they thought was God. The point is they haven't met the real God yet, because if you meet the real God you can't possibly not love Him. So hurrah for atheists.

What is your attitude towards death?
As a child I looked forward very much to dying. I thought how wonderful it would be to leap into the arms of God. Now I see it as the one chance to make a great act of faith, because we all go into the darkness in death. God says, 'Though he slay me, yet will I trust in him.' When God puts the knife to the throat, and I go into the darkness, I will be able to make an act of faith that I've never made before so in that sense I'll be very glad to die.

Sister Wendy died on 26th December 2018.

KIRKER HOLIDAYS
FOR DISCERNING TRAVELLERS

Kirker Holidays provides carefully crafted tailor-made holidays to over 140 destinations in 40 countries - including 70 classic cities and 250 relaxing rural locations throughout Europe and beyond. The Kirker Concierge can arrange opera and ballet tickets, pre-book museums, galleries and private guided tours, and reserve a table for a delicious dinner at a recommended restaurant.

We also provide a series of escorted Cultural Tours & Music Holidays, including opera weekends in Milan, Venice, Vienna and New York, tours to leading music festivals and events, and exclusive Music Festivals on land and at sea.

SPECIAL OCCASIONS

If you are celebrating a special birthday or anniversary, Kirker can tailor make an itinerary to help you to celebrate in style. For the ultimate experience why not travel on the Venice Simplon-Orient-Express?

ADDED VALUE

We have a range of special offers to include complimentary nights and room upgrades at some of our favourite hotels, and in many destinations we also offer complimentary extras such as tickets to museums and galleries or private walking tours.

UNIQUE CONCIERGE SERVICE

Kirker's Concierge will arrange opera and ballet tickets, pre-book entrance for museums and galleries, book private guided tours, and recommend and book restaurants to ensure that you can sit back and relax whilst Kirker ensures the smooth running of your holiday.

EXTENSIVE BROCHURE RANGE

Our collection of brochures includes Italy, France, Spain & Portugal and Cultural Tours & Music Holidays, as well as South Africa and India & Sri Lanka.

CULTURAL TOURS

Join a group of like-minded travellers in the company of an expert tour lecturer. Carefully designed itineraries include visits to renowned gardens, historic towns and cities, archaeological sites and famous galleries.

EXCLUSIVE KIRKER MUSIC FESTIVALS

Our own exclusive chamber music festivals in the UK and abroad, featuring highly acclaimed musicians in unique settings, from Cornwall and Sussex to Lake Como, Ischia and at sea aboard Fred Olsen's Black Watch.

LEADING MUSIC FESTIVALS & EVENTS

Visits to world-famous concert halls and venues, spectacular music festivals and special musical events. For those who prefer a tailor-made short break, the Kirker Concierge can arrange tickets for every major opera house in Europe.

Speak to an expert or request a brochure:

020 7593 2283 quote code XOL

www.kirkerholidays.com

FOR DISCERNING TRAVELLERS

MEMORIAL SERVICE
NED SHERRIN
Brian Johnston, CBE, MC (1912-1994)
Westminster Abbey, 16 May 1994

An Abbey memorial service which starts with *The Eton Boating Song* and plays you out with *Underneath the Arches* starts and finishes strongly. The Abbey stage managers never let down those it celebrates. You can rely on heart-stopping moments which upstage the rhetoric, the singing and the setting – but never the subject. Sybil Thorndike had trumpets to blow her away to the other side. With Laurence Olivier it was the parade of great actors bearing his emblems and awards. For Kenneth Macmillan it was a child fluting the *Pie Jesu* from aloft.

For Johnners it was the Grenadiers. Two young Guards musicians playing the *Grenadiers' Return* slow-marched the length of the nave, the quire and the sacrarium drumming and piping the tune in honour of a Guards MC. The drummer cannot have been born when Brian turned 60.

Brother Christopher read Psalm 15 – 'Lord, who shall dwell in Thy tabernacle?'. Son, Barry, read his godfather William Douglas Home's *A Glorious Game, Say We*: 'Yes, cricket will live till the trumpet trumps / From the wide, pavillioned sky, / And time, the umpire lays low the stumps / As his scythe goes sweeping by...'

Colin Cowdrey and John Major gave addresses from parallel pulpits. Cowdrey represented the cricketing profession with the eloquence and humour of those memorable amateurs. The Prime Minister well conveyed the affection in which the ordinary man held Johnners.

After Michael Denison had done justice to Cardus on the outbreak of war seen from the Long Room, Richard Stilgoe, our leading occasional versifier alluded to 'the bowler's holding...' without offending Dean, Chapter or Archbishop Runcie, and trumpeted two corking couplets. Of Brian's arrival in Heaven: 'He talks to total strangers, / Calls the Angel Gabriel "Angers" '; and of his new role as a heavenly greeter: 'When St Peter's done the honours, / He will pass you on to Johnners'.

Scattered pearls
Ursula Wyndham

An agony aunt is no use on a monthly magazine. By the time her sage advice is published, Nemesis has overtaken the enquirer. I have one last letter. It says: 'All the people I seem to get on with are older than me. I am 55 and the youngest in my art class and folk dancing sessions. I get on with young people well enough, but their culture seems quite foreign to me.'

Yes, indeed. My contemporary friends are either dead or into Alzheimer's. Luckily the young are most kind and friendly. If their culture seems foreign that is a very sufficient reason for learning more about it. As in every other aspect of life there are no certainties. I was told heterosexual males wear earrings in their left ear; homosexuals in their right.

I waited ages to meet a right-eared ring carrier. Finally I came upon two at once. I told them how glad I was to meet them and why. One replied equably: 'I don't think my wife and his girlfriend would be pleased to hear that.'

So Esther Rantzen is now competing with Oprah Winfrey. Excellent news; since these shows give an interesting insight into people's motivation. Esther's producer should realise that half an hour is just long enough to get interested, but at least a quarter of an hour longer is needed to assimilate the answers. People uncertain where they stand in connection with others should watch these shows to connect with public points of view.

With Oprah the mind does tend to boggle at what couples, who loathe each other, will confess to an audience of millions. It is on the sad side to realise that it is the millions of dollars that Oprah's gang are paying them that makes the ordeal entirely worthwhile. Watching their thick, boorish features one wonders how on earth they could have been drawn to one another in the first place. But that is the Eternal Unanswerable Question.

I wish the psychiatrists who both

Esther and Oprah get in to explain these items of human misery did not, a little too often, look somewhat complacent: as if it could not happen to them. I cannot avoid wishing that it could. They remind me of a psychotherapist of my acquaintance asking me to agree that seeing one's reflection, on horseback, in shop windows gave one a pleasing feeling of riding high (in every sense of the term) above the rest of the populace.

> ## 'Will agoraphobics gather on Thursdays at the ***** Hall.' How, I asked in wonderment, did they get there?

Luckily for her this observation struck me dumb. The lady was known locally as a figure of fun on horseback, both for her awkward seat and hands and the peculiar clothes she thought suitable for the occasion. A too-long coat with matching breeches of a light cloth more suited for use as a dust sheet. Of what use to explain that I rode because I enjoyed the sense of collaboration between myself and the horse. I was reminded of this difference of perception when reading a notice pinned to a wall at Guy's Hospital: 'Will agoraphobics gather on Thursdays at the ***** Hall.' How, I asked in wonderment, did they get there? Nobody knew, while admitting it was a pertinent question.

As one who never feels completely at ease in an aeroplane after it has left the ground, I am further chastened on entering the departure lounge by the sight of my fellow travellers. All, including myself, are obviously totally expendable and might with advantage to others sink into some ocean. The *Titanic* is remembered because she was supposed to be unsinkable, not because any brilliant mind ceased to function in the wreckage.

In the late summer of 1944, the Vienna Opera was closed for the duration. The D-Day landings and the July plot to assassinate Hitler had effectively brought Germany to a state of total war. Festivals were cancelled, theatres closed, concerts severely restricted.

And yet singers, players, repetiteurs, and stage-hands remained under contract to the opera. Those, that is, who hadn't been dispatched to the front. During the winter of 1944-45 rehearsals went on with that almost quixotic dedication to the art which is the mark of musical communities all over the world, in good times and in bad. In any case, with light and heat in increasingly short supply, the opera was a congenial meeting-place. It was also a pretty good air-raid shelter.

By March 1945, Vienna was being bombed by day. At 10 o'clock on the morning of the 12th of March, an orchestral rehearsal was about to start for a revival of Flotow's opera *Martha* – a defiant attempt to get the opera back into production. But it was no good. The sirens went. The company retreated to the depths of the opera house and there was apparently much amused discussion about how they might use the opera's props cupboard to defend the house against military attack. The Valkyrie helmets weren't much use, they were made out of best quality straw. But what the cupboard did have was a set of 50 muzzle-loading rifles left over from the war against Prussia in 1866. 'Complete with bayonets,' added one optimist.

After an hour, the radio reported that the Allied bombers had left the city. So the company returned to the theatre. But the radio was ill informed. Within minutes the Opera House had taken a direct hit – a mixture of high-explosive and incendiary bombs. St Stephen's Cathedral was also ablaze.

Sena Jurinac was just beneath the stage when the bombs hit. Had she been a few feet further forward, the blast that flung a huge steel safety door up into the auditorium would almost certainly have killed her. But as she ruefully admitted to me the other day when I met her in the sweet old, sleepy Bavarian town of Augsburg, there were so many wonderful young singers in Vienna in 1945, her loss

Schönbrunn Palace, Vienna

Vienna's dedication to art

by *Richard Osborne*

would hardly have been noticed!

Nowadays people look back on the Vienna Opera's postwar years as a golden age. On the ground, it was anything but. In April 1945, the Russians arrived and effectively turned bombed-out Vienna into a police state. But they also wanted entertaining, which is how Mozart's *The Marriage of Figaro* came to be performed in Vienna's one semi-functioning theatre, the Volksoper, on the 1st of May, 1945. For all their spirit and optimism, the Viennese thought it was a crazy idea.

'Impossible,' said the Director of the Opera. At which point the presiding Russian general took out a gun, pointed it at Herr Salmhofer and said: 'Possible. Is.'

In some ways the performance was a disaster. In the interval a good deal of elegant gilt, rococo furniture disappeared from the stage; furniture that later turned up in the apartments of various Russian officers. But the Viennese were not to be outwitted. The next work they put on was *La bohème*. They had worked out that there was less to steal from a stage-set involving a students' garret.

Out on the streets, things were still

pretty grim. Even with the war well over, life for the stars of the Opera remained a hand-to-mouth existence. Jurinac remembers the 'tea' her mother used to brew. First, cadge some sugar. Heat till brown. Add water. Tea.

Jurinac's mother was Viennese, but had married a Croatian doctor. When Jurinac landed a job at the Vienna Opera in June 1944, there was endless trouble over documents and papers. To this day, Jurinac doesn't know the identity of the man – a mysterious figure from Berlin – who provided her with papers of employment. What she does know is that in 1945 she was detained by the British on suspicion of being a Nazi spy. It seems they'd seen a reference to her name among the papers of our friend from Berlin.

The worst the British did to her, though, was keep her standing in front of a large desk while a languid interrogating officer finished perusing the *Times*. By contrast, the Russians were altogether more sinister. In 1945 they instituted a purge of foreign residents in Vienna. Jurinac herself had Austrian papers, but her Viennese mother was still classed as a Croatian. They were arrested, herded into a room, and prepared for deportation. Until – in a scene more frightening than anything in Graham Greene's *The Third Man* – Jurinac saw a technician from the opera house in the street below. After several dangerous and abortive attempts to attract his attention, she finally got a message to the Opera. With minutes to spare, she and her mother were reclaimed by the Opera House authorities.

What is so terrible about the story is that, of all the hundreds of people deported on that particular train, not one was ever heard of again.

Happily, Jurinac and her mother were spared, and Jurinac herself was able to come to London in 1947 to take part in the wonderful season of performances the Vienna company gave at Covent Garden.

I asked her what memories she had of that visit. 'Fish and chips in Floral Street! Lots and lots of fish and chips! '

She was also a pretty good Cherubino.

I t's Tuesday night at the Prince of Wales, and in the corner by the fire, at their usual table, sit Dave Stent and his friends Ian, Rob and Keith. The pub's other habitués mill around in search of spare stools and someone to buy them a drink. Regulars greet the bar staff like old friends, in mostly doomed attempts to get served before their turn. The landlady shuffles upstairs to find this week's questions. Tonight is quiz night. £1 per person, no more than six to a team. First price £23, second prize £12. Beer tokens for the winners of the bonus round. The Red Army are here; the Chiropodists From Hell are just arriving; the Brontë Sisters (all men) are late, and may have to stand.

Although it's just seven days since the last quiz at the Prince of Wales, there is genuine excitement in the air. There are at least 30 people in this room who know that Mn is the chemical symbol for manganese, and they all want everybody else to know they know.

At Dave Stent's table, a studious silence reigns. The Flywheels take their quizzing seriously. Keith reads a newspaper, hoping to memorise stray bits of information that could come in useful later on. Rob is staring into the middle-distance, absent-mindedly fiddling with a Biro which, although he hasn't noticed yet, is leaking all over his hands. Ian and Dave are, one assumes, deep in fitful conversation. One of the two has clearly said something in the recent past, and the other is presumably preparing a suitably detailed response, but neither is saying anything at the moment. Perhaps it's the five most capped England footballers (the first four are easy, but everyone forgets Bryan Robson), or the five countries whose vehicle registration letters are A, B, C, D and E. Is it Cuba or Canada? Dave never can quite remember.

It is a companionable silence. None of the Flywheels is entirely comfortable in conversation, unless that conversation is about facts. In fact, although they have only met recently, the four have much in common. Dave and Ian both read chemical engineering at red-brick universities. Keith and Dave both live at home with their mothers, Rob and Keith both steal leaky Biros from their work places, and keep them in their top

Robert Geary

Other People

The Flywheels

by *Marcus Berkmann*

pockets. Ian and Rob share unarticulated and deeply buried yearnings for Patrick Swayze.

And they all love quizzes. They are good at them, too. Keith was once on *Fifteen-To-One*, and got as far as the final three, before he was asked in which year the Duke of Edinburgh was born. Most weeks they win the Prince of Wales quiz, although their weakness on literature habitually lets them down. Poetry is a particular problem, which may be why the landlady has a couple of stinkers about Wordsworth and Keats up her sleeve tonight.

Ian goes to the loo. Rob buys another round of drinks: half of lager, half of lager top, Coke, lime and lemonade. The quiz is to start in five minutes. Dave Stent, as team captain, prints the words 'The Flywheels' in careful, methodical script at the top of each answer sheet. Keith thinks he has spotted someone with a mobile phone, and warns his team mates to keep an eye on him. Unscrupulous teams often ring friends for answers. The Flywheels

stare disapprovingly at the potential miscreant.

The first question is read out, and the four friends lean conspiratorially over their answer sheet, mouthing the answers so no rival teams can hear. Finland. Vernissage. 1967. Coracle. Not a difficult one tonight.

At the end of the first round, Ian goes to the loo. Keith buys a round: half of lager, half of lager top, Coke, lime and lemonade. They hand the answer sheet in and sit back, beaming proudly. No one else notices. Last week they took part in a quiz tournament in Letchworth, and came eighth. There, everyone looked at bit like the Flywheels: thick glasses, suits that don't quite fit, polyester ties, Biros, Biros and more Biros. The winning team included two ex-*Mastermind* champions. The Flywheels had underestimated the competition. Next year they will be prepared.

At the end of the second round, the Flywheels are four points ahead. Ian goes to the loo. He washes his hands thoroughly for the fourth time that evening. A short queue forms behind him at the wash basin. It's Dave Stent's round. He buys nothing for himself, having nursed his most recent lager and lime for the best part of an hour. Since he lost his job, this is the only night he can afford to go out.

They don't win the bonus round this week (special subject: the 19th-century novel), but they win the quiz proper by nine points and collect their winnings. The jackpot is down this week. Teams tire of losing all the time, and some have defected to the rival quiz at The Wrestlers down the road. The landlady eyes the Flywheels with suspicion. They come in here once a week, nurse their drinks, win the quiz, and make a small but consistent profit on the evening. This is not what a quiz is for, especially if it is beginning to deter other teams.

Dave Stent and his friends Ian, Rob and Keith suspect none of this discontent. They are in their mid-twenties; they find adult life a wild and terrifying mystery; they are sexually inexperienced, and resigned to staying that way. But they all love quizzes, and they are good at them. It's something, when there's not really anything else.

The world according to
Enfield Senior
Sniping at satellite dishes and nobbling balloons

If I were a magistrate, which I am not, and if any small boys over whom I had jurisdiction (though it seems that nobody has much jurisdiction over small boys any more) – if, as I was saying, any such boys were brought before me for the offence of catapulting television satellite dishes (or whatever you call those big ugly things with which people deface the outside of their houses) then (to bring this sentence to a conclusion) I should take a serious view of the matter.

I should not accept their pleas, however heartfelt, that they were performing a public service by simultaneously doing Rupert Murdoch in the eye and reducing the flow of pornography from outer space. Seductive though this argument might be, it would cut no ice with me, as vandalism in all its forms must be resisted. I should admonish these boys in the strongest terms, with phrases

All vandalism must be resisted

such as 'This is unacceptable behaviour' or even 'This is out of order'. Persistent offenders I should punish most severely, in a way to gladden the heart of the Home Secretary, by confiscating their catapults for long periods, such as 24 hours, or in extreme cases 48.

It is fortunate that a proper catapult, such as would wreak havoc in the hands of William and the Outlaws, is a difficult thing to come by. Toy shops may offer a pathetic thing made of plastic if they have anything at all, and luckily it is not generally known that a good stainless-steel catapult with a powerful elastic and a proper leather pouch can often be obtained from the better class of gun-shop. Should this information leak out, a serious outbreak of satellite-dish-potting might result, which is why I thought it best to

warn *Oldie* readers not to mention the matter in the hearing of any small boys of their acquaintance.

But I am not an unfeeling man. I can quite understand the temptation these lads would be under, as certain things always appear to me in the guise of targets – notably hot air balloons and big ugly buildings of the sort built by a man called Rogers. We get quite a lot of hot air balloons coming within range of our garden, sometimes just one or two, sometimes whole galaxies of 20 or more when they have a rally. The sight of them takes me back to my National Service days and in my imagination I am in a Centurion tank calculating the range for the machine gun to send a burst of tracer bullets though the air bag. I mean no harm to the balloonists, I just want the pleasure of seeing them sink softly to the ground.

Similarly if I see a Rogers-type building in the distance, I imagine myself lobbing high-explosive shells from the Centurion's 20-pounder gun through the windows of each storey in succession. But these pleasures are to be indulged only in imagination, and I dare not allow myself to possess any weapon capable of bringing down a balloon, let alone a building, which is why it is so important to keep catapults out of the hands of small boys.

Edward Enfield died in 2018, aged 89

DOWN ON THE ALLOTMENT
FIONA PITT-KETHLEY

Late summer is one of my favourite times on the allotment. There's always something to bring home for the pot. I disliked tomatoes as a child and only became fond of them once I grew my own. Some allotmenteers eat tomatoes all day while they tend their plots. Personally I prefer to take mine home and slice them into wholemeal sandwiches, smothered in black pepper. Damaged ones, together with courgettes, form the basis for allotment ratatouille.

This year I grew St Pierre and Harbinger from seed. Like Marmande, which I grew last year, the St Pierre tend to reroot themselves if a stem rests against the ground for a day or two. It tends to make for untidy plants, but the fruit is a good traditional French variety with more taste than the bland Moneymaker that you find in every garden centre. Harbinger crops early and St Pierre late, so I should have a good supply.

Courgettes seem to do well on all plots, but he-of-the-Old-Testament beard has excelled himself. He built up a massive heap of earth and compost, so high that it looks like a small cottage. If it had a chimney I'd suspect that poteen was being manufactured inside. But no, this heap, nicely squared off, is crowned with courgette plants. He just stretches up and picks a supply as they ripen. They get all the sun, seven feet or so above the rest of the soil. They had huge orange flowers while the rest of us were only thinking about putting our plants out. Maybe I'll try his trick next year if I find the energy or earth.

My potatoes are coming in thick and fast. As ever, I failed to get the plants in early enough for new potatoes in June – perhaps next year. A large proportion of my current crop seem to be Desirée, principally because they were potatoes I bought that ran to seed. The local WI has a sale every Friday morning at the bottom of the road. The WI does a lot of Desirée (sounds like one of their members). The rest of my crop sprang from supermarket Maris Piper or the delightful pink fir apples – my favourite salad potato – I grew last year.

An End to Getting Frustrated with your Smartphone

Finally discover how to get it to do what you want, easily (and find out what else you can do with it, too)

At last, using your smartphone can be easy, simple and stress-free.

Find out how...

Modern mobile phones - smartphones as they're called - can do so much more than just make phone calls.

From browsing the web wherever you are, checking train times, acting as a sat nav... And best of all they can make it so easy to keep in touch with family and friends – in so many ways, from sharing photos to making video calls.

*Suitable for iPhones, Android smartphones and Doros.
(Not sure what phone you have?
Best send off for the free info pack)*

But using them isn't always as easy as you'd want – and that's putting it mildly!

Do the manufacturers do it on purpose?

Sometimes it can seem like the manufacturers deliberately make them complicated - and how you do things is often hidden away. It might be easy once you know, but until you've been shown the easy way, it can drive you mad.

In fact only yesterday I was talking to someone whose Mum had got a new all-singing-all-dancing phone – but she couldn't work out how to answer a phone call on it! She's not daft - it's just that it's different from what she'd used before and the phone didn't come with a manual telling her what to do.

Whether you have similar problems or you're trying to do something slightly more advanced, the thing is, it can be easy to use them... once you know how. But until you've been shown, it can be like talking a different language.

That's why I've published two new books: *iPhones one Step at a Time* and *Android Smartphones One Step at a Time*.

Plain English... and that's not all

They explain how to use the phone, in plain simple language with pictures of the screen showing you exactly where to tap or slide your fingers. No jargon!

What's covered?

I can't list it all here. But amongst other things, you'll discover:

- The basics of controlling it - swiping, tapping, opening apps & so on.
- How to use it as a sat-nav... in the car or even on foot.
- Send emails from your phone.
- Most phones have a good camera so you can take photos: here's how to use it properly (and for videos).
- Share photos with friends around the world - quickly and easily.
- See updates, photos and video clips from friends and family - as soon as they "post" them.
- Instant messaging & how to use it.
- Make it easier to read the screen.
- Video phone calls - a great way to keep up with family who live a long way away
- Browse the web at home or out and about.
- Choosing and downloading apps.
- And obviously, you can make phone calls and send and receive text messages. ("Voicemail" is covered, too)

All explained nice and simply. (Find out more in the free information pack - read on...

What one reader had to say:

"Thanks for a fantastic smart phone book. Very pleasant staff as usual.

I think this book should be sold with every smart phone. I have learnt so much from it, the info you get with the phone is non-existent.

Smart phones are quite complex, and your books speak in plain English."

Only half the story

That's only half the story but I don't have room to explain here. I've put together full information on the books - who they're for, what they cover and so on.

What's more the books also come with a free gift - no room to explain that here either.

Don't buy now, do this instead

The books aren't available in the shops or on Amazon. Instead, send off now to get a completely free, no-obligation information pack. It'll explain what the books cover, who they're suitable for and so on – showing you just how it could help you.

Just call 01229 777606 and talk to Emma or Jade. Email your name and postal address to OL0019@helpfulbooks.co.uk or post the coupon to The Helpful Book Company, 13B Devonshire Road Estate, Millom, Cumbria LA18 4JS today to get your full Smartphone infopack - we'll put it in the post to you straight away (and we'll keep your details private).

Even if you don't know what type of smartphone you have, the information pack will show you how to tell.

Best order your Smartphone infopack now and soon you could be getting so much more from your phone – with much less hassle.

Batman and butler: George Clooney and Michael Gough

I was Batman's batman

Michael Gough recalls his time in service for the Caped Crusader

I am a very old actor. One of the more memorable moments in my career was a scene in a film where I said to a massive ape, who happened to be carrying me at the time in his hairy fist, 'Put me down, Konga.' Many years ater, Tim Burton happened to be watching a Tony Award ceremony in New York on TV when I won a prize for a performance in *Bedroom Farce*. 'Put me down, Konga' appeared in a bubble over my head as I made my grovelling acceptance speech. As Tim was casting the first *Batman* film at the time, he offered me the role of Alfred the butler. 'Why me?' I asked him. 'Because you made me believe the impossible,' he replied.

By way of preparation for the role, I spent a day with Mr Radcliffe, the butler at Hatfield House, where part of the first film was made. He was kind and helpful. Then my son found a book, *A Practical Guide to the Routine of Domestic Servants by a Member of the Aristocracy*. There is a chapter on The Butler's Duties, and another on The Duties of a Single Handed Manservant and Page Boy. This is even more relevant because Wayne Manor, home of Batman, only employed me – not even a page-boy. I quote from it: 'The class who keep this order of servant possess fairly good incomes yet keep but little company, prefer to keep one manservant only, in or out of livery. A single-handed man servant is not a liveried servant, although he is allowed two suits of clothes a year, or extra wages to find his own clothes.'

Alfred is never liveried and, although the duties of the single- handed manservant are indeed relevant to his task, it tells but half the tale. For not only does Alfred 'have to rise early so that before his breakfast he may have completed the rougher work of the day,

such as getting in coals and wood, cleaning the knives and boots etc. His duty is to valet the gentleman, brush his clothes, put them out for dressing, lay the breakfast, get dressed to carry in the breakfast; to wash and replace the breakfast things in the pantry cupboard, to lay the luncheon, to wait at luncheon, to clear away luncheon, wash the glass and silver used, attend the sitting room fires; be in readiness to answer the drawing bell – and so on all through the remaining hours of the day, through tea and dinner and see the doors and the windows are properly secured.'

For Alfred this is mere bagatelle. (In all my years of butlering at Wayne Manor I have never caught sight of a footman, a cook or a page-boy.) So not only does he perform all these duties he is also chauffeur – only the Rolls-Royce (never the Batmobile) – handyman, nanny, keeper of the Batcave and Batsuits, and computer operator for the most complex of projects.

For further research I, of course, bought many of the *Batman* comics,

indeed became addicted, but the true history of Alfred Pennyworth I gleaned from Jonathan Ross who knows it all and was very helpful.

Both Tim Burton and Joel Schumacher who have shared the direction of the four *Batman* films were patient and supportive and let me get on with it, and both were kind enough to agree that the fewer words I had to utter the better. Occasionally I would refuse to follow the script when such phrases as 'My pleasure. Sir' or 'You're welcome, Sir' were asked for. 'No! No!,' I cried and stamped my foot. 'Alfred would never say that!' However, Joel's butler Andrew argued that perhaps as Alfred is living and working in a foreign country he should conform to the native customs. Perhaps he was right; he had been a butler at Buckingham Palace.

Alfred has worked under three Batmen, and all very different. Surprisingly, my performance is virtually unaffected, indeed unalterable come what may. Alfred Pennyworth has cared for Bruce Wayne since he was a child, therefore, over the years, he has been nanny and teacher, and guru and servant, and he has laid down the rules. Our relationship is, if you can believe it, curiously medieval.

Just as Batman's adventures could be almost chivalric, so the butler/squire has his place and is proud of it.

The stock question I am always asked is 'Who is the best Batman?'. Michael Keaton and I had a good working relationship and Val Kilmer and Alfred got along fine. But George Clooney is my friend.

Alicia Silverstone, who plays Batgirl, was very endearing and her trailer was always crammed with dogs she had rescued from the dog pound. Chris O'Donnell (Robin) is a really nice regular guy, and as he, George and myself are all sort of Irish, that may be why we got along so well. Peter MacGregor Scott, the producer, is a Celt, so that helped, and Joel I found adorable.

All in all, spending 18 months in California during the last five years has been wonderful fun and I am grateful that at the age of 80 I am not only alive, just, but also earning some dosh.

Michael Gough died in 2011.

God

by *Alice Thomas Ellis*

When the Red Guard of the Church, in the wake of Vatican II. had more or less completed the work of destruction begun in the Reformation, I wondered whether they might now ask themselves a few questions. After all, their stated aim had been to 'let air' into the Church, encouraging, presumably, new adherents who might previously have been frightened off. Since the result of their endeavours has been an unprecedented drop in Mass attendance, a near terminal decline in vocations, the closure of religious foundations and schools, and widespread despair among the faithful, one might have expected some soul-searching, or, since the concept of soul is also in doubt in certain circles, at least a little perplexed head-scratching. Surely this could not have been what they intended?

But who knows? Theologians, bishops, elderly nuns, busybody laymen, the army of religious termites seem smugly content with the damage they have wrought. And it is the modernisers and the liberals from whom we have the most to fear. The liberal stands smirking in the midst of ruin, insisting that all is well. Guilt belongs to the past. While the technically blameless fly around apologising for matters over which they had no control, since the events occurred in a different time and climate and were perpetrated by others, no one in the present will accept responsibility for anything.

Holiness is in disrepute. Sanctity is personal and therefore, by definition, elitist and exclusive. We are all only human and for anyone to aim high in anything but worldly terms is demeaning to the rest. Simply admit to being only human and you can do more or less as you like without censure, but do not aspire to be more than usually good. This is regarded as unhealthy. Poverty, chastity and obedience, for example, are particularly abhorrent, both to the leaders of fashion, secular and religious, and to the herd.

Beauty is out of style and distortion is in vogue. Once the churches might have been expected to withstand the trend but now they are entranced by innovation. The C of E is still busily hacking away at its own foundations although it has already more or less demolished itself and the heretical element in the RC Church is not far behind. Instead of doing what they are supposed to do, which is to lead and inspire, the church authorities scuttle to the rear of the crowd, adopt the latest poodle cut and cravenly follow the trend. You'd think the least we could expect would be an 'oops, sorry', but we'll never hear it. Not until the present is in the past and only then if the devil hasn't got us all. I would apologise for this Jeremiah-like stance but the personal *mea culpa* is so un-chic at present that I cannot bring myself to do so.

SPORT
FRANK KEATING

A happy golden rule was never to bother with so much as a glance at soccer's league tables till the clocks went back. Scarcely possible now – triumphs and disasters, goal-less draws and calamities screech at you for attention by the day, by the hour.

October used to be a reflective month. Change of seasons: a mellow summing-up of summer, a keen anticipation of the muddy slog ahead. Like the man in the pulpit said, 'To every thing there is a season, and a time to every purpose under the Heaven.' Not any more there ain't.

Since his team went out of the World Cup on penalties – so lamely, so wastefully – England's soccer coach, the moppish mystic Glen Hoddle, has not only seen his ghosted memoir run into two or three editions in a clatter of recriminations, but he has already begun his sequel. In the European championships, England have lost to Sweden and imminently take on Bulgaria and Luxembourg. Further disasters or calamities then and the tabloids will begin tossing their turnips and other assorted fruit 'n' rotten veg. There is no love lost between old Fleet Street and modern maharishi Mr Hod.

Not that the cricket season had anywhere near finished by the time another of soccer's monosyllabic messiahs had his job taken by a ring-a-ding ringleted PR officer for Ego United. Poor Kenny Dalglish muttered some inaudible words of protest as the toy-boy Ruud Gullit promised Newcastle a season of 'sexy' soccer in return for a couple of million nice ones. Whether there is an ounce of substance in all the Dutchman's glitter and gloss, we shall know once the mud comes and the clocks go back.

There was, however, a ton of gold-bar substance under the gloss and glitter of the utterly glorious performance by the Sri Lankan cricketers in the solitary Test match that England granted them at The Oval. When was there ever such a resplendent riposte to haughtiness?

I was at Sri Lanka's happy inaugural Test, in Colombo in 1982, along with no end of freebying bigwigs from Lord's. In his speech at the celebration banquet, only half-remembering that the country had changed its name from old colonial Ceylon, the England captain Keith Fletcher at least five times referred to his hosts as coming from Sri-Lon. Since when, hard as Sri Lanka tried over the 16 years, the mandarins at Lord's have allowed them only three one-off Test matches in England.

Well, ol' boy, explained the marketing men, who's going to pay to watch them? In the event, the match was a sell-out for all five days. Sri Lanka win the toss at Kennington and every pundit smirks when they smilingly put England in to bat. England score 445, to all intents an unbeatable first innings total; it takes them 158 overs. Sri Lanka go in, and in two overs less – and WOW – they score nine runs fewer than 600. Then they bowl England out for a pallid 181 – and merrily knock off the 36 needed in a blaze of fours and sixes. Game, set and match.

The summer of 1998 might have seemed at the time to have been overwhelmed by soccer, soccer, soccer. But during it was celebrated the 150th anniversary of WG Grace, as well as the 90th birthday of Sir Donald Bradman, a figure of such transcending pre-eminence in his sport that he remains unmatchable in any other ever invented.

But 1998, Great Grandad? Were you actually at The Oval? Did you really see Sanath Jayasuriya bat, and Muttiah Muralitharan bowl? Now that was mysticism all right? It sure was, kid.

Ingratiating smiles soon turned to sneering frowns when *Angela Huth* asked a jeweller if he'd like to invest in some jewellery

Ring cycle

Recently I decided to sell a very large and beautiful aquamarine ring, set in rubies and diamonds. It belonged to my mother who felt that, for her, its heyday was over. On her behalf I approached Bond Street with some confidence.

The ring had been given to my mother in the Sixties; it had cost a few hundred pounds. The jewellers it came from had extolled its beauty and worth, and only recently valued it for insurance purposes at £4,000. It seemed sensible, therefore, to start with them. In the past they had regarded the ring so highly, it was unlikely they would spurn it now. Indeed, I thought, they would be grateful for the chance to recapture it.

So my first stop was this jeweller in the Burlington Arcade, where my mother had made several purchases over the years. They remembered her with a smile. But as soon as they understood I was here to sell, not buy, the smile turned to a perturbed frown.

The ring was examined. Tut tut. Much shaking of the head. The fact is, said the jeweller, aquamarines don't sell anymore. No, they aren't the sort of stones people want any more at all. Why, they could put an aquamarine in the window and it would be there for weeks, unlooked at, unwanted, he added, with an air of immeasurable superiority. As for its worth – well, £ 1,000 would be good: £1,200 would be a miracle. What? In 40 years the ring had scarcely doubled in value? 'That's how it is, sorry to disappoint,' said the jeweller. He offered to keep it for a while, to see if anyone with an unlikely penchant for unsellable aquamarines might fancy it. I declined the offer. By now I felt defensive; I had no wish for the ring to suffer any further snub.

All the same, off I went to a palatial showroom in Regent Street where I was offered a chair in a thick hush rising from thick carpet. In my new coat and London hat I felt I didn't give the impression of someone flogging stolen goods, but there was no denying the same rictus smile as

adopted by the first jeweller. When I mentioned I had something to sell, 'Not for us' was all I got. Tantalisingly, there was no explanation as to why it was not for them. I supposed it was something to do with the strange new abhorrence of aquamarines.

Inspiration, then. The ring, my mother had been told, originally came from Tiffany's. Perhaps, then, Tiffany's...

No such luck. Only the very slightest arch of an eyebrow when I explained its New York ancestry – sceptical, perhaps? I was afforded the glimmer of a sympathetic smile, but my invitation to acquire was firmly declined. Perhaps I'd like to try... across the road?

I re-crossed Bond Street feeling a sudden chill in my mission. Still, the first shop actually said 'Jewellery Purchased' outside: hopes rose. There I met the first friendly jeweller in three hours. He had the decency to suggest the ring could do with a quick brush in washing-up liquid, and came back with it sparkling. Not sparkling enough, though, to appeal to his buying instincts. He offered to put it in the window, just in case that almost extinct creature, an aquamarine lover, passed by; £1,200, he said, would be a handsome price for it.

Angela Huth, with her daughter Eugenie, left, in the film of *Landgirls*, adapted from her book

At the next shop, also a firm of jewellery purchasers, the salesman couldn't quite put his finger on it, but the ring wasn't for him, 'Lovely though it is. It's a buyer's market,' he said, showing me the door. 'Never regard jewellery as an investment. Not even diamonds.' As for my 'lovely ring', I should consider £1,200, from 'somewhere', a bonus.

In the last shop I was prepared to try – another long-established place of old standards – I found a loquacious man who (there being no buyers in the shop) was kind enough to explain why I was having such a lack of response.

'It's not that it's an aquamarine as such, he said. 'It's the size. We do sell aquamarines, but it's the small aquamarines we sell. This is a showpiece. Only a – how can I put it – a special person would be attracted to it. And, yes, £1,200 to £1,500 is a fair price, I'd say. Very poor return for the investment 40 years ago, but jewellery is a commodity, should never be thought of as an investment. I'm sorry.'

At least he agreed with his neighbour on that. But how strange, I thought, pocketing the rejected ring for the last time, that whenever I had dallied with buying a minor piece of jewellery I had been assured by the seller that it was the one thing that was absolutely bound to increase in value.

I had not experienced so humiliating an afternoon since I took a bundle of scarcely worn fine clothes to a second-hand shop near Oxford, and the snooty woman asked me how on earth I expected them to sell such lapels this year. 'We know what our customers like.'

So, it seems, do Bond Street jewellers; how naive I was to have thought they might have shown some respect for my mother's ring. I have no intention of subjecting myself again to the sellers who have quite a different approach when you suggest they might like to be buyers, and write this only to warn others bent on selling the family jewels that they might be in for a disappointing experience. In the meantime, the snubbed but sparkling ring remains for sale, should a lover of aquamarines be interested.

Berkshire flora

Unwrecked England by *Candida Lycett Green*

In Farnborough Village church there is a beautiful stained-glass window by John Piper in memory of his great friend, and my father, John Betjeman. To see it on a summer evening with the lowering sun shining through makes your spirits soar. In richest blues and greens, it is set with butterflies and flowers as the downs around once were. It is hard to find any unwrecked patches of wild flowers now. The agri-farming chemicals have drifted everywhere.

From the south door into the churchyard the view from this, the highest village in Berkshire, 720 feet up into the downs, falls away across undulating country in one breathtaking sweep to the blue distance of Watership Down above Highclere on the edge of Hampshire. I head out towards it. The hedges have long gone along the lane which leads down from Farnborough to the small farmhouse called California. There are prairie-like acres of cereals stretching away on either side. You notice every change of hedgerow and verge vegetation if you are walking, bicycling or, lazy like me, travelling in a horse-drawn cart. Here along the verge only the toughest weeds survive the sprays and seem to thrive on the fertiliser. The hogweed grows as tall as apple trees above the head-high legions of nettles, and the tough old docks rocket up between. Sometimes there may be a patch of the wonderfully dull mugwort. The monotony, if you are travelling all day, is relentless. Perhaps the answer is to learn about the dock (*Rumex*) family – there are 20-odd kinds, after all. I could be differentiating between Sharp Dock, Red-veined, Fiddle, Curled or Broad-leaved.

Further on, past Brightwalton Church with its stained-glass window above the font by Ford Maddox Brown (which John Piper particularly loved), past the Wesleyan chapel converted into a home and the thatched cottage with imitation butterflies settled on its walls, past Oakash Farm, suddenly an island of well-husbanded shooting country begins.

The hogweed grows as tall as apple trees above the head-high legions of nettles

Towards Leckhampstead thicket hedges edge the road and shield you from the wind. Where there are gaps, new hedges have been planted and there are small woods on the sides of mild valleys, and here in the lee of a roadside spinney is a bank of the wild flowers which used to be everywhere: bladder campion, lady's bed-straw, knapweed, agrimony, rock roses, bird's-foot trefoil, lady's-slipper, scabious and St John's wort.

Then as suddenly as the vision of flowers appeared it ends and the sprayed wilderness begins again after Nodmoor Corner. Near Court Oak Farm and the tunnel under the thundering M4 the verges are mown to earth revealing hundreds of old foil crisp packets tossed out of car windows months ago. There are lush gardens in brick-and-thatched Boxford and Hoe Benham and willowy meadows beside the Rennet on a beautiful little lane to Marsh Benham. Here the river, canal and railway run beside each other in the valley bottom and the long hill up passes the grandest gate piers in England leading to a long-lost great house at Hampstead Marshall. On the lane leading towards Holtwood there is normal-sized hogweed on the banks and cranesbill, rosebay willow herb, pearlwort, hedgewoundwort, woody nightshade and purple vetch and honeysuckle in the nut-filled hedges, and high oak trees and briony and white dog rose.

Beyond Burghclere, where the Primitive Methodist chapel is for sale, a sweet disorder begins again below the lines of Downs. Nettle-leaved bellflower spills out of coppiced woodland, and just before Ecchinswell there is a bank thick with pyramid orchids and dotted with the strange primeval-looking broomrape. Like John Piper's window, the sight of it is enough to make the spirits soar.

'Don't call me, text me, email me, visit my blog, join me on Facebook or follow me on Twitter!'

'Well, at least we've got you talking'

'Have you forgotten, Thompson, this is hair-shirt Thursday'

'It never fails to stop him crying – handing him the phone'

'Must do Munch'

Holy Moses – it's deep-vein thrombosis

Dr Stuttaford's Surgery

A 68-year-old reader from Wiltshire and his wife are hoping to visit their family in Victoria, British Columbia. The flight to that part of Canada takes nine and a half hours, rather longer if they land at Edmonton en route. They are very anxious to see their new grandchild, but the reader tells me that he has recently had surgery for cancer of the colon – is it safe for him to make a long-haul flight?

Our reader's question is a very important one. He has obviously read about the risk of deep-vein thrombosis in air travellers, a risk which became greater after the distance between the rows in the economy seats was reduced from 34 to 31 inches. The reader doesn't tell us how tall he is but unless he is well below the average height he is going to find that he is very cramped.

A particular hazard for long-distance air travellers is developing a pulmonary embolism following a deep-vein thrombosis in the leg or pelvis. A thrombus – a clot – forms in the vein; sometimes part of the clot breaks off and is carried to the lungs, where it can block the pulmonary artery. This prevents the lung tissue from receiving its essential blood supply. As a result, starved of oxygen and nutrients, it dies in the same way as heart muscle after a coronary thrombosis. If enough of the lung is destroyed the patient may perish – pulmonary emboli account for 18 per cent of sudden deaths on aircraft. The effect of a deep-vein thrombosis is usually not so sudden. More often it doesn't give rise to a pulmonary embolism until days, occasionally even a couple of weeks, after the flight. Fortunately, although deep-vein thromboses are comparatively common – the Health Aviation Institute estimates 30,000 a year – only a small minority develop a pulmonary embolism as a result and few of these are fatal.

Our reader has an increased risk of suffering a deep-vein thrombosis because he is over 50, the flight is more than five hours, and he has recently had cancer. The risk would be further increased if he landed at Edmonton, as it is greater in flights of over 12 hours. All cancers

increase the tendency for patients to suffer thrombotic phenomena, whether in their legs, cerebral vessels, coronary arteries or lungs.

The good news is that there is nothing which would cheer our reader up more after his recent surgery than meeting his new grandchild – who, incidentally, is named after him. Although he should go and meet his namesake he should take reasonable precautions. He should have a good night's sleep the night before – no last-minute packing. He, and his wife, should take low-dose aspirin. Nu-seal aspirin (75mgs) is a very convenient way of taking aspirin in the strength needed to prevent thromboses. He should avoid very fatty food before he flies, and he must take plenty of fluids: it is important not be dehydrated.

Once in the air it would be all right to accept the first complimentary airline whisky, but perhaps it would be as well to avoid the second, and certainly the third. He should try for an aisle seat. He and his wife, while awake, should walk up and down the aisle at least once. It is also possible to exercise while sitting. If our reader did National Service he will remember how to repeatedly clench and relax the calf muscles in order to maintain circulation. He can regularly work his ankle joint by moving his foot up and down. In-flight magazines also advertise other exercises.

Millions fly every year; only 30,000 develop a deep-vein thrombosis. This reader, like all our other readers, should keep moving during a flight.

A reader from Islington has written to tell us about her older sister, and to ask

how she can avoid suffering a similar catastrophe. The sister, who is apparently a slightly built 53-year-old, fell in some recent heavy rain. Anxious to keep dry, she was rushing back from posting a letter when she slipped on the wet pavement. After the accident she suffered severe back pain, radiating to the arch of her right foot. X-rays showed an unstable fracture of one of the vertebrae. They also showed that her bones were osteoporotic – this presumably was the fundamental reason why her vertebra collapsed. Our reader's sister is not alone. As the result of osteoporosis there are 150,000 fractures a year in the UK, or one every three and half minutes; 45 per cent of all postmenopausal women have some evidence of osteoporosis and, sooner or later, one man in 12 will also develop fragile, thin bones. Fifty thousand, a third of these fractures from osteoporosis, are of vertebrae.

I have always been a great advocate of HRT for middle-aged women, and this remains the gold standard by which other treatments for osteoporosis are compared. I can, however, understand the reluctance of women in whom there is a family history of breast cancer to take HRT. I have, for a year or two, been recommending Evista, raloxifene, for these women.

Evista is an interesting preparation classified as a SERM – selective oestrogen receptor modulator. These preparations have a different side-effect profile to HRT. They have the good effects of oestrogen on the skeleton, the heart and the central nervous system, but unlike oestrogen-rich HRT they have no effect on the lining of the womb and, some trials have shown, actually reduce the likelihood of developing cancer of the breast.

Unfortunately a few women develop cramp and hot flushes with Evista. This is, perhaps, a small price to pay if it maintains bone strength without increasing the risk of breast trouble. A huge study recently published shows that the number of fractures in women known to have osteoporosis was halved if they took Evista.

Thomas Stuttaford died in 2018, aged 87

Barry Cryer's
PIN-UPS

1. J B Priestley
The writer's writer – I got to know him and my idol survived the ordeal. Surface Yorkshire grit concealing a raging romantic.

2. Billy Connolly
The heavyweight champion – the thinking woman's naughty boy. Deadly charm as the boot goes in.

3. Humphrey Lyttelton
Grace and style under pressure. Don't look up 'gentleman' in the dictionary, it's spelled 'Lyttelton' (is that all right, Humph?).

4. Marti Caine
One of the most funniest and sexiest women I ever knew. Her incredible sense of humour triumphed over her final days. I miss her terribly.

5. Thora Hird
The North's answer to Edith Evans. Funny, indomitable, a superb actress, and after a hilariously bawdy phone conversation I fancy her rotten.

6. Mo Mowlam
It's all been said and it's true. A politician who actually speaks her mind. The novelty is breathtaking. Another woman shouldn't follow Betty Boothroyd as speaker? Why not?

'Bloody call centres'

Eggheads at the Shed End

I was a Chelsea supporter, admits *John Moynihan*

Hardly a trace remains of the old, cumbersome Stamford Bridge ground which once housed those great unpredictables of soccer, Chelsea Football Club. The somewhat shambolic stadium off the Fulham Road, SW6, which I remember with great affection from schoolboy days in bomb-ravaged, postwar London, has been swallowed up by all-seater stands and the posh hotels, penthouses, restaurants and shops which make up the glitzy façade of Chelsea Village.

In one small but poignant space near the Village entrance are two blue plaques on a slice of ancient concrete wall which once separated Chelsea's renowned Shed End from the more bohemian world of Chelsea studios. It was here that the fans climbed the steps to watch their beautiful 'game'.

Ken Bates, Chelsea's often abrasive, success-orientated chairman, was in a more cuddlesome mood when he proudly showed me the plaques after a fish-and-chip lunch at one of his favourite Village restaurants. He pointed to one, which was inscribed 'CHELSEA FOOTBALL CLUB – THE SHED END – THIS IS THE ORIGINAL SITE OF THE SHED TERRACE'. 'We could have knocked the wall down – it would have cost £400,000,' Bates said, as boys charged past to invade the club's megastore. 'But it's part of Chelsea's history, isn't it, John? You must have stood up there yourself.'

'Yes,' I replied, sounding like Captain Charles Ryder in *Brideshead Revisited*. 'I was there, many times.'

Bates couldn't wait to show me round the new Stamford Bridge, at the start of what he thought would be a prosperous new season. His mood would change in a matter of weeks when, after a poor start, Bates fired his popular Italian manager Gianluca Vialli amid massed protest – the eighth manager he had sacked since he bought the club for £1 in 1982. But that acrimonious melodrama was to come as we walked through rows and rows of blue seats. Inevitably, my thoughts turned back to the years when there was magic to be had on the Shed terracing.

Reactions from the Shed End as Chelsea miss an open goal against West Ham in 1961: in the foreground (from the left), John Moynihan, an unimpressed James Michie, and Karl Miller (arms aloft)

One rainy evening in September 1946, I paid one shilling to enter Stamford Bridge through the Boys' Entrance to watch one of Chelsea's first home games in the first postwar Football League season. Chelsea took a battering from Manchester United that night, but I was hooked by the display of Chelsea and England's high-springing centre forward, Tommy Lawton. He may have refused to sign my autograph book after the game, but we became firm friends much later on.

The Shed terrace looked pretty unsociable at that austere time. The asymmetrical overhanging roof had not been built for the convenience of Chelsea supporters in 1932, but by the fellow hosts at Stamford Bridge, the Greyhound Racing Association. It was meant to protect bookies and punters from the weather on Saturday race nights, which continued until the 1967 season. Chelsea fans viewed the roof with disdain because it was hardly weatherproof, with large slabs of open terracing surrounding it. But somehow it had survived constant bombing during the Blitz, and if you were lucky to find a space its shelter could be welcome.

What, I wonder, was the attraction of standing behind the south goal in those days of terrible winters and rampant chilblains, watching two teams of Brylcreemed professionals kicking a large leather football about? It was obviously worth putting up with, because the crowds were enormous and the atmosphere was electric during the build-up to kick-off. On one memorable afternoon, a crowd of over 70,000 filled Stamford Bridge in the expectation of seeing some epic dribbling from Stanley Matthews. It was a scary occasion for schoolboys like myself, pressed against barriers and almost panting for breath until we were picked up bodily and hauled down to the greyhound track for safety. Stanley didn't let us down – but Chelsea claimed a draw, bless them.

One favourite companion during the Old Shed days was a garrulous character called Shortie, who used to bring a soapbox along so he could watch matches. This dwarf had a caustic wit: 'I always f***ing know that if I can't see the game, I won't be missing anything, the way Chelsea play.'

There were many boisterous characters like Shortie on the Shed terraces: ex-servicemen, National Servicemen, peanut-munching gas men – 'I'm going to put my head in a gas oven if the Blues lose' – bus conductors, café owners. Players were lucky not to be barracked at some stage of the season if their performances weren't up to scratch – even the high and mighty like Lawton.

The 1950s and 1960s saw the Shed throng become far more cosmopolitan, with a scattering of intellectuals suddenly hooked on the game. Much of it had to do with my father Rodrigo and mother Elinor running a salon up the Fulham Road, where artists and writers would meet for lunch before Chelsea games. The Irish publican, Sean Treacy, ran two fashionable ale houses along the Fulham Road, Finch's and the Queen's Elm, and many of his customers downed pints before being lured away by their juniors.

Artists often paraded at the Shed End – John Minton, Rodrigo, Carel Weight, Peter Blake, Elisabeth Frink and Michael Andrews. A duffel-coated David Sylvester was a resident art critic, driven sometimes to bleak despair by Chelsea's displays – so much so that one day he told us he was becoming a Spurs fan. He had a fervent new White Hart Lane companion in the philosopher Freddie Ayer. Laurie Lee and an often unimpressed James Michie represented the poets; a truculent Jeff Bernard, Karl Miller and Alan Ross, when he wasn't in the press box, the writers. Then there was the world of showbiz, led by such talented actors as the Old Vic's Tony White. Sometimes the old guard found it hard to fathom.

There was a lot to celebrate in 1955 when Chelsea won their first and only First Division championship. At a society wedding in the morning, I had to leap into a taxi outside St Margaret's, Westminster, and speed towards the Bridge. Chelsea won 3-0. And there were loud cheers for the manager, Ted Drake, captain Roy Bentley and the players.

After Chelsea won the FA Cup in 1970 and the European Cup Winners' Cup in 1971, the club went into a financial decline, until its rescue by Bates in April 1982. By then the sporting Shed End was a place to avoid, controlled by Chelsea's lunatic hooligan fringe. The owners of Chelsea Studios complained of violence and vandalism. In a moment of inspiration, the new chairman suggested electrifying the terrace fencing.

Chelsea have remained in the news, even if the Shed is mere history. I don't know what Shortie would have made of the Vialli affair, but he would certainly have kept his head down.

Goon to Hollywood

Clive Donner worked with Peter Sellers on *What's New Pussycat?* Then came the last of the *Pink Panther* films – and the end of an extraordinary life

Silence in the recording room. A green light flashes twice. From the loudspeaker come the familiar tones of Winston Churchill broadcasting to the nation. The rhetoric rolls around the room. When the speech is finished there is a moment's pause, then a voice says, 'Excellent. No one would know it wasn't the boy himself.' A curly-haired, plump, 35-year-old man turns away from the microphone. 'Are you sure, mate?' he asks. 'I'd be happy to do it again.' He is reassured that it's perfect. 'Oh, good. In that case, mate, do any of you know if there's a film being made in the studio with a part I'd be right for?'

The Goon Show, with Spike Milligan and Harry Secombe, had given Peter Sellers a taste of success – once a week they were stars on the radio – yet although Sellers came from a music-hall family, moving around the country with his mother and father, nobody for a moment considered him as a film actor. He was in great demand for recording film voices – and in the case of Churchill he actually impersonated the great man for a film during the war – but nobody thought of him as having any serious film potential. Boy, were they wrong. But there was a flaw beneath the affable clown, a deep vein of unresolved unhappiness.

David Niven said of him: 'He joined us among the stars and was one of us, but he looked down and got giddy.' He gradually picked up small parts, and by the end of the 1960s he was famous throughout the world. In 1964 he was working with Billy Wilder on *Kiss Me Stupid*. In the middle of shooting he had a series of life-threatening heart attacks. Production was stopped; Peter was replaced and returned to England to recuperate for six months. I had known him since his voice-recording days and from *The Goon Show*. I was working in Paris with the Hollywood producer Charles K Feldman and badly

Herbert Lom and Peter Sellers in *The Revenge of the Pink Panther*, 1978

needed a strong comedy actor to play against Peter O'Toole in Woody Allen's first film, *What's New Pussycat?* Feldman was delighted when I suggested the possibility of getting Sellers, and I flew to London to coax Peter into taking the part of a sex-mad psychoanalyst. He was still recovering from the heart attacks, but he liked the script and wanted to get back to work. 'Why do you want me to play this part?' he asked. 'Because you can play it better than anyone else in the world,' I said. He accepted the offer, which goes to show that in show business nothing succeeds like excessive praise.

Before we started shooting Sellers came to see me. 'What about this O'Toole, then? I mean, I'm a comedian, and he's a serious classical actor.'

'Don't worry, he's a pro,' I told him.

Soon afterwards O'Toole asked: 'This man Sellers, can he really act?'

'Don't worry, he's a pro.'

I kept my fingers crossed, and they really hit it off. They respected each other and shared the skills that are needed for comedy.

Sellers was obsessed with cars, and tended to fall in love with his female stars. He believed that Sophia Loren would marry him after they finished filming *The Millionairess*. After a riotous night out, he and Liza Minelli announced to the ever-present paparazzi that they were to be married, but that didn't survive the light of day either.

Peter did some of his best work with Stanley Kubrick, whose working methods were quite unlike Hollywood. Days could

be spent working out a scene, without any pressure of time, and might then be totally revised: this didn't suit all Kubrick's actors, but was perfect for Sellers. His invention of the German scientist whose damaged arm kept involuntarily giving the Hitler salute was a perfect example of creativity working within a flexible schedule.

Many years later, United Artists called me. Blake Edwards, who had directed Sellers in all the *Pink Panther* films, decided he had had enough of working with him; they had had some great successes together, but had come to the point where Peter's unpredictability, changes of mind, dissatisfaction with his own work, continual retakes and heated arguments with Blake had become too much. But United Artists wanted one more film. *The Romance of the Pink Panther*. Would I be prepared to direct what was intended to be the last of the *Pink Panther* films?

I thought hard. Peter had made some wonderful films over the years and become very rich, but his deeply superstitious, moody side and his phobias had become more pronounced – he wouldn't work on a set with green in it, for example, and he was very influenced by clairvoyants. Was he mad, I sometimes wondered. But we had remained friends: in spite of Charley Feldman, whom he called 'the Prince of Darkness', our previous film together had been amicable and successful.

Peter had just finished *Being There*, directed by Hal Ashby. Production had gone smoothly and he arranged for me to

see a private screening. It was a brilliant and serious film in which Peter played an idiot savant whose gnomic utterances were seized upon by a world eager for certainties. He played it in a quiet, low key, yet still brought out the ironic humour; there were no slapstick jokes, and the word from the set during production was reassuring. So in spite of Blake Edwards's gloomy messages, I decided to go ahead.

Although Peter had recovered from his attacks in the Sixties, he still needed to take care of his heart, but a frenetic lifestyle, drugs and sex had made him very vulnerable. Against his doctor's advice, he had had more plastic surgery for his part in *Being There*. Visiting him at his house in Gstaad, I could see tiny pin tucks underneath his chin where he'd had surgery to make his face smooth and enigmatic for the role of the Gardener. He had always taken great care with costumes, make-up, voices and visual props, so a facelift or two was par for the course.

Shirley MacLaine, who starred with him, was much involved with spiritualism, reincarnation and New Age mysticism, and they worked well together. He was, I decided, an oddball, but a gifted one. We dined, we were 'mates'. We received a phone call from United Artists in New York; they'd read the script and liked it, and a production executive would start on the preparation straight away. Ideas flowed, and we went through the script revising and fine-tuning it until we were satisfied. I was flying back to London the next day, and Peter gave me a lift in his private plane.

As we were making our separate ways from the airport into London, Peter passed me in his limo and gave me the traditional royal charming wave. We'd overcome some serious difficulties with the script and made some important casting decisions. Peter was to have lunch the next day with Spike Milligan and Harry Secombe before going on to Los Angeles. I left the day before he did. Everything seemed set fair.

I was met at Los Angeles airport with the news that Peter had had a final heart attack and died while in the air. People have asked me if he was trying to die. I don't think so, but he certainly pushed himself very hard: he was only 54 when he died.

Still with us

John McEwen visits the photographer and painter Humphrey Spender

Humphrey Spender will be 93 on 19th April, so it was a surprise to find him waiting for me by his car at the station. He looks far from frail – he has the same boyishness that his late brother, the poet Stephen Spender, retained into old age – but it was cold and the train was late. 'It's usually late but you can't rely on it,' he said, with a chuckle on the infectious verge of a giggle.

His country retreat was an even bigger surprise. Designed by Richard Rogers in 1968, it is a rare example in England of hard-line Modernism: a glass and steel cube framed by canary-yellow I-beams. Nearby was its smaller skylit companion, which doubles as a studio and garage. 'The only problem is, he forgot about insulation, so it heats the whole of Essex,' Spender told me. As a result, the heating comes in various improvised and added forms: 'It looks hi-tech but it's actually extremely low-tech.' It is easy to see why he likes it. The uninterrupted glass walls place the garden at your feet and bring the birds at the feeder so close they might be in your hand – a perfect house for an artist. 'Richard [his son] thought that being a painter I'd want the same for the studio, but I said I'd never get any work done.' Yet, if he is a painter today, it is for his photographs that he is famed.

Why Humphrey Spender is not in *Who's Who* goodness knows, because in the world of British photography he is a legend. Best-known are the pictures he took for Mass Observation, the idealistic sociological survey of the working class in Bolton in the late 1930s. But he was also a pioneer contributor to *Picture Post* and an official war photographer; he was a tutor from 1953 to 1975 in the influential textile department of the Royal College of Art (Zandra Rhodes was the hardest-working pupil), and has always painted.

He still works in his studio daily from 10 until 7, and was completing a

Humphrey Spender and his paintings *Greek Café* **(top right) and** *Stem 1*

forthcoming exhibition when we met.

His photographs could not make a starker contrast with his gentle and fanciful paintings. In photography, Spender's intention, learned from his scientific eldest brother Michael, was to be as detached and factual as possible, whereas in his current paintings people do not appear and fantasy is allowed full rein. Views of Mykonos – the absence of life accentuating the modernist accent on form – vie for attention with surrealistic collages and formal inventions. 'People complain that I don't have an identifiable style, so they can say, "That's a Humphrey Spender." I once did a lot of paintings based on the sea-wall in the Maldon area and they were a success and always sold, but I stopped. I didn't want to become formulaic.'

He has a fund of stories, mostly funny and against himself; but his life has had more than its share of sadness. Both his

parents were dead by the time he, the youngest of four, was 16; his first wife, Margaret, died of cancer in her youth, and Pauline, his second wife, is now in a nursing home. Michael and his best friend were killed during the Second World War.

Spender's father, a Liberal man of letters, was notably altruistic and, with Arnold Toynbee, a founder of the Boys Club movement. It is to him that Spender attributes the social conscience that guided his photography and made him a 'semi-communist' in his youth, though never a card-carrying member like his brother Stephen.

He could not find an architectural job when he graduated from the Architectural Association, so in 1934 he opened a photographic studio with a friend. Michael had 'taught him the basic chemistry', and he knew the latest European developments. His starkly modernist style was in deliberate opposition to Cecil Beaton's fashionable rococo opulence.

He did all kinds of work and soon came to the notice of the *Daily Mirror*, whose editor asked him to launch a series of special photo features under the name of 'Lensman'. The art editor's demand for sexual fantasies, 'including Windmill Theatre stuff, where, incidentally, none of the girls was completely naked', soon dashed his altruistic socialist hopes, better served by an assignment for *Left Review* to cover the Jarrow hunger marchers. It was then that the 'charismatic devil' Tom Harrisson rang him, reduced him to 'a jelly of hysterical laughter', and persuaded him to work (unpaid) for Mass Observation. 'Everybody said, "You're absolutely daft doing it for nothing," but in fact it proved one of the best investments I ever made, because much later I sold all the negatives to Bolton Museum for a large sum.' Spender's Mass Observation negatives were not printed until historians caught

up with them in the 1970s, since when images like *Wash on the Lines* and *Catapult Kids* have become classics.

Bolton made him 'more depressed than appalled. We lived at 85 Davenport Street, which was falling to bits. There were generally about four other disciples of Tom Harrisson staying there. They all smoked like chimneys. The food was absolutely dreadful and the place caught fire from time to time.' The object was to catch people unawares and this snooping aspect was always an embarrassment. One Labour MP fulminated in the *News Chronicle*: 'If I catch anyone mass-observing me, there's going to be trouble.'

Mass Observation was a short-lived experiment but led to his being offered a job with the new photojournalist magazine *Picture Post*, then about to be launched. This was well paid and, if less purely altruistic than Mass Observation, a great deal more principled and inventive than the *Mirror*. Nonetheless it confirmed his opinion that press photography is endemically falsifying – even his own decision to show poverty 'to the exclusion of the success side of the story', introducing, he now admits, a questionable bias.

War followed and, after basic training in tanks, he served as an official war photographer, but every time he took an interesting and therefore indiscreet picture – such as an exhausted George VI having a cup of tea, or the dead and wounded (including a general) in a VIP enclosure after a weapons demonstration went wrong on Salisbury Plain – he had the dispiriting experience of a top brass chap, usually covered in medals and scrambled egg, confiscating the offending film. His most rewarding war work was interpreting photo-reconnaissance pictures. 'I think the only good thing I've done in my life was to prevent the Americans bombing a POW camp,' he says – making light of his identifying VI rocket sites or helping construct the

Spender's most rewarding war work was interpreting photo-reconnaissance pictures

maps for the D-Day invasion armies as a member of Theatre Intelligence Service, which had requisitioned the corset department of Peter Robinson's in Oxford Circus.

After the war he continued to work for *Picture Post*, which once resulted in his being arrested with the irascible Geoffrey Grigson in Warminster on a suspicious publican's assumption that they were Burgess and Maclean – a reward for the spies' arrest having been offered by the *Daily Express*. The farce was compounded by the fact that they were actually compiling a feature on 'High Summer in Ageless Wiltshire'. A jammed gear meant that they crept all the way to the police station in reverse, and, on their release, they were promptly rearrested for driving through Warminster backwards. 'Oh no, not you two again,' groaned the duty sergeant when they were dragged before him.

We ended the interview in the skylit studio, where the blind walls force him to focus on the painting or collage in the making. I asked him the secret of an evidently enjoyable old age. 'Love,' he said, and then after a slight pause, 'combined with work. I am cared for by a companion younger than me by 55 years. The nice thing about being old is that you can allow enjoyment to interrupt work.' By the look of things, such interruptions have always been welcome.

Humphrey Spender died in 2005

Living the good life

I don't recall Felicity Kendal having to put up with bossy chickens or psychotic geese, says *Paula Youens* – and she certainly didn't have to dismember her own pig

In the Seventies I lived in an old half-timbered, moated farmhouse with vast draughty rooms, rattling sash windows and brick-tiled floors. There were spiders in the bedrooms, mice in the hall and rats in the coal-shed. In the dismal downstairs loo, slugs held parties behind the cistern and developed a taste for pink Andrex.

The village called us the 'commune' but we were just a group of twenty-somethings, too poor to buy and too gregarious to fester in damp Cambridge bedsits. Pond Farm was rented from two eccentric sisters, one of whom was married to Dr Griffith Pugh, a medic on the Norgay/Hillary Everest ascent.

Soon we got permission to keep animals. The chickens came first. Then the ducks, which wouldn't lay and were too cute to kill. The geese didn't either and were too damn scary to attempt capture, let alone killing. George, the gigantic gander, bit the postman's backside and the milkman refused to come past the farm gate.

Someone came home one day with that iconic Seventies' bible. *The Self Sufficiency Handbook*, by John Seymour. It had nice drawings of animals and bearded men plodding about in wellies and hand-knits. We thumbed through the chapters. Food for free? We'd tried shaggy inkcap mushrooms, long and pale as a dead man's unmentionable, floating in black liquid. Hedgerow jam, chewy with hawthorn and elderberries and tasting of wet cardboard. Nettle soup, a green gloopy sludge. Homemade wine and beer? The place was full of bottles of my elderflower champagne and demi-johns of bubbling dandelion wine. Upstairs, the airing cupboard reeked of booze, where marrow rum oozed sweet brown syrup into a jug. Goats? We had one of those too.

But what about the chapter on pigs? Meat was what we needed. A phone call was made to a neighbouring pig farmer and a deal was done. He delivered a young 'weaner' to one of the brick outhouses, slipped the wad of notes into his overalls, climbed back in the pick-up and drove off laughing. We stared at Piglet over the wooden door, who stared back with gimlet eyes. Neighbours came. Kids came. Soon every nosy bugger in the village was leaning over the door, giving advice. 'Don't get too fond,' they all said, 'you won't want to kill it.'

Piglet blossomed and grew and seemed happy enough, shucking the earth back and forth in the new pen. It even went for walks. Using a rope harness, like a giant pair of kiddies' reins, we set off across the fields. But pigs are sociable creatures and ours was getting lonely. One afternoon a lady came dashing up the drive shouting, 'Your pig! It's escaped!' I charged downstairs to see it galloping across the village green. Strung behind was a line of squealing kids. If you want to look stupid, try chasing a pig in skirt and Wellington boots. Each time I got close, it took off with a flounce. Twice round the green we went, with the pig screaming blue murder and all the kids cheering. I

Paula and Piglet go for a walk

grabbed both ears and clung on. We spun to a halt and the audience clapped. On the pig's ears the imprint of my hands remained, red and glowing, for hours.

Pig was confined to barracks and after more escapes, acquired a new name. When the day came for Colditz to go to the abattoir, none of us shed a tear. After the evil deed was done, I'd drawn the short straw to make the collection. At the big metal door I handed over the paperwork. What I got back was our pig... huge, white, cold, and neatly sawn in half, straight down the middle from tail to snout. It's an image that remains with me still. I carried the two carcass pieces back to the car, along with a gigantic plastic bag of innards.

That night we got out the Seymour book and set to.

I still don't believe what happened. But there are colour slides to prove it. The pine kitchen table covered with bones and flesh. Liz grinning, holding half a head. The glitter of a knife blade reflected in Simon's specs. Richard sharpening an axe. John attacking a rack of ribs. We chopped and sawed and measured and sliced. We juggled intestines and extricated kidneys. We cut chops and haunches and shoulders and joints we couldn't name. We even boiled the head and made brawn, though nobody touched the mottled pink mass that crouched in the fridge for weeks.

Usually you see pigs' livers in small, delicate slices. Ours was vast and slippery, the size and shape of a strange, dark continent. It smelt like one too. Of putrid jungle swamps and blackened pools of stagnant water. It yielded trays and trays of pâté. Knobbly bits of meat were ground up into sausage-meat. We drew the line at cooking the feet. Hours later, using just Seymour's diagrams on pig butchery, we'd finished.

These days I hardly eat meat. Especially pigs' trotters. I know what they walk around in all day.

We have the way: Do you have the will?

I have seen a little bit of ZANE's work on the ground and from what I have seen it is very, very impressive . . . ZANE is one of those lovely organisations that make a little bit of money go a long, long way. ZANE is a good cause and the money is properly and well spent.

John Simpson CBE
World Affairs Editor of the BBC

Please help ZANE with a gift in your will.

ZANE: Zimbabwe A National Emergency looks after 1,800 destitute pensioners, including over 600 war veterans and their widows. Without ZANE they would die a lonely death, hungry and without the most basic medical aid.

Making a will and keeping it up to date is one of the most important things you can do to protect the people you love and help the causes you care about. A gift in your will to ZANE will provide a lasting legacy for the most impoverished people in Zimbabwe.

ZANE: Zimbabwe A National Emergency

Z

Reg Charity No 1112949

ZANE does fantastic work looking after vulnerable people in Zimbabwe and showing servicemen and women that they are not forgotten. They are professional, passionate and scrupulous about how the money is spent.

HMA Melanie Robinson
UK Ambassador to Zimbabwe, Former Executive Director of the World Bank

To request a free copy of our wills guide, call 020 7060 6643 or email legacies@zaneinfo.com

www.zane.uk.com

The literary racket

It's not just sports journalists who feel uneasy with Dostoevsky, says *Miles Kington*

One of the moments I remember best from this year's Wimbledon came after an epic struggle in the men's singles between the Spaniard Gonzales and the Serb outsider Janko Tipsarevic. Gonzales was seeded and expected to win, and nearly did so, but Tipsarevic, a craggily handsome man with a corsair's beard, which gave him the look of someone from an old Rafael Sabatini book or film, had thrillingly wrested victory back in the last few games. Then Tipsarevic appeared to be interviewed.

Before Tipsarevic started answering questions the BBC interviewer confided something to us, the audience. 'I must tell you,' he said, in that tone of voice which means we are about to learn something quite unnecessary, 'that Tipsarevic is the king of tattoos here at Wimbledon and has a variety under his shirt that would make you gasp. For instance, Janko, I believe you have a tattoo on you that says "Beauty will save the world". What is that all about, then?'

'Well,' said the bearded (and pierced) Serb, 'it comes from one of my favourite books. I very much like the Russian writer Dostoevsky and one of the books I like most is called *The Idiot*. This is one of the things that the main character often says, and I think it is quite profound.'

That was the moment I remember.

It was the moment when the interviewer realised that he might be getting in too deep. That he didn't know what Tipsarevic was talking about. That he couldn't remember having read any Dostoevsky. That he should not, perhaps, have raised the subject of tattoos. That it was time to move on to tennis...

'Well,' said the interviewer, 'you've certainly raised the bar since Cantona. Still, moving on to tennis...'

I am not sure if Tipsarevic caught the reference to Eric Cantona, the French footballer who starred for Manchester United a decade or more ago. Occasionally Eric would stun the sports reporters by referring to French poets

they did not know about and even quoting lines of poetry he himself had written. On the whole, British sports writers do not always have an available mechanism with which to deal with art, literature and philosophy (why should they?), so they tended to back off from that side of old Cantona and treat him as some kind of holy loony. It came as a

> At that moment the interviewer realised that he might be getting in too deep. That he didn't know what the tennis player was talking about

great relief to all concerned when one day the player left a football match, climbed into the crowd and attempted to flatten a heckler with a kung fu kick, thus suggesting that all this poetry lark was just a cover-up for the real big hairy sports chap beneath.

At which point I have to own up. I make it sound as if, were I to be faced

with Tipsarevic's tattoo, I would be immediately ready for a Dostoevsky conversation. In fact, apart from remembering the names of some of his books, having a dim memory of his style and knowing that he was on about evil quite a lot, I do not think I would stand a chance of bluffing my way through. I have never read *The Idiot*, and I cannot remember now, so long after, which of his novels I did start and fail to finish.

I wonder how many of us well-read people this would also be true of? I have considered myself to be fairly well read over the years, but only because I have never been put to the test. Well, sometimes I have been put to the test and failed dramatically. I once agreed to go on a television literary quiz in which Stephen Fry and Phill Jupitus were also taking part. A great error. Fry had read all those books and could remember the details. Jupitus had not read the books, but he had lots of jokes to make up for this fact. I had neither, and came out afterwards thinking, I must never do that again. The nearest I have ever got to that since then is appearing on Radio 4's *The Write Stuff*, and although team captains John Walsh and Sebastian Faulks are more knowledgeable than I am, at least the gap was not so wide as between me and the empyrean heights occupied by Stephen Fry.

So I was very encouraged to read some words of wisdom in the *Independent* on 29th June this year, written by Tom Sutcliffe. He was reflecting on the lists you often see published with titles like '100 Films You Must See Before You Die' and how irrelevant they are to most of our lives. And then he said: 'To be well read may not be a matter of having read nearly everything; indeed, quite the contrary. It's more likely to be about reading well – and an endless burgeoning list of essential texts is actually hostile to that, given the great truth that this particular gimmick acknowledges, which is that we only have limited time.'

Amen to that. I might even have it tattooed on me somewhere.

'No more for him, he's driving!'

I first met Arthur Marshall at the house, in Chester Street, Belgravia, he shared with my theatrical agent, Philip Pearman, and his wife, Coral Browne, the profane and outspoken Australian actress. He was awaiting several crates of Christmas wine from Fortnum & Mason. 'You're a Trump!' Arthur exclaimed, as he confronted the Fortnum's delivery boy, who had arrived with a vanload of seasonal Christmas wines. 'You're an absolute Trump! You're a Trumpetta!'

I met him again when I was making a TV programme on ENSA, the wartime Forces Entertainment Units, popularly known to the troops as Every Night Something Awful, and its successor, CSE, known as Chaos Supersedes Ensa. I interviewed him about his experiences in the Circle Bar at Drury Lane Theatre, and he explained how he had entertained himself by imagining high-ranking officers as sporty mistresses at a smart public girls' school. 'There was Miss Gort, and Miss Allenby, and that spanking little gym mistress, Miss Montgomery.'

As a member of the Intelligence Corps, he was attached to the British Expeditionary Force during its retreat from Dunkirk. 'Just back from breezy Dunkirk, dear ...' he told those who had wondered at his absence from his usual West End and theatrical haunts.

According to Philip Pearman, however, who knew Arthur very well indeed, at some point in the proceedings, when the defeated and demoralised Expeditionary Force was desperately trying to dig themselves in on the beaches while the troop carriers remained patiently offshore and an armada of pleasure steamers and Sunday yachtsmen urged the defenceless soldiers to wade out towards them where they could ferry them on to the larger ships and away to England, a huge landmine exploded, showering sand and debris into the dark grey sky, and Arthur Marshall alone rose to his feet, a solitary figure in khaki with a captain's pips on his shoulder.

'That silly old Mrs Goering has missed again,' he said. 'Come on, boys! Follow me, and the first one into the bum-boats wins the Grace Darling medal!' And he strode out to sea towards the awaiting pleasure boats. As one man, it is said, the soldiers rose to their feet with a cry of 'Good old Arthur!' and followed him into the sea in impeccable order, patiently queueing to take their places in the little

Marshall the troops

The understated charm of Arthur Marshall bewildered Nazis and won him fans young and old, reminisces *Patrick Garland*

boats – a scene later to be immortalised on film and in the history books. When I asked Arthur about it – with some discretion, because I knew of his genuine modesty – he roared with laughter, and strenuously denied it.

Still stationed in London and devoting much time and energy to the demands of CO HQ, Arthur was engaged, early in 1943, to appear in the weekly BBC comedy *Take It From Here*. Frank Muir told me that the programme was stuck for somebody to fill in at a Sunday recording, so the producer suggested that Arthur, an old Cambridge friend, should do one of his comic monologues as Nurse Dugdale, a hearty and bossy nurse in a local hospital. I vividly recall an account of a girls' school bug-hunting expedition, and how the botany mistress led her party

Arthur Marshall, far right, with Frank Muir and Robert Robinson on *Call My Bluff*

with a cry of 'Steady girls, steady, killing botts ready.'

At the end of the war, Arthur found himself in Flensburg, the Baltic port where the German High Command had finally halted and were waiting to surrender. Arthur arrived with a delegation from Supreme Headquarters Allied Expeditionary Force; they had flown in from Frankfurt on a mission to discover the whereabouts of Reichsfuhrer Himmler, the head of the SS. Among the German officers assembled were General Alfried Jodl, Field Marshal Wilhelm Keitel, Field Marshal Albrecht Kesselring, and Hitler's successor, Reichs president Grand Admiral Karl Doenitz. All were immaculately turned out in full dress uniform greatcoats, peaked caps and ceremonial swords.

Arthur was part of a fairly scruffy delegation, which consisted of himself (a former schoolmaster from Oundle), an art teacher in a corduroy jacket and a couple of naval officers in weather-worn duffel coats. The Nazi commanders gazed at them with eyebrows lifted in astonishment and a considerable degree of distaste. Arthur said it was difficult to know quite how to address them. He thought of asking 'Anyone for ciggies?' or 'Is that sofa comfy?', but nothing seemed adequate under the circumstances. He remembered how, as these stalwarts of Nazidom were being politely interrogated, they exchanged looks of complete non-comprehension 'that an elite super-power like them, disciplined, impeccably uniformed, meticulous to the last detail, could possibly have been ignominiously defeated by an army so frivolous, scruffy, and down at heel, as us'.

Gently down the stream

Ben Mallalieu reminisces about the childhood idyll of growing up by the river near Hampton Court

One of my strongest memories of the time I lived near Hampton Court is of going to sleep, in my father's office on the second floor, listening to the sound of his typewriter and watching the sky slowly turn a deep shade of royal blue. From his desk in front of the window, he would have seen the whole length of the garden to the river. He would have also seen the heron that perched every evening on the cedar tree halfway down the garden, and its mate sitting on top of the weir.

To the right of the cedar was a small rose garden separating the two lawns, which were both cut in neat stripes. When asked at school what her father did for a living, my older sister, Ann, who was then about five, said: 'He cuts the grass and sometimes he writes articles.'

He cut the grass wearing an increasingly tattered Oxford University or Harlequins rugby shirt and, if it was hot, a straw boater. Once, instead of cutting straight lines, he cut Ann's name in the bottom lawn, but when she saw it, she ran back crying into the house.

On the far right-hand side, by the river, was a line of weeping willows, where people from the pleasure boats would stop to pee when they thought no one was looking, and where my mother once found a couple making love. Now there is a high, chain-link fence along the whole length of the garden bordering the river, which deters intruders but spoils the view.

To the left of the house were the garages, some greenhouses and, below them, a kitchen garden and, eventually, a

> From his desk, my father would have seen the heron that perched every evening on the cedar tree halfway down the garden

row of copper beeches leading to the river. The gardener once caught an eel in the river and put it in the water tub by the greenhouses. Later that morning, my mother went to dip a tray of bedding plants in the tub and got a nasty surprise.

I often dream about the house we lived in then. Sometimes, the river has broken its banks and the water is lapping against the steps of the veranda. Often, I am wandering about the house in the middle of the night, to the consternation of the current owners. Once, on a cloudless night by the river, I dreamt I met the gardener, who told who told me to go away as I didn't belong there any more.

In dreams, the house becomes a living, conscious entity, watching the proceedings almost with the expression of a chess player who has just made the winning move and is waiting to see how long it takes you to realise. The house is not a source of comfort. Perhaps it is a place where something terrible once happened or will one day happen?

It was, at the time I knew it, a very unlucky house. The previous owner had gone bankrupt, and it took my parents a year to get vacant possession, so that, when we moved in, the grass on the lawns was waist high. My father's political career and his personal life also both came badly unstuck during the time he lived there.

As well as being what the columnist Paul Johnson later called 'the last true amateur in the Parliamentary Labour Party' (I think that was meant as a compliment), my father wrote parliamentary sketches for *Tribune* and the *New Statesman*, and sporting essays for the *Spectator*, forms that he effectively invented or reinvented and are now found in every newspaper. But journalism, even the best, rarely lasts and now his work is almost entirely forgotten. Occasionally, I find old copies of *Lilliput* with articles of his, still as fresh as ever.

At Hampton Court, he was at the high tide of his creativity, when written words came easily (which was just as well, as he

> We lived well and there were plenty of parties. At night, I would often be woken by the sound of laughter drifting up from the dining room. In summer, socialists and literary figures played cricket on the bottom lawn

ILLUSTRATIONS OF THE AREA TODAY BY NICK BAKER

was probably not capable of sustained effort at anything other than manual work), but none of his work paid much and his debts multiplied as chaotically as the cats that overran the house and garden (at one time we had 24).

But we lived well and there were plenty of parties. At night, I would often be woken by the sound of laughter drifting up from the dining room two floors below. In summer, socialists and literary figures from Chelsea and Fitzrovia played cricket on the bottom lawn. Michael and Jill Foot came to dinner and stayed for six months.

Out of sight from the window in my father's study, there was a path that snaked its way through the shrubs and trees to the right of the top lawn. Halfway along the path was an air-raid shelter, where we kept chickens and where the gardener once caught a rat – it was caught alive in a 'humane' trap, a galvanised wire cage with a door that opened inwards but not out, posing a problem of how to dispose of the contents. The rat was enormous and not afraid of anyone, and it stared through the bars with a look of defiance. The largest of the tom cats was brought, but on seeing the rat, it walked slowly backwards, never taking its eyes off the cage until it was at a safe distance to turn and run. Then the gardener brought a tin bath and began to fill it with water, whereupon the rat lost its bravado and began to scream.

The weir on the opposite bank from our house looked like a flight of steps covered in deep green moss, and the water flowed over them so evenly that it looked like glass. Only at the bottom step, where the water reached the river, was there any sense of movement. To a child who couldn't swim, they were fascinating: it seemed impossible to walk down the steps without slipping to certain death in the deep water. More fodder for dreams, perhaps?

Pugin's progress

GAVIN STAMP

*God's Architect: Pugin and the
Building of Romantic Britain*

By Rosemary Hill

Allen Lane/Penguin

'I never worked so hard in my life for Mr Barry, for tomorrow I render all the designs for finishing his bell tower & it is beautiful & I am the whole machinery of the clock.' So ran one of the very last of the thousands of expressive and manic letters hastily scribbled by Augustus Welby Pugin. Written in February 1852, it referred to his design for that national landmark which contains the bell 'Big Ben', but while the architect of the Palace of Westminster, Charles Barry, got his knighthood, Pugin's crucial role in creating that most splendid of Gothic Revival buildings was suppressed. Seven months later he was dead. He was a mere 40 years old.

In his short life, Pugin transformed the built landscape of Britain. A Roman Catholic convert consumed by a personal vision of Medieval England, he argued that Gothic architecture alone was Christian and national, real and true. As well as writing influential books, he built cathedrals, monasteries, convents, schools and houses, and designed stained-glass, furniture, wallpaper and metalwork. An only child of doting parents and an infant prodigy, Pugin once described himself as 'a locomotive being'.

In this, the first full modern biography of this extraordinary, exasperating, brilliant and lovable man, Hill brings Pugin and his world to life. Part of the secret of his success was that he could get people to do just what he wanted, whether it be the Earl of Shrewsbury or workmen on a building site. He was entirely without snobbery. He was also often unkempt and dishevelled, and dressed like a sailor. He loved the sea and had his own boat (often used for the dubious activity of 'wrecking'). And then there was sex. Without female company, Pugin was bereft. He married three times, had seven (possibly eight) children and probably died of syphilis. A product of the Regency, he never really fitted into the more serious world that emerged in the 1840s.

Hill liberates Pugin from coteries who have jealously claimed him for themselves: not only the Roman Catholics but also the architects and architectural historians who insist on seeing him as a proto-modernist influenced by French rationalist theory – merely because his artist father was French. In fact, as Hill demonstrates, Pugin was an autodidact who read little and was astonishingly ignorant – he had never heard of the Reformation when he published his notorious cartoon attack on modern architecture in which he ridiculed the work of ageing Classicists like Sir John Soane.

The religious politics of the time are handled with aplomb. The irony was that the Roman Catholics – especially converts like Newman, who wanted to be more Roman than the Romans – eventually distanced themselves from Pugin's English Catholic vision, while lesser men scooped up the work. Several years before his death, his career seemed to be in decline – until his triumph as a designer in the Great Exhibition of 1851,

> ## Pugin was an autodidact who read little and was astonishingly ignorant

when Pugin alone was given a whole section to himself, called the Medieval Court.

The end was terrible. Hill gives a moving and tactful account of Pugin's collapse into madness and how his third wife had to battle with friends as well as doctors to get him out of the Bethlem Hospital and back home to Ramsgate – only to die the same night as the Duke of Wellington, who eclipsed Pugin's obituaries. Recompense is done this year with the publication of this magnificent biography and the opening of The Grange, Pugin's house at Ramsgate, superbly restored by the Landmark Trust.

Robert Geary

ILLUSTRATION BY BOB GEARY

Fired up by tango

After watching the professionals at work, *Maureen Lipman* braved an after-show tango class. Could she get her legs and feet to follow her heart?

The show was called 'Tango Fire', the company was 'Estampas Portanas', and once I'd negotiated the gridlock that is Holborn, given up banging on the door of the wrong theatre and finally found the right one, I was hot to trot. The Peacock Theatre is a tucked away treasure and tango audiences are like no other theatre crowd. They are the converts from fox-trot and flamenco, the secretaries who salsa round the water cooler in their lunch hour and the heavy set, brilliantined aficionados, possessively clutching their sloe-eyed consorts. They cheer and stamp and whoop out their approval and the whole atmosphere buzzes with shared mystique.

I was watching the show with Christine Denniston, the writer of *The Meaning of Tango – The Story of the Argentinian Dance* and a teacher of the dance on five continents. She has a neat black bob, a sensible rather than exotic manner and a degree from Cambridge in theoretical physics. After the show, she would give me and any other willing member of the audience a basic tango class in the upstairs bar.

The last tango class I'd attended had seen me walk out in a strop because the teacher treated me like a moron and the pupils treated him like King Herod. Perhaps I'm not good at relinquishing control. After all, when I learned

ballroom dancing in Hull, anyone over four-foot high was classed as a man, so I rapidly became a leader and, in fairness, I've found following a bit of a challenge ever since.

The show was hugely entertaining. The four-man band, 'Quatrotango', of piano, violin, double bass and bandoneón, created the throbbing, drifting sound required for the milonga of the first half. They had a quiet diffidence which lured us seamlessly into their salon. The tango singer, Javier di Ciriaco, was tall, dark and wearing a suit which seemed to be made from hand-reared moleskin – and he appeared to have a private affair going on with every female in the house. The dancers were frankly more *Strictly Come Tango* than the glory that was *Tango Argentina*, which is not to deny their skill and the dazzling mastery of the steps, but it was showbiz razzle dazzle rather than the choreography of the Golden Age of tango, which was inspired by the social mores of the time.

In *Tango Argentina*, which, ten years ago, revived the dance for a whole new generation, the hairs on my neck stood up as the well-past-their-middle-years dancers came on. Here, I had just a couple of moments where my heart leapt into my throat, and they concerned one particular pair of dancers whose hearts, suddenly, mysteriously, became one before our

eyes. The ending was pure Las Vegas and, rightly, had the crowd roaring on its feet.

Christine talks a lot about dancing with our hearts in the after-show class and in her book. It's not an easy concept to convey; indeed the backstory of tango is as impenetrable as an enigma code. Hearts have legs attached to them and feet which dangle from them – it's a wieldy metaphor – and the careful diagrams of footwork make understanding even harder.

The tango singer, tall and dark, appeared to have a private affair going on with every female in the house

I do love the fact that tango was originally a dance for two men, springing from the lonely émigré workers who came to find work in 1920s Argentina. Those who became the finest dancers got to court the finest women. I love too the seemingly rigid choreographic ritual which allows for extraordinary interpretive freedom. Most of all, I love the startling intimacy which the dance can engender, with a total stranger, in a few shocking moments. 'You can let go of tango,' says the programme note, 'but tango will never let go of you.' I'm edging tentatively back to class. It sure beats Pilates, but is my heart in it?

Genius crossword 224 by Antico

Clues are given according to alphabetical order of their answers, which should be entered jigsaw-fashion in the grid. (Clues to three-letter words are definitions only.) Clues to entries at 27, 41 and 8 are without definition parts. 27 and 41 are definitions of two unclued entries, and 8 is defined by an unclued entry; the unclued entries, which solvers should shade in, combine to form a person's name. Four words of a quotation by the person read clockwise round the perimeter; the quotation's fifth word is 27. Solution is on page 53.

CLUES

More skilful sailor on liner, not at home (5)
Commercials (3)
Old editor after silver (4)
Trouble insect endlessly raised in old car (6)
Moving on, say, occupied by new troubles (6)
Ace artist and son in field (4,3)
Song from star I admire (4)
Sheep's cry (3)
Gamble and answer letter (4)
Give up strange creed, not right (4)
Fish, bearing north, twist? (5)
Pleasing gig held wildly entertaining element (10)
Dreadful to confine last pair of inmates (6)
Moisture (3)
Catholic dignitary's title (3)
Insect, I wager, agitated (6)
Revise bad diet (4)
Moose (3)
Period of history (3)
Avoids end of joke with companion in stitches (7)
Watched part of parade yeomen brought about (4)
Payment (3)

Not as many sheep kept by father (5)
Golfer's name in note following blank page (7)
Loud and also upset (4)
A judge put in greeting for pilgrim (4)
One fine, singular love provided that's true (2,2)
Representation that is to receive publication (5)
Play nit wrongly, not suitably (7)
Anger not entirely about press (4)
Criminal trial, never unimportant (10)
All excited about inclination mostly concerning lips (6)
Messy mud on hill (5)
Dazed, heart broken by maiden (4)
Fibre, mass behind tree for all to see (5)
Individual catching copper at the right moment (2,3)
Whale in error caught (4)
Clear hesitation in extra clause (5)
Horse raced round ring (4)
Mass of eggs (3)
Stamp sale arranged (4)
My tale unravelled feebly (6)
Welsh river (3)
Reject oxygen after check (4)
Used to be (3)

WORLD'S WORST DUMPS

Marrakech

Heaving with vulgarians and complacent second-homers from Notting Hill, *Jeremy Wayne* has finally written off Morocco's 'Red City'

I first went to Marrakech in 1978 and rather liked it. In the mornings, before the sun grew too hot, I would visit the souk, searching out beautiful pots and painted chests that had not yet been seen in Blighty. In the afternoons, I would mooch around the gardens of La Mamounia, lanky and affectedly world-weary for one so young, listening to a song called *Golden Brown* on my new Sony Walkman. A lovely song, I thought, about a lovely sun-tanned girl; years later, when someone told me the song was about heroin, it lost its lustre and I threw the cassette away.

I continued visiting Marrakech through the '80s and '90s, trying to ignore the fact that Marrakech was in terminal decline. La Mamounia had a much-vaunted refit and added a casino, which attracted a lot of very vulgar French people – even more vulgar than the ones who had been going there previously. And, soon after, Thompsons started flying 'holidaymakers' in for something called 'Winter Sun', or even 'Winta Sun'.

Then came the palace restaurants, quite glamorous in their day, 'in their day' being the operative phrase, because now these médina (old city) restaurants have

become parodies of themselves. You pay £70 a head to eat six courses which all taste exactly the same and to hear a group of manky 'musicians' sitting on the floor playing Gnawa music which – to the Western ear – sounds like nasty cats fighting. The luxuriant Majorelle Garden, once an oasis of calm, has become a sort of theme park, chock-a-block with Birkenstock-wearing Austrians and sun-burnt English mums and dads trying valiantly to avoid baby-stroller gridlock.

The médina, which once felt vital and exotic, now feels like Westbourne Grove

In Djemma el Fna, Marrakech's famous central square, the snakes are now too indolent to be charmed out of their baskets by a few off-key notes on the flute. And the acrobats, who used to give the square a sort of macabre but oriental charm, have all left for better-paid jobs serving dirty martinis in the city's new five-star hotels.

But nothing has ripped the guts out of Marrakech quite as much as the riad-refurb movement. Once, these traditional Moroccan townhouses – built around a central courtyard – were the preserve of government ministers, middle-class merchants and a tiny handful of colourful ex-pats (usually disinherited). Now everyone has a riad – lawyers, accountants, hairdressers, your daily woman. Every second family in Notting Hill has a second home in Marrakech, and the médina, which once felt vital and exotic, now feels like Westbourne Grove, or Balham. Marrakech always teetered on the brink of dumphood, but its colours, its alleyways, its smells and its African exoticism redeemed, or at least excused it. Nowadays it's the worst dump of all – a dump with attitude.

On my last – and I do mean last – visit, a punkish, pink-haired German woman cosied up to me in the bar of La Mamounia, the city's last, safe-ish haven. 'Are you coming here often?' she enquired. 'Madam', I replied, 'I have been coming to this bar once or twice a year for the last 30 years, but now that I have met you I shall never, ever, set foot in here again.'

Marrakech – your time is up.

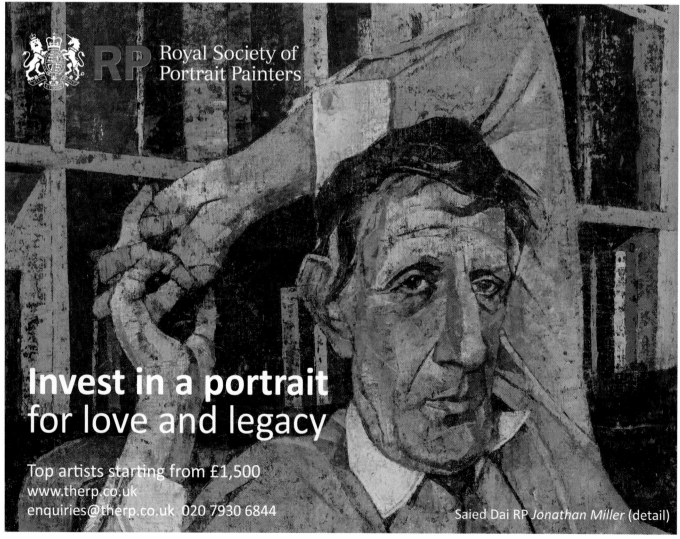

Confessions of an infant firebug

As a tot, *Geoff Waterhouse* was an enchanting little chap.
He was also a pipe-smoking pyromaniac

This, sadly, is a true story. It concerns an event that has lived with me for 60 years. I was six and, like many children, I was fascinated by matches. I can recall pinching them and sneaking off behind the garage to burn bits of paper. My first attempts at smoking were also around this time. I used a pipe made from a hollow hemlock stem, blocked at one end with clay and pierced with a length of straw. My pipe was filled with my own version of Ogden's Nut Flake in the form of tea leaves – and lit of course with a stolen match. In some ways I was a clever little fellow but this experiment left me feeling so sick it was a lesson learnt very early. Not so my fascination with fire. My small bonfires began to escalate with a search for more combustible materials.

Way back then, children in rural areas had a fairly free rein: paedophilia was not yet a household word, the war was just over and people had worried long enough. Across the field from my home was Mr Parry's farm, our playground. We would jump from the barn beams into mountains of hay and wander through the cowsheds to watch the milking. Farmer Parry would dump all his obsolete milk delivery wagons and tractors in a compound and we would spend hours clambering over them – an adventure park without a single plastic padded bar or pit of sterile coloured plastic balls.

It was on this farm that my incendiary interest reached its climax. Mr Parry had another barn for straw bales, an open affair with supports made from telegraph poles and a curved, galvanised tin roof. The outer bales would protect the inner ones and the tin roof would keep out the rain. No protection from three six-year-old boys with a box of matches though – the only guard was a cock turkey that would charge at children with its tail feathers fanned, emitting its high-pitched gobbling squawk. The turkey was off-duty so we clambered our way up the mountain of bales to the top. There we lit our fire.

Our little pile of straw was soon ablaze but the fire quickly spread and we couldn't put it out. We were soon left with only one alternative – to bale out. Three frightened little souls tumbled and scampered down their straw mountain and made their escape.

We ran through the farmyard and off down the lane, covering a good mile in a time that would have beaten a similarly aged Roger Bannister. I heard the clang of the fire-engine bell as it raced to the farm. I made it home, but alas, not home and dry. I entered the kitchen and my mother took one look at the sorry, black-faced figure before her.

'What have you been up to?' she asked. Mother was a teacher and even at that age I knew that 'nothing' would not be an adequate response.

'I've been drawing a moustache with a burnt cork,' I offered.

At six, I was already an arsonist – and now a liar. Pretty adept at one but less convincing at the other. She looked across the field and saw a huge plume of smoke filling the sky and emanating from the farm. She walked past me to the phone. I'd been rumbled.

Later that afternoon she took me over to the farm and I stood trembling and tearful before Mr Parry, several police officers and the firemen. It was like a re-enactment of the painting *When Did You Last See Your Father?* Farmer Parry looked down at me and in a quiet but stern voice he explained the consequence of my flirtation with flame: 'All the straw to feed the animals this winter has been burnt. They will have nothing to eat.'

His simple words and the manner in which he uttered them left quite an impression on me. The enormity of my folly had been well and truly explained. No shouting, not even a smack from my mother. I had destroyed not only the barn but the animals' food: that awful realisation was punishment enough.

We kids continued to play for years on Mr Parry's farm and never once did he caution the little chap who had caused him so much trouble. A remarkable man. Recalling the event some years later, my mother said she had been quite impressed with the creativity of my lie and the speed in which it had been delivered. The fact that I had lied though was not forgotten.

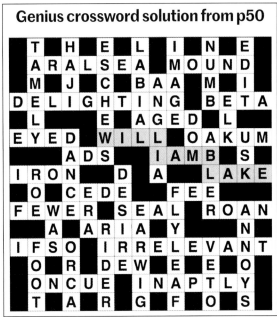

Genius crossword solution from p50

John Sweeney
ROVING REPORTER

When the going gets tough...

Fleshpots, navigation and mountain-climbing: *John Sweeney* reveals his rugged, masculine side

The stag night from hell started bleakly when Andrew, the stag-ee, as it were, punched the wrong co-ordinates into the satnav. Round and round Bangor's one-way system we drove, going slowly bonkers, impaled on Andrew's 'garbage in, garbage out' human error. He says he's a TV reviewer for a grand paper but judging from his command of technology he would be doing well if he empties the bins at *Knitwear Weekly*.

Eventually, we reprogrammed the satnav, moaned at the foolish A and hove-to at our lodgings, sandwiched in the middle of a road-widening scheme, with a fine view of the brick wall base of the railway station and two funeral parlours. Handy for passing over to the other side, see?

The North Welsh hills looked down on us miserably as a steady drizzle set in. I got the attic, where even the Twa, the more vertically challenged pygmies from Equatorial Africa, would have found their work cut out not banging their heads on the roof-beams. Not being a Twa, it hurt.

Not for us the swanky cosmopolitan delights of, say, Aberystwyth, or the sun-drenched beaches of Barry, the jewel of the South Wales coast. We were holed up in the gem of Gwynedd as it was handy for our planned ascent of Snowdon the next day – but that night we were determined to engorge ourselves on all the sinful pleasures the slate-roofed, giga-chapelled town could offer.

It was always a tall order. The lowering presence of Bangor Mountain throws such a gloomy shade over the downtown area that from November through to March chunks of the High Street receive no direct sunlight. True, Bangor is the smallest city in Britain. Fascinatingly, 76.7 per cent of the population speak Welsh – mountains preserve languages, flatlands don't. Praise be to the city that boasts the oldest bishopric in our land. And, oh yes, the city has the ninth-longest pier in the United Kingdom.

Having listed all its charms, it would be fair to say that Bangor is no Las Vegas. At least, not yet.

In search of devilry, we retired to the Fat Cat, and hunched round a table in fear as groups of tough, mega-bellied, hard nuts swaggered and slugged down bottles of beer. And they were just from the Bangor Women's Institute.

Frightened of getting roughed up by Bangor's belles, we opted for la-de-dah conversation, more *Newsnight* than anything else: the growth of the Chinese economy, blah high-falutin' blah. Soon, a hen party of Welsh rarebits – geddit? – had sniffed us out and Andrew posed for a shot with the chicks, him donning a bridal veil, sandwiched between two cliffs

> That night we were determined to engorge ourselves on all the sinful pleasures the town could offer...

of Celtic cleavage. One of them promised to do a table-dance, but she didn't.

That was the highpoint. For the rest of the evening, we just got expensively drunk on alcoholic jelly and retired to our beds, me wishing I was a Twa.

The next day the ascent on Snowdon began extremely badly when Andrew's younger brother, Nigel, got lost in the breakfast room and then all five of us got in our cars and got lost again because of a second satnav co-ordinate misfeed by Andrew. Finally I got everyone lost in the car park. I pointed due north at some other geological monstrosity, whereas our goal was pretty much due south, to Snowdon.

We turned 180 degrees and set off, huffing and puffing as the car park slightly tilted uphill. I'm not the worrying kind but as the ascent proper started I began to wheeze like an old man of 90. Gasping for air, I staggered to a halt. Far ahead Andrew and brother Nigel were lolloping along like spring-born lambs, and ahead of them was the ultra-fit Gethen, a kind of not-exactly-brother-in-law-elect. Only the Boy David – he's pretty-nearly-50-something too, but calling him the Boy still amuses – kept me company(ish), a dozen yards ahead. We were still in the car park.

The long walk began. The sweep of the ridges high above melted into the cloudscape as if we were moving inside a Victorian water colour. It was achingly beautiful. But it's hard to will yourself upwards to an unseen heaven. Unfit, chubby, begging for the pathologist to lend a hand: these are the kinder phrases that describe my physical condition.

The others waited for me on the steep bits as we slogged onwards. Halfway up there was a caff, where we guzzled tea and felt human. Visibility reduced, the weather got grimmer, and suddenly we were battling against foul winds and marching on snow. It was extremely cold and had we not been wrapped up in our hi-tech gear we might have ended up in one of those 999 TV docs which begin: 'Pot-holing Dave...'

We turned back. Pointless to go on, really. And I might have expired. But – as we summed up – not dead yet.

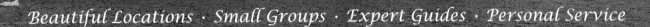

Bearing witness

Helen Bamber has spent her life working on behalf of the violated. Now in her eighties, she continues to support survivors, helping them rebuild their lives. Interview by *Melanie McFadyean*

Helen Bamber is poised, humorous, welcoming. She is used to being interviewed; her reputation as a champion of human rights spans the world. She has received many awards – European Woman of Achievement in 1993, an OBE, an award for a Lifetime's Achievement in Human Rights in 1998, honorary doctorates, degrees from half a dozen universities. But there is another kind of testament to her work, one that can't be hung on a wall, lodged in the memories of thousands of people who remember her as someone who listened while they told her of their experiences of torture, rape, murder, human trafficking, genocide.

She isn't worthy or self-satisfied; she creases up with laughter, likes a bit of a gossip. She is always beautifully turned out, hair and make-up perfect. 'I'm very interested in clothes, make-up and hair – it's a part of my defence. If I have a difficult telephone call to make I comb my hair or put my lipstick on.' This stylishness comes from her mother who, as the bombs were falling, would make sure she was elegantly dressed before

going to the air raid shelter in the garden of their home in North London.

She turned 83 in May but it seems meaningless. She's at work by 7.30. She lives on her own, 'I lead such a crazy life that nobody would put up with it for very long.' She has two sons and one young grandchild. She and her husband Rudi, a Jewish refugee from Nazi Germany, parted many years ago. 'I have immense energy, more now than when I was young. I need less sleep and can work a seven-day week. I feel one day it'll go whuff! and I'll be on the floor and it'll all be over.'

Her parents were Jewish of Polish descent, and her father, obsessed with the Nazi threat, would read to her from *Mein Kampf* or articles by Goebbels. As a child she feared the Nazis would invade and she and her family would be eliminated. She grew up with the miasma of persecution familiar to many Jewish children, perhaps the source of her capacity for compassion. It was to be crystallised by her first job when, at 20, she worked with survivors at Bergen

Helen Bamber, Belsen, 1945

Belsen in Germany, shortly after liberation.

Back in the UK she was appointed to the Committee for the Care of Young Children from Concentration Camps, working for the welfare of 722 young children and adolescents suffering from the effects of violence and loss. She worked in collaboration with the Anna Freud Clinic. She then took a number of hospital posts before joining Amnesty International. In 1985, she and others established the Medical Foundation for the Care of Victims of Torture. In 2005 she left and set up the Helen Bamber Foundation, which offers medical consultation, therapeutic care, human rights advocacy and practical support to survivors of human rights violations. They help some 1,600 asylum-seekers and refugees from more than 70 countries.

Her office is light and welcoming. We sit at a small round table. On it is a bowl of smoothly polished stones. 'Some people I see really cannot speak and we talk about very simple things that have nothing to do with what has happened to them to help them to communicate with me. We'll begin sometimes with the stones. I will ask them to take a stone and hold it, then I will hold it and then I will give it to them: it's this awful phrase in the trade, a transitional object, something from me to them.' Her voice is soothing, slightly husky, her delivery mesmeric.

From early childhood life threw experiences at Bamber which drew her further into the person she became – a witness, a listener, her unsentimental empathy never dimmed. She remembers a woman clutching her and desperately rasping out her story just after the war. She said: 'I cannot bring back the dead but I can be your witness. Your story will be told.' When she came back from Germany having witnessed the immediate aftermath of the Holocaust, she was driven by a 'need to bear witness to man's cruelty and inhumanity, the

banal cruelty that we see sometimes in our own society. That has stayed with me.'

We talked about the UK's 10 immigration detention centres where some 2,500 asylum-seekers, including families with children, are locked up indefinitely without charge. Most of us know little about these places out of which come reports of hunger strikes, self-harm, suicide and neglect. Bamber and her team hear detainees' horrifying stories which most of us would choose to walk away from.

Bamber is rarely sad, more often angry, a slow-burning anger, no ranting or swearing. The anger gives her energy. So when she fell silent and cried, it seemed we should abandon the interview. She said nothing for some time and then spoke for 20 minutes seamlessly, in her slow deliberate way, picking her words with care, editing herself as she goes along – 'No, I didn't mean it quite like that, change that.'

She talked about asylum-seekers whose claims have been rejected and who are living rough, of people whose claims failed partly because 'When you've been violated, you're in shock and you can't speak about what torture really is – the threat to one's sexuality, about lying in your excrement and your urine, screaming, begging for them to stop, you can't talk about that. So you say, "They beat me." And that word beat doesn't sound so bad.

'It's about violating a woman and laughing at her plight and that woman being unable to say what happened to her because most women find it difficult to talk about rape. It's about a woman who's been subjected to female genital mutilation and when they rape her they split her open with a knife in order to enter her because she's sewn up. Women and men can't speak about these things, so they don't give an easy account of themselves.' Bamber wonders why many officials charged with the responsibility for making informed decisions with such damaged people 'have not been trained in the sensitive facilitating manner in which you can really identify trauma. Is it perhaps that they don't want to identify it? Is it perhaps that it is it easier not to hear about these things?'

She talks of people whose stories are 'catalogues of banal neglect, lack of understanding and compassion'. With everything stacked against them, her many clients say they don't know why

Thousands of people remember her as someone who listened while they told her of their experiences of torture, rape, murder, human trafficking and genocide

they go on living, they've lost their families, their homes, everything. 'And then somehow through our therapeutic relationships, together we find reasons for them to go on living.'

Her sadness, she said, came from thinking of the continuum of that banal neglect and abuse of human rights. 'At the end of the war when all the human rights covenants and declarations were being fashioned we had hoped a new world had been born. It was perhaps naïve. I was young at the time and many of us felt a sense that there was now a framework for the protection of those who had suffered

at the hands of others – international agreements about violence, atrocity, torture and genocide.'

That global ethic dependent on a collective sense of compassion has, she says, to be recreated by successive generations. 'Each generation has to fight for its morality, its compassion and to be able to help people to whom they owe nothing. I listen to people talking about asylum-seekers and refugees and I sense danger; it doesn't take much more to cross the boundary into hatred and violence. I have to keep saying to the public, walk in their shoes.'

She feels encouraged when she visits schools and universities, and meets students who ask intelligent questions. 'I'm not without hope, I've seen people can make change. But it is such a painstaking exercise. I can see where we as an organisation have been able to change lives and change decisions.'

When you have been with Helen Bamber, you leave with a feeling that if more of us had her qualities, the world would change and be a much better and less cruel place.

Helen Bamber died in 2014 but her foundation continues. For more information: www.helenbamber.org

Bound by water

Patrick Reyntiens revels in the downtown delights of Seattle, a city in the Pacific Northwest that is almost entirely surrounded by water

How did it get its name? It's an odd one. But what a surprise when you get there because, although Seattle is in the United States, it displays a character, independence and authority all of its own. This is not a city of bigger, better, higher, taller and richer. Leave that to Chicago or New York. No, Seattle has very few skyscrapers, no down-town 'hugies', and blocks, blocks, blocks.

You can walk around the city centre with ease, relaxed in the certainty of being able to make your way on foot without being continuously pushed by traffic, police and passers-by. Compared with many other American cities, the centre of Seattle is remarkably small and compact and you can find things you want without much difficulty. There are at least 15 art shops and galleries that merit a squint.

And then, of course, Seattle is the birthplace, workplace and resting place of most of the hot-glass hand-blown glasses, urns, bowls and other vessels – squeezed, drawn out, expanded and squished into extraordinary and unbelievable silhouettes and shapes in a myriad different colours. The hot-glass phenomenon is, in many ways, unique to Seattle in the States – and almost in the world. Go there and grab some. (Careful, it's brittle.) You'll not regret it.

The city isn't on the sea. It feels like it is, but it isn't. Seattle is protected by the misty loftiness of the Olympic Mountains some 30km to the west, on the other side of the wide stretch of water that enables comfortable navigation round the city. The water is all around the city, but not in the centre.

You always feel free to escape the city whenever you need to. And it's worth it, for just a few kilometres away, fringing the water in many of the gullies and miniature lochs that surround the place, are marvellous restaurants whose main attraction is, fairly obviously, fish. Delicious. And there are oysters. Marvellous. And calamari, calamaretti, clams and mussels, not to mention salmon and, I think, bass, and all sorts of other fish that can be found in the waterways around the American-Canadian border. 'Catch 'em and eat 'em' seems to be Seattle's motto. The rest of the food is pretty good, too, and eclectic: Japanese, Italian, Mexican – you name it, it's here.

> ## When, usually towards evening, the clouds move away and the sun comes out, nowhere could be more alluring

Then there are the suburbs. Far from being uninteresting, they have enormous character. You can find a Benedictine monastery in one of them. Everyone seems in the best of health. Perhaps because there are leafy suburbs all around – each with its little local lake rimmed with jogging and walking paths. There are tracks for cyclists – and you do see some very odd sorts of cycles here: one-wheel, big-wheel, no-wheel-at-all –

or so it seems. Within 400m of the lovely house in which I was staying there was a run-walk around a freshwater lake (scullers and other boats on it), which provided two miles of exercise before breakfast. And there were a lot of people of all ages, from 6 to 84, at 7.30am, exercising before the day's activities commenced.

The weather of Seattle is, for a few too many months of the year, 'in parenthesis'. That's the north-west for you. Grey clouds, not too heavy but spread all around, mooch over the divine landscape. And they occasionally produce little splats of rain that sometimes gently dribble down for the whole day. It doesn't take long to realise that the climate in Seattle is not the slightest bit Mediterranean. But when, usually towards evening, the clouds move away and the sun comes out, nowhere could be more alluring.

Time has to be found to go to the opera. Wagner has a very special significance here and it's worth going to Seattle just to experience this one phenomenal achievement. In spite of the high price of seats, the *Ring Cycle* is always completely sold out. I think it takes place every two years or so. I only wish the producers would commission Dale Chihuly, the world's most accomplished blown-glass expert, to design the stage sets for *Siegfried* or *Götterdämmerung*. Wow, what a stunning experience that would be. It would doubtless double the price of the seats, but if Dale can do it for Kew Gardens, why not for Wagner's *Ring*? Perhaps Bill Gates could pay for it. He lives in Seattle after all – the lucky man.

The Oldie Competition

by Tessa Castro

IN COMPETITION No 102 you were asked for Clerihews beginning with the name of a television programme. Goodness, I laughed! Thank you for so many and such good 'uns. There were lots of deserving runners-up. Congratulations to those printed below, who each win £10, with the bonus Taylor's of Harrogate tea and cake set going to Donald Parker.

Last Choir Standing
Is best heard on the landing
With the volume turned low
On a set far below.

Songs of Praise
Seeks different ways
Of avoiding affinity
With the Trinity.
*Donald Parker,
Wakefield*

TV's Naughtiest Blunders –
Well, really, one wonders!
Is half an hour's fluffing one's lines
and swearing
So terribly funny and daring?
Michael Brereton, Dublin

The Bill
Eventually will
See every actor we ever knew
Pass through.
Keith Norman, Oxford

Inspector Morse
Is no longer on the force.
Now, when a don's killed, what they
do is
Call Lewis.
Adrian Fry, Swindon

The Apprentice
Is worse than going to the dentist:
Setting a bad example if
viewed
By youngsters
who'll think it
clever to
be rude.
*Philippa Lawrence,
Salisbury*

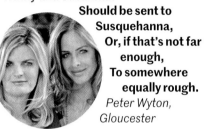

Location, Location, Location
Enthralled the house-buying nation
Till the Crunch, like a trampling
elephant
Made it completely irrelevant.
Pam Harris, Ilkley

The Flowerpot Men,
Bill and Ben,
Started a trend they could not check –
The one that brought us Ant and Dec!
Sarah Hill, Shepton Mallet

Are You Being Served?
Featured blokes who are
completely
unnerved
To the point of being
wussy
By Mrs Slocum's
pussy.
*Basil Ransome-Davies,
Lancaster*

Fiona Bruce
noticed her blouse had come loose
as she warned the nation
of rising inflation.
Kate Williams, Cardiff

Trinny and Susannah
Should be sent to
Susquehanna,
Or, if that's not far
enough,
To somewhere
equally rough.
*Peter Wyton,
Gloucester*

Friday Night with Jonathan Ross
Makes me exceptionally cross
Since, having always shunned it,
I help to fund it.
John Robinson, Desborough

Final Score
Is a monumental bore.
It's weird that some men get excited
If they hear that Blackburn Rovers
have beaten Manchester United.
David Rundle, Cheltenham

Inspector Morse
Is never coarse
What a pity
One cannot say the
same of *Sex and
the City*!
*Paul Griffin,
Southwold*

Sharp end of knife crime

BLOG NIGEL SUMMERLEY, 2019

Knife crime is something that you read about in the news and tend to forget about until the next one. But not when you see its victims up close. Acute nocturnal pain from a suspected kidney stone gave me the unexpected opportunity to do just that.

At 3am on a Friday night, I waited while A&E staff at a south London hospital patched up a have-a-go-hero who had made the brave mistake of standing up to some men making homophobic comments outside a nightclub. He wasn't gay – he just thought it was wrong to abuse people who were. He paid for his intervention with being punched and then slashed across his hand with a knife.

But that wasn't the worst of it. When I was leaving A&E at 5am, an ambulance crew was bringing in the second knife crime victim of the night, also from a nightclub altercation. The young man sat on a gurney with a bloody red spot decorating the right side of his bandaged chest. If that spot had been on the left side, it would have coincided with his heart. He was lucky to be alive.

He looked like a casualty of war – and, of course, he was. The offensive and defensive use of knives is turning our streets into a battle zone – and one that could so easily touch any of us.

And the violence doesn't end with the victim and those close to them. It has a knock-on effect on already overstretched A&E departments, where staff have to deal with the injured, and where emergency patients have to wait even longer while the wounded are brought in from the front line.

This was just one night, in one hospital... But it's a sorry snapshot of what is happening across our country.

A singular woman

Dervla Murphy talks to *Dea Birkett* about travelling, writing – and doing it on her own

I found Dervla Murphy bent over in the cowshed. It's where she stores her papers, and she's having a clear-out, sifting those she'll keep from those she'll discard. There are piles of old newspapers going back decades, colourful issues from Africa, Asia and the Americas. There are folders of letters and boxes of photographs. I note there's a small stack of *Oldie*s on the 'to be kept' shelf.

Dervla is excited to have discovered the typescript of a novel she wrote when she was 13 and a half. *Royalty Rides the Sky* is a stirring tale of imperial endeavour, part Blyton, part Biggles. 'It's 43,000 words,' she says proudly. 'I spent my pocket money for somebody to type it, so I obviously wanted to have it published or I wouldn't have paid.'

Over 60 years and 20 books later (but not one published novel), she types up her own manuscripts. The first, *Full Tilt: Ireland to India with a Bicycle*, published in 1965, established her as a young, feisty, fresh voice in travel writing. Her reliance on simple modes of transport – either with four feet or two wheels – was her trademark. She also took on subjects other travel writers shied away from as too political, including Northern Ireland and race relations in Birmingham. This October, her new book *The Island That Dared: Journeys in Cuba* is published. It was first written, as all her titles, in longhand at her desk in another cold, damp shed, just a few yards away from the cowshed, reached over worn cobbles sprouting weeds. The scattering of ancient stone sheds, with their bare walls and floors, resembles an African compound. But this compound is behind the Credit Union on the main street in the small Waterford town of Lismore, Dervla's Irish home.

'Tea? Coffee?' She grimaces as she offers them. Then cocks her thumb towards her mouth and smiles. 'Beer?'

'I'll have what you're having,' I say. It is mid-afternoon. She cocks her thumb again – 'Beer!' – and pulls a six-pack of Bavaria from the fridge. I can spot little else inside. She pours my beer into a glass, but not hers. 'Tastes better from the tin,' she says. 'Slainte.'

Now *The Island That Dared* is

> Now, the tall, black, iron gates protecting her compound are propped open. But for the three to four months it takes to write a book, they are permanently padlocked. 'No one comes through – I won't have a conversation with anyone'

Cuba 2007: Dervla Murphy in the grounds of Fidel Castro's family farm (above) and with her three granddaughters, the Trio, about to board a ferryboat (right)

finished, Dervla Murphy is in a social phase. The tall, black, iron gates protecting her compound – the sort that appear at the start of a winding drive up to the haunted house in a horror film – are propped open. Anyone is welcome to walk in. But for the three to four months it takes her to write a book, they are permanently padlocked with a heavy chain that could have featured in the same horror film. 'During that period, no one comes through,' she says. 'No one at all. I won't have a conversation with anyone. I like that. I like being alone entirely.'

During her writing retreats, she refuses to answer the phone, 'otherwise you have someone outside the gate telephoning and saying they're from Australia and want my autograph and have come all the way to Lismore just to get it. So I don't answer.' The only calls she makes are to 'the Trio' – her three young grandchildren, who live with her only daughter, Rachel, in Italy. 'Every Sunday morning I ring the Trio. That's routine.' It's the only way she keeps in touch with them. She has no computer.

She keeps convent hours, in bed by 9.30pm and up by five, eating a big cooked breakfast – 'home-made muesli, home-made bread from spelt flour, lots of cheese, maybe a boiled egg'. From then on, it's mostly beer.

Her company is four dogs, a cat and

thousands and thousands of books. Each shed is heavy with the must of old volumes, suggesting ancient libraries and accumulated knowledge. Dervla, I decide, smells wise. Her appearance, however, does not suggest scholarship but hardiness. She has a very masculine square jaw, short grey hair that isn't so much cut as hacked off, and a face that looks as if it's been subjected to a good daily scrub for several decades. (It probably has.) Her T-shirt is covered in cat hairs. Her posture suggests she's permanently at the point of embarking on a journey. Even walking between the kitchen shed and the sitting-room shed, she tilts her head slightly forward, as if taking the first step in a trek across the windswept steppes, striding purposefully forth, almost colliding with the fridge door from which she pulls another can of Bavaria. The overall impression is of daunting, single-minded determination.

As we settle down with a couple of cans in the largest shed – her study – she briskly brushes aside any attempt at small talk, even about the atrocious Irish weather, unless it concerns the recent floods that have prevented her taking her daily swim in the Blackwater River. We quickly become embroiled not in a conversation about Cuba, but on literary matters more generally. I mention footstepping the Victorian traveller Mary Kingsley, of whom I know Dervla Murphy is an admirer. 'I don't think in the footsteps is a very good idea, really,' she says. 'Of course, HV Morton is worth reading, and he's always in the footsteps of somebody. But that's St Paul or Julius Caesar. But I don't think on the whole it's a very good idea. Too constraining.'

Being constrained is something Dervla Murphy has striven, for most of her 76 years, to avoid. As a teenager, she looked after her mother who was disabled by rheumatoid arthritis. 'I never saw her standing. She got about in a bathchair,' she remembers, as a plain fact, not a complaint. 'I wanted to get going from the age of eight. It felt like being imprisoned.' When she wanted a child, she had one, by Terence de Vere White, an *Irish Times* journalist, without ever bothering to get married.

Apart from raising Rachel, who went

to boarding school at 11, Dervla has lived by herself. The order she has created is entirely her own. The books, which cover every wall in every shed, are strictly arranged by geographical location. Each of her books has its own section – Ethiopia for *In Ethiopia with a Mule* (1968); India for *On a Shoestring to Coorg* (1976); South America for *Eight Feet in the Andes* (1986); the Balkans for *Through the Embers of Chaos* (2003). There are sections for unwritten books, for example on China. 'I thought China was just too big to handle.' There are even

sections for books that are, possibly, still to be written. Korea is one such area.

'I was going to go to Sri Lanka. But something put me off.' She tries to remember exactly what.

'Civil war?' I offer.

She guffaws. 'No – civil war wouldn't put me off. I think it was because I thought there'd be too many hotels.'

Dervla Murphy hates hotels. She only accepted the invitation to this year's Toronto's Harbourfront literary festival on the condition that she didn't stay in a hotel but a B&B. 'They like to keep all the writers in the same zoo,' she says.

There is something of the nun in the firmness and clarity of her convictions. She is vehemently anti nuclear power and passionately in favour of legalising all drugs. Although she was a single parent at a time when such families were frowned upon, she does not approve of adoption by same-sex couples. She rails against 'ruthless multinational corporations'. 'They don't care what they're doing – the profiteers – as long as they're making money ... what we need is the younger generation to come to their

senses and realise that this utterly materialist way has the seeds of destruction within it. One of the most pernicious ideas is that it's all too big a problem, and individuals can't do anything about it. As individuals, you can change things. It can be done. It is possible.' She drowns these disappointments in another Bavaria, accompanied by a cigarillo.

We leave her compound to walk up to her friend's house. Her friend is on holiday, and Dervla is feeding the hens while she's away. We set off at a startling pace, as if about to tackle the Karakoram, not walk past Michael McGrath Victualler and Sweets 'n Things in Lismore's Main Street.

She's lived in Lismore since she was born – her father was the local librarian – so everyone knows her. Each passer-by greets her, but no one stops. She's walking so fast, head thrust forward against an imaginary wind, that to halt her would require almost making an arrest. Perhaps she's deliberately walking that way to avoid having to engage in pleasantries with her fellow townspeople.

Or perhaps she's trying to shake off the shadow of me. 'I really don't suit travelling with other people. I just can't do it,' she says firmly. Her readers get little of her inner journey. Her books are very matter of fact, detailing the course of her travels, blow by blow. Gate numbers and flight times are all given, and I'm convinced they are correct. Unlike almost every other travel writer, she isn't tempted to massage the facts or make things up for the sake of a good story. When Dervla tells us she has met a man on the 2.22pm from Cairo to Alexandria, you can be certain she actually did.

She is an honest sage. And as we part, I have a strange longing to receive her blessing: for her to send me on my way from Lismore with a mission in my heart and wind in my sails. But I can't keep up with the redoubtable Dervla. Soon she's gone, disappearing around a corner, head down, chin out, spirits up, on the next lone journey.

'The Island That Dared: Journeys in Cuba' by Dervla Murphy, Eland Publishing

Gossip and fun

PIERS BRENDON

Grub Street Irregular: Scenes from Literary Life

by Jeremy Lewis

Harper Press

It may seem improper, if not downright incestuous, for an *Oldie* writer to review a book by *The Oldie*'s Commissioning Editor, some of which deals with goings-on at *The Oldie*. Yet why should *Oldie* readers be deprived of, say, Jeremy Lewis's priceless description of trying to hold back an avalanche of paper from the adjoining desk, while its occupier, Richard Ingrams, eats a lunch consisting of potato crisps washed down with orange juice from a large plastic container? Why, indeed, should they not be told about the funniest, best-written and most enjoyable slice of literary-bohemian autobiography since Julian Maclaren-Ross's *Memoirs of the Forties*?

Lest this verdict be reckoned too cosy, let me set out the worst case against *Grub Street Irregular*, the third volume in a kaleidoscopic trilogy. Lewis is too hard on himself and too nice about others, too much Betjeman and not enough Waugh. He portrays himself as a 'superhumanly flatulent' bumbler and he is supremely indulgent towards monsters such as James Lees-Milne and AL Rowse. He is politically incorrect. He makes the occasional involuntary error (for example, confusing 'Jackie' Fisher with Jellicoe) and he admits to improving his stories for effect. Hearing that the publisher Mervyn Horder had been surprised in a public lavatory wearing a full frogman's outfit, complete with flippers and goggles, Lewis adds 'a trident to complete the ensemble'.

Whatever the embellishments, no one has described more brilliantly the fringes of workaday publishing and jobbing journalism as they have existed over the last 40 years. Like Smollett and Surtees, two of his heroes, Lewis conjures up a raffish, picaresque world rich in character and anecdote. Thus Mark Longman confesses that he doesn't actually read books. Derek Verschoyle, literary editor of the *Spectator*, shoots cats with a .22 rifle from his Gower Street window. Victor Gollancz inspects himself for symptoms of VD in full view of the

Jeremy Lewis: a very affable cove

houses opposite his Henrietta Street office. Penelope Betjeman sets off for the Himalayas with 'a team of hand-picked lesbians'. Iris Murdoch refuses to be edited, though she thanks Lewis for pointing out that Hyde Park Corner is not on the Circle Line. Nirad Chaudhuri wears Indian or English clothes to suit the language in which he is writing. André Deutsch appears as a 'boiled canary'; Richard Cobb resembles a 'freshly skinned rabbit'; John Lehmann looks like 'a blond, bad-tempered eagle'. Alan Ross asks Sidney Nolan if he could improve the dental state of a one-toothed lion in a picture of his that Ross has bought. Auberon Waugh congratulates Lewis on his biography of Cyril Connolly: 'You are a wonderful man. I hope nothing dreadful ever happens to you.'

Lewis himself lives from pen to mouth. He flits from Gastons, purchasers of review copies, to the Old Piano Factory, where Duckworth serves cocktails 'with the colour, consistency and flavour of lighter fuel'. He goes on travel freebies and hobnobs with writers such as the late-lamented Rob Neillands. He assists Connolly's tempestuous ex-wife Barbara Skelton and her two neurotic Burmese cats to move from France to England, a marvellously Pickwickian episode. He reflects uneasily on his father's alcoholism and recalls that his mother briefly managed a troupe of midgets.

Above all he relishes the gossip and conviviality of literary life, while noting that gregariousness can all too easily become a substitute for writing itself. Lewis somehow manages to combine enthusiastic party-going with successful authorship. *Grub Street Irregular* is hack work raised to the condition of fine art.

'There's something of the night about you, Dennis'

It's bah to goats – but some humbugs would be nice …

by *Virginia Ironside*

I have discovered something rather interesting about time. I am going away for a week to Scotland next month, and when I say to friends that I'm dreading it – because the older I get the more stressful I find going away from home, notwithstanding that, like a child at a party, I often 'love it when I get there' – they say: 'But it's only a week! Now we're older it passes in a flash!'

In one way they're right because a week is only 1/3328 of my entire past life – rather small. But when I see it in terms of my future life, say ten years, it's 1/520th – incredibly long.

Same problem with Christmas. When I think that I've already experienced 64 Christmases, it seems potty to get into such a tizz about it, and where I will spend it or who will spend it with me. And yet when I think in terms of there perhaps only being ten more Christmases left, the whole event becomes ludicrously important.

Yet the truth is that Christmas does seem to come round with alarming regularity, and as I'm still sweeping the old pine-needles from the cracks in the sofa, I can't think why I didn't just get a tree in a pot and keep it up, decorated, for the whole year. The prospect of staggering up a ladder and putting up those wretched old decorations yet again, only to pull them down the following week, seems dotty. And there's the entire crib carved out of balsa wood by my father, not to mention the irritating little brass Austrian tinging thing with angels going round and round when you light the candles. When I said to someone that 2009 was round the corner, he replied, with an agonised sigh, 'Oh dear, is there no end to it?' I knew how he felt.

As for Christmas cards, I gave them up years ago, but unfortunately they haven't given me up. There was a period when I kept two baskets by my front door at Christmas time. One was for the cards that came in and the other was full of stamps, envelopes and cards which I'd send to anyone who sent me one. Then came the usual 'I'll only send cards to old

> I have my own charities thank you, and don't want people deciding which one I'm going to give to

people, people I never see and people who live abroad' decision, and finally I decided to give the whole thing a miss altogether. I no longer have to worry about 'which Clare?' when I get a card from Clare because Clare, whoever she is, never gets a card in return.

However, nothing could get me out of the dilemma I had last year – another year in which I sent nothing out at all – when I received a card from yet another 'Clare' which read: 'Dearest Virginia, What a gorgeous card you sent me! You know that my great loves are the forests of Canada, and the sweeping skies on your card and the little girl with the pony-tail in the foreground (me?!) filled me with joy! All love… Clare.'

I haven't yet got to the point when I don't give presents, my friends will be glad to hear. Though I do give rather more eatables and smellies than I used because, like most of my generation, I can't cope with any more 'things'.

And I'm very pleased to receive them, too. As long as no one dares to give me goats. Goats (as in goats to Africa) aren't really a present at all. They're a charitable donation on the part of the giver to an African village, in which you are just inserted as an unwitting – and, if you believe that aid to Africa is a Jolly Bad Thing, unwilling – middleman. It's so patronising, too. It's like offering a child a fiver and then snatching it from his hand and saying he must give it to the poor.

Anyway I have my own charities thank you very much, and don't want people deciding which one I'm going to give to. For reasons of my own I don't like giving to Cancer Research or Shelter, and would hate anyone to give them money on my behalf.

When I get a present I want it to be a present for me and me alone. Whether it's a bottle of ginger in syrup or some Badedas for the bath (hint hint). Or even, I have to say, a humble walnut whip.

Welcome to Arcadia

Paraguay is no longer a disreputable destination but a country fit and ready for tourists. It's absolute heaven, says *Hugh O'Shaughnessy*

Arcadia, anyone? A pleasurable weekend in Utopia, a real *terra incognita*, madam? Perhaps a few days in the Lost Paradise over the New Year for you, sir? Paraguay, once a place of fable but latterly struck off the tourist map, is coming back from the unknown for the curious and enterprising traveller. There is little glitz and the cost of living is ridiculously cheap.

For many years Paraguay was not a place where respectable people went. For decade after decade this landlocked country in the remote heart of South America, squeezed between Argentina, Brazil and Bolivia, was seen as full of dictators and conmen, smugglers and white slave traders. Types whom you would not want to be seen with at the Waitrose checkout, never mind in your golf club. It was, like the republic of Haiti, an ideal place for Graham Greene to site some of his more exotic novels.

Yet no oldie need be ashamed any more about getting on a plane and having a few days in the country which wise men in the 17th and 18th centuries long regarded as somewhere really special, possibly even the original site of the Garden of Eden. Earlier this year the voters were allowed to choose their own ruler for a change and the new President, Fernando Lugo, who had served for years as a bishop with his own diocese, was elected with a massive majority in a free election. He's cleaning up the corruption and Paraguayans are rallying round the man they chose.

Almost unknown to the outside world, Paraguay was closed to visitors for years at the beginning of the 19th century. It still receives few tourists, and only a tiny

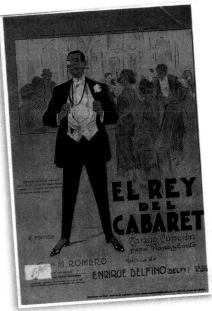

Left: the Río Iguazú, where Paraguay, Argentina and Brazil meet
Above: Mennonite brother and sister in Paraguay's Rio Verde
Right: the 'quincho', or covered barbecue area, in the Santa María Hotel in the village of Santa María de Fe

PHOTOGRAPHS COURTESY OF WWW.SANTAMARIADEFE.ORG, ALAMY/ © EDITH DORSEY RAFF AND GETTYIMAGES/CHRISTOPHER PILLITZ

number every year from Europe. Its natural phenomena and surprising history are, therefore, a closed book to most travellers, though that indefatigable bird-watcher Kenneth Clarke enthuses about its wildlife.

In the south, Paraguay is a gentle place of ranches and cowboys. In the wilderness of the Chaco in the west, there are strange colonies of German-speaking Mennonites, distant cousins of the Amish people in Pennsylvania, living their exclusive religious lives and producing excellent dairy products.

In the far eastern corner there is the new metropolis of Ciudad del Este, raw and vital and with more tall buildings than the capital, Asunción. From Ciudad del Este it only takes a few minutes by taxi to travel east across the majestic River Paraná into Brazil and it's a short way on to Argentina to view the Iguazú Falls – 300 magnificent cascade waterfalls nearly three kilometres across.

In the surrounding forest, yellow toucans with huge beaks fly through the trees where monkeys screech. Or you can go a similar distance in the red earth to the Itaipú Dam, built with the Brazilians and still the largest generator of electricity on the planet.

The most Arcadian of places in

In the surrounding forest, yellow toucans with huge beaks fly through the trees where monkeys screech

Paraguay must be the village of Santa María de Fe, a former mission set up by the Jesuits for the Guarani people. Santa María has a museum with a collection of more than 40 gilded and painted statues, carved in local cedar in the 17th and 18th

centuries for the local church. The arts of carving and playing the harp, first brought by the missionaries, are still common more than two centuries since the fathers were sent into exile, and visitors to the tiny but exquisite Santa María Hotel, which is run by the English scholar Margaret Hebblethwaite, can hear the harp, see the work of local craftsmen and get to know village life. Perfection.

And your stock will go up at the golf club back home.

Hugh O'Shaughnessy is a prize-winning journalist who has written on Latin America for over 40 years

Off for a buzz!

Oliver Bernard proves that flying a plane is like riding a bicycle
– a skill you don't lose, even after a 63-year break

My memory is not what it was. At least I don't think it is. Names are difficult, of course. But my most humiliating defeat to date is that I've forgotten the phrase which signifies the hut or room in which we trainee pilots sat and played poker and smoked and aimed friendly insults at each other while waiting to climb into our Tiger Moths, Cornells and Harvards.

'Are you dicing this morning?' was a common greeting at breakfast. Or someone would enter the room with a worried expression and say, 'Has anybody seen a little yellow aircraft?'

We were all so anxious to get our hours in and emerge as operational pilots that we even went in for flights of imagination, thus: 'There I was at 20,000 feet. Nothing below me but the moon. Nothing on the clock but the maker's name. And 3,000 pounds of aircraft strapped to my legs ...' I was once delighted to hear a chap called Reg Hartlebury, a Birmingham man, calling a trainee a 'Middlesbrough-faced twat'. But most insults were less baroque.

My training took a long time because as a former 16-year-old Communist I kept being 'investigated' by the authorities and held back from drafts. I was told this by a WAAF typist to whom I'd sold several copies of the *Daily Worker*. She had typed letters about me from the Group Captain to the Provost Marshal (RAF Police).

So on VJ Day in Calgary, Alberta, I had about 75 hours in, including solo aerobatics and low flying, but no more wings than a day-old chick. No more flying unless I signed on for another five years after my release date: no rank, no pay, no celebrating on leave in New York. I was, however, alive.

Sixty-three years later, just outside Bristol, I was taken by the son of an old friend for a Sunday morning joy ride in a small Piper aircraft by no means new – I think it was called a Vagabond. It cruised at 80 miles per hour and felt like riding on a large leaf. My last flight had been in a Harvard, which takes off at 90.

After a quarter of an hour I'd got used

Piper PA-15 Vagabond, built in 1948, and Oliver Bernard at the age of 17

to not sitting on a parachute, and Nye asked me if I'd like to take control. I saw straight away that my eyes had deteriorated. I stared at the misty horizon – there was no artificial one on the instrument panel – and concentrated on flying straight and level, aware that I was failing to keep a sharp lookout all round as I'd been taught to do. Still, it was a most beautiful morning. The Severn Bridges looked good, Wales looked good. I was beginning to enjoy it when we – or rather I – turned back.

In the mobile home they use as mess-room and control tower on that grass airfield, there was the old familiar laughter and leg-pulling, and the unmoving floor under one's feet. Nye told the other flyers that I'd 'had' the aircraft for 20 minutes. It had felt like 10.

It was like getting on a bicycle again, only rather more glorious. Dicing!

PHOTOGRAPH OF PIPER VAGABOND BY TIM VICKERS

Another kind of haven

Jersey has changed a fair bit since the 1950s, but for *Rosie Boycott* the nearby Ecréhous islands retain the haunting charms she remembers from her childhood

When I was born in Jersey in the early 1950s, it was a cheap holiday destination, one much favoured by honeymooners on a budget who'd hole up in caravans or take refuge in the string of boarding houses which dotted the south coast of the island. My mum's family had been on the island since the 1300s and they'd made their livings in various nefarious ways – one did a stint as a wrecker, luring boats onto the rocks and then stealing whatever washed ashore. By the time mum was born, they'd settled into respectability – my grandfather was the island's first vet and the owner of one of the first cars to zig-zag his way through the miles of small lanes that connect the little villages and hamlets of the tiny island.

When we were young we spent our holidays at my grandmother's house on La Roque beach, where the tides are enormous, moving in and out every day, exposing almost a mile of rock pools and gulleys – a paradise for children since we could scavenge for shrimps and crabs. If you studied the sand at the bottom of a pool for long enough you might even glimpse the occasional plaice, moving softly as it breathed, stirring the sand into little eddies and whirls.

But the best place of all was a tiny group of rocks, situated mid-way between Jersey and France, called the Ecréhous. For centuries, this little rocky outcrop had been a lay-over for fishermen who erected tiny huts – most about the size of a caravan – on the highest part of the islands. When the tide was up, the water lapped at the windows; when it was down, there was about a mile or so of rocks and pools, full of shrimps and crabs and myriad shells.

Its ownership was always in dispute: were the islands French or English? It wasn't an issue anyone debated much until the late Sixties, when a Jersey man named Alphonse chose the Ecréhous as a hideaway after he'd been accused of a series of grim child rapes. Alphonse settled into one of the huts and, over the

The Ecréhous islands

years, he became a regular fixture: he'd mend your fishing nets, catch you lobsters, help pull a boat ashore and tie it securely if a storm was on its way. As teenagers we slept in little camp beds in the attic room of the hut belonging to family friends, but if we happened to be there when there was a full moon, my mum and her friends would take extra special care that we were all safely upstairs before night fell. It was wildly exciting; no one knew for certain whether Alphonse was actually a rapist or just a harmless and innocent man who had been wrongly accused, but mum and her friends always believed that – like a werewolf – he might rise up when the moon was full.

He survived on the islands through fishing, and when the summer visitors like us left – or the winter fishermen who still used the islands as a stop-over – we'd leave behind copious quantities of canned food to keep him going.

One winter, during a severe storm, he fell and broke his leg on the rocks. Somehow, he dragged himself back up to his hut, set his leg with bits of wood and string and mended the break himself.

> These small rocks are probably the most magical place I know in the world. Nothing but you, the sea, the ever-changing tides and the noise of gulls screeching

He taught himself law and for years engaged in a long struggle to prove that he was the natural owner of the Ecréhous, a battle that he never actually won, but then again, no one ever tried to evict him.

It wasn't until the 1990s that his name was finally cleared: the real rapist confessed and a flotilla of boats carrying a variety of judicial big-wigs sailed out to the islands to ask him to come home. He wouldn't – at least not for about another ten years, by which time he considered himself too old to cope with his solitary existence.

Last summer, after a gap of some 40 years, I set foot on the Ecréhous again. Nothing had changed – except that Alphonse no

St Brelade's Parish Church

longer came limping down to help you tie up your boat. The tiny huts – squashed together like a child's model village, separated by narrow paths, their paintwork battered by the salty winds – were still just as they had always been. I sat on the bench at the top of the island – Jersey to the west, the coast of France to the east – and still thought that these small rocks were probably the most magical place I know in the world. Nothing but you, the sea, the ever-changing tides and the noise of gulls screeching.

Nowadays, it is possible (and easy) to hire a motorboat to take you out there for the day and for anyone planning a trip to Jersey, I can't recommend the trip too highly. Jersey itself has changed. Locals complain that it is horribly built up, a victim of its success as a tax haven, but the caravans have left (it became cheaper to head to the south of Spain once the £50 limit had been lifted) and as a result the tackiness which once characterised much of the place has gone.

Last summer I stayed in L'Horizon in St Brelade's Bay, a perfect crescent-shaped sweep of sand surrounded by wooded hills with an old fisherman's church to one side (where I was christened and many of my family are buried). I fell asleep to the sound of the sea and woke up hearing the waves surge slowly on the beach below. This summer, fingers crossed, we've managed to rent a hut on the Ecréhous (a very tricky business as there's only one not in private hands). I can't wait to go back.

Great Bores of Today

'... you won't believe what I paid for this ticket the normal price is 900 dollars but I only paid 25 of course it means that instead of flying direct to Paris I have to take a flight to Kennedy then go over the pole to Schiphol that's Amsterdam then to Johannesburg and then back up to Milan where you spend the night and get up at 3 o'clock in the morning but who wants to pay 900 dollars when you can get it for 25 ...'
© Fant and Dick

The rise and rise of Geoffrey Palmer

Geoffrey Palmer served a long theatrical apprenticeship before achieving national fame in *Reginald Perrin* and *Butterflies*. Now 82, he has no desire to retire. Interview by *Sandra Smith*

From post boy at the Central London Electricity Company in Carnaby Street to Corporal Instructor in the Royal Marines, Geoffrey Palmer readily admits that he had a few false starts before hitting on a career in acting. He simply 'had no ambition and no idea what I wanted to do' when he left school more than 60 years ago.

At home now in a tranquil location in Buckinghamshire (within commuting distance of Pinewood and Elstree Studios and London), where he has lived with his wife for the past 45 years, this recipient of an OBE for services to drama is remarkably down-to-earth about his success. 'In my life I'm grateful for my wife and family and for having been fortunate enough in a difficult business to find work,' he says. 'My greatest achievement is that I'm still working.'

The younger of two brothers, Geoffrey was born and grew up in North Finchley, where he enjoyed Greek and Latin at Highgate School but felt he 'wasn't bright enough to achieve an awful lot. I had no careers advice and anyway grew up thinking I would go to war. One of my greatest regrets is not having had the opportunity to go to Oxford or Cambridge to study English.'

To counter his disappointment, Geoffrey joined the Royal Marines in

May 1946 ('if you've got to go into the armed services then the Royal Marines is the best outfit to be in'). Two years later, his service complete but with no idea what line of work to follow, he obtained a government grant for a year's business training and joined an import/export firm. Fortunately, as it turned out, he quickly discovered a loathing for office life – 'so I just left, drifted about for a while then got an unpaid job as a trainee assistant stage manager at a small theatre by Kew Bridge. Up to then I'd done a couple of plays at school, but never thought of becoming an actor.'

His father voiced concern about the insecurity of acting only once, says Geoffrey, but 'he would never have stood in my way' and both parents were quietly supportive as he immersed himself further in the profession. 'Formal training wasn't really necessary then. The basic way into the business was to be an assistant stage manager in one of the dozens and dozens of repertory companies. That way you got to play small parts.'

In one of his early roles he played a young extrovert in *Junior Miss*, an American high school play. 'I had the right reaction from the audience so I knew I must be doing something right. By then I had joined the Grand, a beautiful old Victorian theatre in East Croydon, now sadly pulled down, and stayed there for two or three years.

'I had a number of small parts during that time but just took the roles I was given. In weekly repertory theatre the general line-up always included a juvenile character man – not the good-looking one. I enjoyed playing these comedy roles.'

By this time Geoffrey was living in digs and had to survive on modest wages. Not that this troubled him: 'I didn't need a lot of money. I was a medium fish in a very small pond and was happy to be carried along.'

After serving his apprenticeship for several years, a couple of successful TV sitcoms – *The Fall and Rise of Reginald Perrin* and *Butterflies* – launched him into television. Geoffrey considers himself lucky to have been in programmes written by Carla Lane, whom he greatly admires. And he knows how difficult a writer's job is: 'I tried

Far left: as Sir John Crowder in *Margaret Thatcher: The Long Walk to Finchley* (2008); above: with Leonard Rossiter (left) in *The Fall and Rise of Reginald Perrin*; left: as Dr Warren in Nicholas Hytner's *The Madness of King George* (1994)

writing once during a quiet period – it didn't work!'

But though television brought him fame, he lost none of his love for the theatre. 'It is by far the most satisfying,' he says. 'Once you've rehearsed and the curtains rise, it's up to you and the other actors. Theatre is the only medium where you have a real response, where you control the audience. Yes, it's nerve-wracking, but at the same time it gives me a buzz.'

And the unusual characters were always the best: 'In all honesty, I've enjoyed a lot of my roles, but it's better to play someone unlike you. I don't want to be the laconic, middle-class, ageing man next door. A villain or person who is just bloody angry the whole time is

much more interesting.' One dream role did elude him: 'I'm 100 years too old now but I would love to have played, though I have never been offered, Kenneth More's role in Terence Rattigan's *The Deep Blue Sea*. It was the most wonderful, moving part and I saw the play three times in London.'

Now aged 82, he has no desire to retire ('I'll take on a role if anyone asks me as long as it's not particularly strenuous – it's just nice to be asked'). He continues to be involved in the Iain Rennie Hospice at Home charity, where he has been patron for 20 years, and goes trout and salmon fishing. 'If you're fishing in a river in a beautiful place, with luck you're on your own with your surroundings. There's an extraordinary mystery in running water and doing something which is a little bit primeval, like hunting. I wish I had started fishing earlier.'

Acting awards and public honours have not fazed this refreshingly down-to-earth actor, who still talks affectionately of his father as 'an honourable, good human being'. He adds, 'In so far as we all grow into our parents, whether we like it or not, I realise if I've got any of him in me that's pretty good.'

And the advice he gives to his own children? 'You're not here for long, so enjoy it.'

'I had no careers advice and anyway grew up thinking I would go to war. One of my regrets is not having the opportunity to study English at Oxford or Cambridge'

OLDEN LIFE

What was...
a Rechabite tent?
by *Alan Thomas*

Contrary to what one's first thoughts might be, we don't need to go back to Biblical times to find an answer to this question. Well within living memory there were hundreds of Rechabite tents in this country, many still in existence until 1948. They were killed off 'stone dead', one might say, in that year by the introduction of the National Health Act.

The first of these Rechabite tents came into existence on 25th August 1835. They were the brainchild of the founders of the Independent Order of Rechabites, a pioneer of the self-help movement among working men – and created at a time when self-help was about the only kind of help available. It was set up in reaction to the almost universal practice among friendly societies of holding their meetings in taverns, a situation that raised problems of its own, as the abuse of alcoholic drink was widespread. Dissatisfaction led to the formation, in 1835 at Salford, Lancashire, of a friendly society to cater for the needs of teetotallers, called the Independent Order of Rechabites. The name was based on the biblical story of the house of Rechab (Jeremiah, Chapter 35) when Rechab's son Jonadbab is tempted by Jeremiah and responds, 'We will drink no wine.'

The founders were inspired to call their branches 'tents' after the nomadic lifestyle of the ancient Rechabites; the first tent, named Ebenezer, was formed at Mrs Meadowcroft's temperance hotel in Salford. All subsequent tents were established in premises where there was no connection with intoxicating liquors. Within a year, 27 tents had been established in several counties, and it eventually became the largest, wealthiest friendly society of abstainers in existence, with a membership of over one million.

The raison d'être of friendly societies was to provide benefits to members in times of need, whether sickness, medical attendance, medicines or funeral expenses (the latter being curiously described as 'death benefit'). Funds came from the regular contributions made by members. The Rechabites, along with other friendly societies, were run on

Rechabite tents were a fact of life until the National Health Service took off

sound actuarial principles: in fact they were largely responsible for gathering and assessing data on which much actuarial science came to be based.

Monthly meetings at the tents, where contributions were received and new members admitted, were conducted in great secrecy and in accordance with strict rules laid down by the order's founders. Branches were at all times referred to as tents, each being given a number and a distinctive name, such as number 4721, the Hope to Prosper, and 798, the Star of Harrogate. The women's section had separate tents and names – 356 was Faithful and True, and 37 was the Emblem of Purity.

The book of ritual contained an illustration directing the seating position of each officer when business was being conducted, and no deviation was permitted. Passwords and signals were given to the door steward before admittance could be gained, and appropriate regalia and medallions had to be worn at all meetings. The regalia, including aprons, collars, chains of office, sashes and badges, defined both status and duties. Each meeting commenced with an ode to the hymn tune of *The Old Hundredth*, *Boston* or *Wareham*:

Each effort to redeem our race,
Who by intemperance are made
  slaves,
To lead them back to paths of
  peace,
The blessing of our God receives.

New members would be sworn in at these meetings only after the candidate had completed and signed a declaration that henceforth he/she would abstain from intoxicating liquors. Exceptions were only allowed when required by religious ordinances or prescribed by a qualified medical practitioner during sickness. This form of declaration, known as the Pledge, was signed by the candidate and countersigned and witnessed by officers in the tent.

Each tent meeting closed with a departing ode, the final lines of which – 'To dry the springs which banish peace' – provided a thoughtful conclusion.

Sadly, the Rechabite tents that for nigh on 80 years played such an important part in the lives of thousands have disappeared without trace. However, evidence of membership of the Independent Order of Rechabites was carried to the grave by some, those who have the initials 'I.O.R.' carved on their headstones – an inscription that must have puzzled many.

Flights of fancy

As the former political editor for Channel 4,
Elinor Goodman flew around the globe with various
prime ministers on the hunt for a story...

They were the best of trips and the worst of trips – travelling with different prime ministers as they flew round the globe visiting other world leaders. The political hacks were bottled in the back of a VC10 in great comfort, the Prime Minister and the Downing Street entourage sat in the front. Food and drink were served from the moment you got on board. You didn't even have to sit down when the plane took off.

Every now and then Alastair Campbell, or whoever was the Prime Minister's spokesman at the time, would come back to try and make the most of a captive press corps. But, desperate to justify the huge expense of sending us on the trip, we would usually agree among ourselves a better story than the one being offered. In the vacuum-packed atmosphere of the cabin, stories bred like germs. It was when Alastair Campbell was still political editor of the *Daily Mirror* that he managed to persuade the rest of the flying pack that he had distinctly seen John Major's shirt tucked into his underpants. From that flight a myth was born.

I never understood why prime ministers came back to the press cabin. It was started by Mrs Thatcher, but in those days the pack was far friendlier. I am embarrassed to say that we serenaded her, with a *Sun* wordsmith writing a song for each trip. The song was usually a bit risqué but, not surprisingly, she loved it, and it did wonders for her relations with the press.

Despite having witnessed so many of John Major's unhappy jousts with journalists on the plane, Alastair Campbell duly escorted Tony Blair down the gangway. Blair would often complain that his words had been taken out of context, and vow never to come back again. But he needed us as much as we needed him. I remember once being woken by

Tony Blair standing above me – I was stretched out across four seats – and wondering why on earth he didn't try to sleep himself.

We went to some wonderful places – South Africa, and of course the Azores for Blair's 2003 summit with George W Bush. My main preoccupation was not the rights and wrongs of the imminent war with Iraq but how to get across a field of cows to where I was supposed to do a piece to camera. For a television journalist logistics are everything. You arrive at a destination, help the crew gather up their gear, then drive like the clappers to get to where the Prime Minister is. There would then be a few minutes for a bit of filming, followed by several hours of hanging around for a press conference. The press would then get on their phones and file their copy. But we had to edit a piece for television, which takes much longer.
Sometimes we would go to the

local television stations – in Saudi Arabia I remember recording a piece under a plastic palm tree. On other occasions we huddled in the backs of vans or slumped on beds in hotel rooms. It was always a rush to get on the plane. The press corps would already be on their second glass of champagne as we hurtled up the steps.

One of the most exotic trips with Blair was to Libya to see President Gaddafi in May 2007. We were driven out into the desert where he had set up his tent. The centre of Libyan government is always

> Rather than listening to Blair, Gaddafi seemed more interested in us – political editors struggling to record pieces to camera with a background of burping camels

where the President's tent has been pitched, and it was apparently moved even as we were arriving at the airport. But nobody had told our bus driver, so after speeding along for half an hour, he suddenly screeched to a U-turn and set off in the opposite direction.

Gaddafi had brought along his camels to show Tony Blair, though Blair didn't seem very interested in them and the camels showed a haughty disdain for all of us. The two leaders sat in the tent in full view of the cameras, supposedly negotiating. But most of the real work had almost certainly been done by officials. Rather than listening to Blair,

ILLUSTRATION BY BOB GEARY

Elinor Goodman in Saudi Arabia

Gaddafi seemed more interested in us – political editors struggling to record pieces to camera in front of the tent against a background noise of camels burping. All this without over-running our allotted three minutes of satellite time.

I went to places I would never otherwise have visited. I nearly got left behind in the spectacularly beautiful Umayyad Mosque in Damascus because the Prime Minister's motorcade moved off through the souq without me. I saw leaders like Nelson Mandela in the flesh. But I am ashamed to say that I found the trips very stressful – partly because they were so expensive. I felt I should be giving Channel 4 something extra for its money.

I had the added – and now, I realise, ridiculous – preoccupation with what I looked like. Nick Robinson didn't have enough hair to ruin it by sleeping on the plane. I was supposed to look presentable when I did the mandatory piece to camera in front of a landmark to prove that I had left Westminster and wasn't just voicing over somebody else's picture. I would borrow the flight attendant's Carmen rollers, while on the other side of the divide, Cherie's hairdresser gave her the full works.

There was also the worry that a colleague might come up with a scoop, or that the political editors of the Sunday papers would invent one of their own. As a result I would get horrific indigestion, burping like one of Gaddafi's camels, and be desperate for a decent night's sleep. But nowadays, strapped into economy class with my knees pressed against my chin and a howling child beside me, I do reflect on how times have changed. I now have more time to explore countries than on those trips when a long stay was a day. But I do miss the VIP departure lounge, and the chance of being in on the making of history.

Simply the best

ANTHONY HOWARD

Best seat in the house: The wit and parliamentary chronicles of Frank Johnson

JR Books

On the day of Frank Johnson's death in December 2006, the *Evening Standard* had billboards all over London declaring, 'Fleet Street Genius Dies'. That may have been pushing things a bit, but this nicely balanced volume at least serves to remind us just how big a gap the absence of the Johnson byline has left.

He was, quite simply, the best parliamentary sketch writer of his generation, and given that his contemporaries include Simon Hoggart and Matthew Parris, that is no mean claim. Frank was a classic example of the autodidact in journalism. He knew about Italian opera, Russian ballet, English literature, and American as well as British politics. Best of all, despite being a right-winger, he always followed Lord Beaverbrook's advice to 'make

mischief'. If anyone has written anything funnier or more irreverent than his description of Mrs Thatcher campaigning in a chocolate factory during the 1979 election, I have yet to find it.

Frank's career was mostly confined to two papers, the *Telegraph* and the *Times*. He was briefly editor of the *Spectator* but, like most first violins, his metier lay not as conductor. Nor, though he sometimes hankered after it, was he a natural heavyweight columnist: he tried that hat on with Sir James Goldsmith's ill-fated *Now!* magazine in 1979-81, and it did not fit.

It was then, incidentally, that I did him a singularly bad turn. Detecting that he was far from happy, I mentioned his possible availability to the then new editor of the *Times*, Harry Evans. Evans snapped him up – a week or so before *Now!* folded, thus depriving Frank of a quite lavish redundancy payment.

Frank became the great ornament of *Times* parliamentary coverage. The flip comment, no doubt, would be that he resembled the clown always wanting to play Hamlet. But that is unfair. He was an outstandingly witty writer who, in the end – he was only 63 when he died – wisely gave up the temptation to write the kind of ponderous pieces most of us turn out all the time.

A groping Claus Bülow

BLOG ELISABETH LUARD, 2017

Claus Bülow – as he called himself when I met him in 1959 – was not a nice person. I was a deb at the time.

I foolishly accepted a lift from Bülow back to my family's flat after a deb dance - he was far too old to be there unless as somebody's dad. He drove a sports car – maybe an E-type – and it didn't occur to me he was anything but a kindly uncle till he parked somewhere off the King's Road (outside John Sandoe's, as I remember, when I was supposed to be dropped in Palace Gate).

He locked the car door and made a determined lunge (not easy

across the gearbox). I yanked the door and yelled so loudly that he unlocked the door and accelerated away as soon as I jumped out, leaving me without the fiver I carried in my bag for taxi-money, and I had to leg it home in my ball gown and high heels.

I never told anyone – Nanny let me into the flat. But, when the business of his trial, conviction and acquittal for the attempted murder of his wife, Sunny, came up, I wouldn't have put anything past him.

Thank God for my Hartnell dress (dark red satin). It had a whaleboned bodice, petersham waistband and full-net underskirt – pretty good armour, actually.

And I also carried a paperback in my knickers, so that I could read in the loo and avoid the debs delights I was supposed to be dancing with.

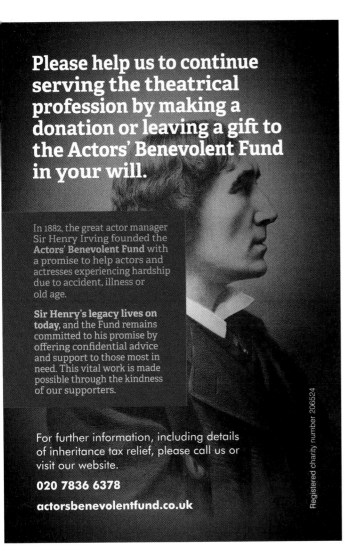

Christmas with Tyrone Guthrie

Novelist *Joseph Hone* recalls a miserable, penny-pinching childhood that changed utterly when he was fostered and began sharing family holidays with the extraordinary cast of characters at magical, moated Annaghmakerrig

Looking back, I can be pretty certain where the turning point came, showing me where my proper future lay. It was when the famed theatre director Tyrone Guthrie, whom we called Tony, entered my life. It was at Christmas, when I was about nine, when Tony, then head of the Old Vic, arrived with his wife Judy for their annual Christmas visit to Tony's mother at the old family home, the big house of Annaghmakerrig in the north of Ireland. I was then with my Butler foster-parents, and Peggy Butler was Tony's sister, so Tony had become a sort of foster-uncle to me. I was an unhappy, difficult boy, abandoned by my real parents in London in 1939 and initially put in the care of sad, penny-pinching grandparents in Dublin, before being farmed out to the Butlers in their house in the south of Ireland. But this was the making of me in that I, with other children, came to spend summer and Christmas holidays at Annaghmakerrig, where the house became the stage set for my conversion.

Annaghmakerrig was a wonderful house, moated by lakes, remotely distant beyond its three avenues, inviolate behind fir-clad hills, boggy fields and small brackish canals; a dream kingdom, and at Christmas, once up the steps and into the big hall, with the smell of Aladdin oil lamps and candle wax, you had the first intimation of the pleasures to come. Settled and secure, the house offered both mystery and comfort – the soft-carpeted, lamp-lit rooms warmed by log fires, where pools of rose-gold light ran away into shadowy spaces, down long corridors into ghost-haunted nooks and crannies, hidden rooms and attics filled with

novelties, secrets. And here we waited for the central drama of Christmas day. But the prelude was almost as good: children's parties, dumb crambo and charades in the drawing room, getting dressed up in the hall from boxes of Victorian tat and finery, musical chairs to the tune of *The Dashing White Sergeant* from the cabinet gramophone, and *Oranges and Lemons* with nervous procession through a pair of arched arms, where you could be trapped on the last words of 'Here comes a candle to light you to bed, here comes a chopper to chop off – YOUR HEAD!' And later, on Christmas day in the evening, the presents piled around the tall fir tree in the study, the magic of candles and the smell of melting wax and warmed fir needles. And finally the heart-stopping moment when the brown-paper parcels could be set upon and fiercely unwrapped. Christmas at Annaghmakerrig, with its silks of Araby, its décor of tinsel and coloured streamers, its warm perfumes of wax, fir and almond-cake icing, had a touch of *A Thousand and One Nights* about it.

And it was here, with Tony sometimes directing us in our charades, that I sensed life need not be unhappy, dull, difficult and penny-pinching, but that with Tony, in the stage setting of the house with its Victorian props and costumes, life could be 'produced' to show a much more exciting side, that in his inventive hands it could be

transformed into all sorts of magic, the workaday world banished in the cause of entertainment and illusion, with Tony master of the revels, alchemist in the dross-to-gold department. Tony was a transforming influence for me.

I was an accomplished liar as a child, and often suffered punishment for this. But Tony showed me how the make-believe was entirely valid, how there was an escape from my sins and glooms through invention,

Tyrone Guthrie

fantasy, creative lies. And this was a message he repeated for me later when I knew him better, saw some of his productions and did some film scripting work for him.

Tony was six foot six in his socks. He towered over everything. Eyes narrowed in the smoke from a dangling cigarette, pondering some dramatic plan – anything, as I see it now, which would kick ordinary life in the pants, or celebrate it, or alter it entirely. There wasn't a moment to lose in this transformation of the mundane, nothing of life that couldn't be tinkered with, re-fashioned by his vital spirit into something unexpected, astonishing, spectacular. Everything was prey to his inventions: evenings at the soft-toned Blüthner piano in the drawing room, when he would sing old ballads with exaggerated relish, a Thomas Moore melody or *The Skye Boat Song*. Or just as suddenly, in his quick military way, he would go to the cabinet gramophone, wind it up, put on a record and bring forth *The Pirates of Penzance*, annotating the songs mischievously, taking different roles, counterpointing the words in a *basso profundo* or in his high tenor voice.

He was a man overcome with endless provocative schemes, of creative or sometimes destructive fever, whether directing us in our charades or leading an attack on the garden scrub, with bonfires, the whole household commandeered, the grown-ups issued with bow-saws and choppers, we children the lesser spear-carriers as the wilderness rapidly diminished, the whole tiresome business made fun, produced as vivid spectacle, like the mob scene in *Coriolanus*. 'On! On!' he would shout, rising up suddenly from behind a bush like a jack-in-the-box, with a mock-fierce smile, urging us on, prophet-like, to smite the nettles and the brambles – storming the barricades of convention, in life as in theatre, setting every sort of hungry cat among the complacent pigeons, to propose and often to achieve the unlikely or the impossible. Life at Annaghmakerrig became repertory theatre for me, a cabinet of curiosities that I could pick through, finger and possess. A time of gifts indeed, and of all sorts of daily theatrical surprises.

Some years later, in my teens, I was standing with Tony in the hall of the big house after breakfast when there was a timid knocking on the huge hall door. It was a summer day, the lake a hazy blue below us. We were surprised. Visitors

> Tony towered over us, eyes narrowed in the smoke from a dangling cigarette, pondering some dramatic plan – anything, as I see it now, which would kick ordinary life in the pants

normally came in through the side or the back door. Tony opened the great baronial entrance and there on the steps was a rather nervous little man in a tweed outfit, with a moustache and a pork pie hat, a fishing rod and net.

'Excuse me, Dr Guthrie,' the man said in a gentle Scots burr, 'I'm Mr McAlmond, over on holiday doing a little lake fishing in the district. I wonder if you'd be so kind as to allow me to fish your lake? I understand there are good roach and perch to be had.'

'Why certainly, Mr McAlmond. You're very welcome. Where are you from?'

'From Glasgow, Dr Guthrie.'

'Glasgow? I know it well. Splendid city. And people. I used to produce plays there.'

'Indeed. I'm afraid I'm not a theatre man. I'm in the bakery business. McAlmond's Bakeries. Soda bread, fruit cakes and the like.'

'And very nice too, I'm sure. And just as valuable as theatre. "Bread and Circuses" – that's all people really need.'

The two of them had some more chat and I had moved away before I heard a roar from Tony and peals of laughter, and a shout of 'Alec! You rogue. I would never have believed it!'

I returned and saw that the little man, minus the moustache and pork pie hat now, was Alec Guinness.

Stanley Baker: the greatest
BLOG ROGER LEWIS, 2019

I often wonder whether Sir Stanley Baker, who died on 28 June 1976, aged 49, wasn't a better actor than Richard Burton.

They were the same age, from identical backgrounds – the coal-mining valleys of South Wales. They were rescued by enlightened schoolmasters, who perceived their talents and packed them off for careers on the London stage.

Yet where Burton remains famous for his marriage to Elizabeth Taylor, and the decadence of his lifestyle – yachts, private jets, jewels – Baker, unfairly, is perhaps a more forgotten figure today, remembered chiefly for *Zulu* (which he also produced, in 1964) and his roles for Joseph Losey.

Where Burton was declamatory Baker, who also possessed a dark voice, had genuine physical presence. He'd fling himself about in action scenes. There was real force behind his punches, the crunch of an elbow in the neck or kidneys. He also had a lanky grace – Baker looked good in those Sixties/early Seventies suits, the yellow or orange ties.

He had a pinched face, with high cheekbones – not beautiful (like Burton), but his slightly slanted brown eyes could be vulpine and handsome, or rodenty, sneaky. Baker often sported a bushy black moustache, which gave his face body, symmetry. He never smiled much. In his last years he did look pasty (terminal lung cancer). But there was never any stiffness about him – he had nobility, strength.

Like Burton, Baker had an instinctive grasp of men who don't belong to anybody. Their characters were men under pressure who had discerned that the rules by which we are meant to live are valueless. Hence, why Baker could suggest crime was virtue – his villains had their own convincing rectitude.

Stanley Baker always had power, menace, and could be undone in a trice by a woman, as in *Eve* (1962) with Jeanne Moreau. 'Bloody Welshman!' she calls him, at the end. The sentiment was echoed by Burton. 'Unless you are Welsh, you couldn't possibly understand him,' he said of Baker when he died. This remains true.

Notes from the sofa
Name-dropping

Written and illustrated by *Raymond Briggs*

It is strange that ordinary trade names can hold such a place in the oldie mind. They have almost the same resonance as nursery rhymes and, like the rhymes, they are part of our memory and our childhood: Golden Syrup, Bourneville Cocoa, Robinson's Lemon Barley Water, Horlicks, Fyffes, Oxo, Saxa, Tizer, Typhoo Tea, and even Vim.

I suppose it is only nostalgia, which, we are told, is bad for us, but it doesn't mean we idealise these products – 'Wasn't life wonderful then?' – it is simply that they are part of memory and are still in our minds today.

Mum's Hoover, our battered, brown Thermos for picnics on the common, the Pyrex kept under the dresser, my Dad polishing our brass stair rods with Bluebell. The home-made wooden box of shoe-cleaning stuff kept under the draining board with tin after tin of Cherry Blossom. Mum's Brownie box camera, Kodak, and Dad's Rolls razor. Hovis, Liquorice Allsorts, Quality Street, Golden Shred...

The fact that these names have been around for so long gives us a sense of continuity and security. Rowntree's Dairy Box, Black Magic, Lifebuoy – even Rinso, Persil and Lux.

Many of these names are now multi-nationals, but it doesn't seem to matter, they still touch us. So much so, that when Alliance took over Boots, they changed their own name to Boots. Probably because it had been around for decades and was held in some affection by everyone.

This is why it was such a shock when Woolworth's disappeared. It had been part of all our childhoods – the Threepenny and Sixpenny Store, used by generation after generation. If Woolworth's could go, anything could go, even the Empire, but then that had gone already, like Rinso.

Camp Coffee with its kilted Army officer being waited on respectfully by his humble, turbanned Indian servant. Oh, dear.

At our local Woolworth's branch it was quite upsetting to see its doors closed, its windows blanked out, the gold letters taken down from the fascia, leaving the ghostly, grey shadows of the lettering still readable.

One old lady looking up at it had tears in her eyes.

Cloud cuckoo land

Superbyways: your guide to digital life, by *Webster*

This is the time of year for reflection and prediction, but as the man said, prediction is a tricky business, especially about the future. Who would have guessed two years ago that the faintly ridiculous Twitter would have become so prominent, or that Facebook and others like it would have become a marketing force to be reckoned with? All over the country, courses are being run to teach business people how to make the most of these gadgets, and they are finding ready pupils among the baffled commercial community.

It's no fad: I already know of several professionals in a variety of fields who derive a very large part of their work from promoting themselves on these social networking sites.

Of course, that's not to say that some other bright idea won't soon pop up to usurp them all; in fact it almost certainly will. Perhaps it will be some means of unifying all the various threads of this strange industry, so that we don't need separate accounts at Twitter, Facebook, Bebo, LinkedIn and others, bringing the certainty that we will forget at least one of the passwords. Google and Yahoo have made stabs at this, but have not really managed it yet.

One social change it has created is the re-introduction of the mobile phone to polite society. The so-called smartphones (such as iPhones) are becoming more affordable; as well as being phones, they allow the user full access to his Twittering and Facebooking at all times. Whereas at the start of a lecture or a conference we used to be asked to turn off our phones, we are now encouraged to keep them on, so that news of what is going on may be disseminated as fast as possible, and reaction sought from around the world. It is still impolite to actually make a phone call, but those are so old-fashioned these days…

What we will also see in 2010 is the increased use of 'cloud computing'. This means running your affairs – business or personal – by using the internet to connect to powerful computers owned by someone else, and on which you have stored all your data. You already do this if you use a web-based email system like Yahoo or Hotmail, when all your messages are stored out there somewhere rather than on your own computer where you can keep an eye on them.

Cloud computing has many benefits, especially for businesses: it's cheaper than owning your own big system, and someone else has to look after the security of the machinery and keep it working.

For exactly that reason, however, it is also a massive accident waiting to happen. I predict that in 2010 there will be a huge failure in some data centre somewhere, perhaps through natural disaster, financial collapse or even criminal activity. This may not matter if the data centre is well run, because there will be back-up systems and complex encryption to protect it all. But if the set-up is cheap and cheerful, with computers held together with sealing wax and string, you'll lose the lot.

Google, and others, are building huge 'server farms' all over the place. These are rows and rows of industrial buildings filled with big computers (called servers) for storing all our data. Many of these server farms are actually bigger than normal farms.

What's more, because it is important to keep them cool, it makes sense to build them in a cold place. So, believe it or not, they are building them in Siberia. Answer me this: how keen would, for example, a large British exporter be to have all their data stored in Russia? Not very, I suspect – but they wouldn't know that was where it was. I have no doubt that we will soon see a major incident involving data loss (at best) or data theft (at worst) from one of these storage places.

The irony is that one of the reasons server farms are economically attractive is that the cost of the equipment they need is falling like a stone – but this means it is also becoming cheaper for companies to create their own facilities and stay out of the cloud. Having your head in the clouds is, after all, no way to run a business.

> I predict that in 2010 there will be a huge failure in some data centre through natural disaster, financial collapse or criminal activity

One of my enduring memories of living in Notting Hill is standing in my kitchen one morning in 1995 watching two prostitutes trying to stab my lodger to death. Luckily for him, he was large with long arms whereas the prostitutes were small and rather unhealthy. He had lured one of them back to my flat and then refused to pay her the measly £25 she had demanded. He was an awful scumbag and I quite enjoyed watching the police throw him and his belongings onto the street. We then tracked down the poor woman and gave her £100 – partly to apologise but also out of deep gratitude for giving me the excuse I needed to reclaim the spare room.

The incident highlighted a shortcoming in security which I rectified by a call to Phil's Grille and Bill Security Emporium (motto: 'We aim to incarcerate you'). In our part of Notting Hill at that time, most of the law-abiding citizens seemed to live behind bars while all the muggers, burglars and assorted criminals ruled the streets: you had to watch your step. Notting Hill Gate itself had always been rather swanky, but where we lived in North Kensington – sandwiched between Portobello Road and Ladbroke Grove – was edgy: the Notting Hill of Keith Talent and *London Fields*, and, not all that long ago, Peter Rachman.

But goodness! Hasn't the old place gone down hill in the ten years since I left? Most nights, my local on Ladbroke Grove was a smoke-filled commotion with drunken old Irish guys scrapping in the corner while a barmaid swept up bits of teeth with a dustpan and brush. Now, snooty hedge-funders boast about bonuses over decent claret or a jar of strawberry Belgian beer. The juke box has gone, along with the overpowering smell of Dettol, and the air is filled with the tap-tapping of laptops.

The old couple next door ran an illegal drinking den; the rattling of dominoes

Notting Hill

What goes up comes down, says
Andrew Hosken

drove me to despair most Saturday nights. They've upped sticks back to Jamaica where they live like kings thanks to the fortune they secured for their dingy basement. Down the Portobello Road the heart would sing at the sight of a Salvation Army captain rattling his tin on a cold wet evening outside the derelict old Electric Cinema. Now someone's done the place up and it teems with brokers and barristers slurping buckets

> **The place teems with brokers and barristers slurping buckets of coffee mocha, the sound of their braying disturbing the peace for miles around**

of coffee mocha, the sound of their braying disturbing the peace for miles around.

In a recent series, Harry Enfield runs a store called Modern Wank that sells loads of over-priced garbage to gullible people with too much money. There's another antiques store called Old Shit flogging pricey antiques. And that about sums up the current retail sector for Notting Hill.

The demise began in about 1998 when the council introduced residents' parking. Few people understand the social-cleansing power of residents' parking: it is a pure avenging fire which dodgy neighbourhoods can't withstand. To get a permit, you needed proof that you paid council tax, car insurance and road tax. Within months, the tarts, pimps, drug dealers, vagabonds and cut-throats seemed to melt away and in their place came the bankers, the trustafarian fops, the dot-com arseholes, the future Tory front-benchers and the greaseball libel lawyers.

What really finished off the place was the eponymous Richard Curtis movie. It completed the transformation from neighbourhood to tame tourist safari park. Even the carnival now seems to throb less menacingly and attract more sponsorship.

A few places hold out. You can still find the odd watering hole with people who seem fairly normal. It probably won't last: here, I'm afraid, it's down Notting Hill all the way.

I once met...

Robert De Niro

When *Jane Thynne* got the opportunity to meet the notoriously private megastar she was keen to discover what his off-screen personality would reveal...

Everyone knows about Hollywood stars. We know that behind their shiny smiles and American teeth there lurk monster egos beset with attention deficit and anger issues, given to babyish tantrums and absurd religious cults. Even if it's all kisses on the red carpet, behind the scenes there are invariably mobile telephones being hurled at cowering assistants. Then again, there are some Hollywood stars so brooding, so suggestive of ill-suppressed anger and psychotic menace, that they barely even manage the public persona part. Jack Nicholson comes to mind, as does Nick Nolte. But right at the top of this category I would have put the scary, saturnine star of *Taxi Driver*, *Raging Bull* and *Meet The Parents*: Robert de Niro.

Back in the 1990s I was on a flying trip to New York, part of an attempt to sell a screenplay to some Hollywood studio. It was my husband's screenplay, so my only function was to be what politicians call 'room meat', which means ligging along to bulk out a meeting. A meeting was being set up with Robert de Niro's production company and, while we waited for it to materialise, all I had to do was hang around in the trendy TriBeCa area of the city, chatting to the junior producers and marvelling at their enormous, picture-window lofts the size of basketball courts, with limed oak flooring and just one sofa right in the middle. I also found myself singing the Bananarama hit, *Robert De Niro's Waiting, Talking Italian*, in an annoying loop.

The producers loved De Niro, and spoke respectfully of his awesome talents, of his ability to produce and direct films as well as act. I have to say I fished shamelessly for gossip. De Niro is known as one of Hollywood's most private stars. He rarely gives interviews and when he does he rules great chunks of his life off-limits. Though most of the roles he

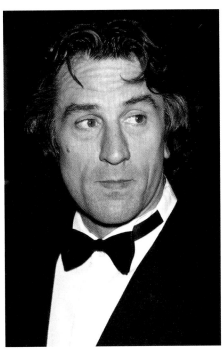

takes are borderline psychotics, little is known about his personal behaviour. Sadly hardly any gossip was forthcoming, except the tale that when De Niro had heard of the Bananarama song, he had rung the group's London council flat and arranged to meet the girls for dinner, but they got so nervous that by the time he arrived, they were blind drunk. Somehow, I knew how they felt.

> Behind the shiny smiles of Hollywood stars lurk monster egos beset with attention deficit and anger issues, given to babyish tantrums and absurd religious cults

De Niro loved the screenplay. He felt the lead part could have been made for him. We were invited to visit the star in his office.

TriBeCa Productions occupies an impressive office block in Lower Manhattan. As we entered reception and waited for his people to come and find us, a commotion occurred. Outside in the street a huge stretch limousine had pulled up and half a dozen frightening bouncers wearing dinner jackets and telephone headsets were thrusting people out of the way. Onlookers gawped. Out of the car stepped a curly-haired, brown-skinned woman in a white trouser suit who proceeded through the protective wall of bouncers to the far end of the lobby where the lift doors were being held open. Quite a crowd had gathered, and in order to facilitate her regal progress everyone else was shoved brutally out of the way. In the crush I was pushed back and felt my foot crunch painfully on that of an anonymous little guy wearing a donkey jacket and flat cap. Apologising profusely, we exchanged wry smiles and he said: 'Looks like it must a real big star!' As it turned out, the woman in the white trouser suit was, indeed, Whitney Houston. The real star, though, was the guy in the donkey jacket – Robert De Niro.

Later, I sat next to him for a meal at the Japanese restaurant he owns. He appeared rather shy, until the subject strayed onto children. He demanded my baby snaps and showed me his. We talked about his father and his love of art. A nicer, more decent and civilised superstar it would be hard to imagine. And when we had said goodbye, he pulled on his cap and donkey jacket, stepped onto the sidewalk and became instantly anonymous, just another slightly shabby little man, melting straight into the crowd. And at no point, I have to report, did he talk Italian.

Being Frank

Frank Field has been an MP for 31 years. Respected on both sides of the House, he says what he thinks. Even when it's not what people want to hear …Interview by *Sarah Shannon*

Frank Field is waiting behind the security cordons at Portcullis House. A policewoman at this glowering fortress of MPs' offices frisks me. A large sign says the building is on amber alert for terrorist threats. Then suddenly I'm inside the light-filled atrium and shaking the cool hand of the MP for Birkenhead.

It's a bit like being met at the door of the Vatican by the Pope. After all, Field has been a backbencher (and briefly welfare minister) for an impressive 31 years and watched the rise and demise of seven governments. He manages the rare feat of being admired on both sides of the House for his fierce intellect, and for sticking to his principles no matter which way the political winds prevail. He's the man who led the rebellion against the government's clumsy attempt to abolish the 10p tax band. He joined forces with an unlikely ally, the Tory MP and Old Etonian Nicholas Soames, to encourage debate about immigration, and most recently he became the first MP to willingly publish his expenses on the internet.

In fact, with a general election just weeks away, the thought of this outspoken maverick probably brings Gordon Brown out in hives. But what does the veteran MP have to say about the Prime Minster? 'I've always felt sorry for him, this combination of intelligence and an inability to see the people side of politics. Unfortunately the public have marked their card on him and nothing will change that now. In opposition I had a meeting with him and I thought, "God, this isn't normal." Sadly nothing's happened to change my view.'

Crikey. This is why journalists love Frank Field – he sings like a canary if it will land him in trouble. Last year he declared that Brown had a 'vile temper' and is 'unhappy in himself'. He later apologised to the House for the personal nature of his comments. Yet here he is letting loose once again.

Field lobbied unsuccessfully to get Brown removed and replaced by Alan Johnson, an MP whom he has admired ever since he defied a whip's instruction to walk out during Field's resignation speech as welfare minister. 'Alan Johnson comes over as a real person. From postman to prime minister – that really would be something. Here we are prattling on about social mobility and here's this guy that symbolises everything we stand for.'

Field's main concern for the looming general election is that voters will be sidetracked by outrageous expenses claims for duckhouses and moat-cleaning and forget the big political issues. Although Field's own expenses were modest in comparison to most (he only

> This is why journalists love Frank Field – he sings like a canary even if it will land him in trouble. Last year he said that Brown had a 'vile temper' and is 'unhappy in himself'. He apologised to the House, yet here he is letting loose once again

claimed 30 per cent of the total sum allowed last year) he was still asked by Sir Thomas Legg's review to pay back £4,000 he had claimed for a housekeeper. He rages against the injustice of the demand because the threshold of cleaning expenses was set retrospectively. 'It's so damn arbitrary. There are those who manage to use up every penny every year. There are those

who have set up property companies or who have flipped three or four times,' he points out crossly. Although he hates being lumped in with the cheats he decided to abide by the ruling and repay the sum. 'It looks as though I feel I'm guilty if I pay up. On the other hand I feel unclean because he's actually said you shouldn't have claimed this money. He's been set up by the House of Commons and however bizarre his judgement, that is his judgement.'

Despite the repayment, Field came out of the row smelling of roses and was even praised by the media for publishing his own expenses. Now he hopes the country will draw a line under the affair and concentrate on the major issues such as the economy. 'Our country is in such a state. We've printed money in order to buy our own debt. It's real Alice in Wonderland politics. We've got to go to the world and ask if they want to lend us money. If we can't shift the debt we're finished.'

This isn't the sort of doom-mongering we read in the national press. Isn't the recession supposed to be over? Field shakes his head ruefully and employs a Phoney War analogy: 'People fled to the shelters but no bombers came in those first early months of the War. That's the same with this crisis. I think this year the bombers are coming and the destruction will occur.'

Field pauses to sip his coffee. He is whippet-slim and dressed in an elegant suit that would have fitted him equally well on the day he entered Parliament. His fine face and slightly hooded eyes give him the look of a world-weary aesthete, but at 67 he shows more enthusiasm for solving society's ills than MPs half his age. He entered Parliament three decades ago after fighting off a right-wing academic and a Trotskyite to win Birkenhead. His own background was respectably working class – his father was a Tory-supporting labourer, his mother a classroom assistant. As a west London grammar school boy he joined the Tory Party but was kicked out for supporting the boycott of South African goods. Despite the best efforts of some Tory MPs, he has never been persuaded to defect back. After a degree at Hull University, he began teaching before becoming the director of the Child Poverty Action Group and the Low Pay Unit.

We chat about his experiences with previous prime ministers. 'Whenever I met Blair I always came away beguiled and convinced that he would do things differently this time. He reminds me of a water spider. It skims across the water but once it's gone you can't tell that it was ever there. He was brilliant at winning elections but then did nothing with it. I don't think he had much idea of how to run the machine.'

Field returns to this idea of the importance of a politician's effectiveness again and again. He says that, unlike most of the world, he has not fallen in love with Barack Obama and his main issue with the American President is that he will be too inexperienced to drive through change. 'I loathed the Clintons but if I had been a Democrat in America I'd have voted for Hillary. She knows the business.'

Field reserves his warmest words for a prime minister whom most Labour supporters abhor – Margaret Thatcher. Much of this admiration stems from first-hand observation of Thatcher's ability to make things happen. He was not afraid to seek help from Thatcher, or Mrs T as he calls her, despite their diametrically opposed politics. 'Here was a prime minister who was the most powerful PM we'd had in years, punching well above her weight on the world stage. It would seem barmy not to lobby her.' His many meetings with her created a bond between them. When he realised that she was about to lose the Tory leadership, he was concerned that her Cabinet wouldn't tell her it was time to step down. So he went to Number 10 to warn her himself. When she walked into the room he was taken aback by her appearance. 'All the previous times I'd had with her she was the big momma. This time it was like my gran coming in. I imagine that's how you'd look if the doctors were telling you that you had inoperable cancer.' She said, 'Why have you come, Frank?' Field told her the truth: 'You can't go out on a top note but

you can go out on a high note. And if you don't go tonight they'll tear you apart tomorrow.' After they spoke, Thatcher had him escorted out of another passageway to Whitehall, away from the cameras, and she never mentioned Field's visit in her memoirs for fear that it would damage him. This curious affection across a political divide clearly cuts both ways.

These days Field is most concerned with what he calls the 'politics of behaviour'. He thinks that Britain is becoming a less civilised nation and blames a breakdown in good parenting for the rise in bad behaviour. The results of this lack of family structure became clear to him one day in his constituency surgery when a group of smartly dressed

pensioners came to ask for help with local children who were running across their roofs and peeing through their letterboxes. 'At that point I thought, "I've got to accept that the world has changed. I can't just keep brushing these things off as random – this behaviour is becoming the norm."' As a result he began a campaign to tackle anti-social behaviour, lobbying that those affected should be allowed direct and fast access to justice.

As he escorts me to the exit, Field alternates a rapid fire of political ideas with questions about my views and experiences. 'I'm still learning so much,' he tells me with genuine zeal before shaking my hand and disappearing back into the busy political throng.

GARDENING
DAVID WHEELER
CROCUSES

'There is a widespread idea that Autumn Crocuses are hard to grow, and so there is many a well-furnished garden that still lacks their special charms. I cannot believe, however, that there is a garden in England that can produce a healthy cabbage and a Marigold in which *Crocus speciosus* and *C. zonatus* would not become so thoroughly at home after a few years that it would be as hard to entirely eradicate them as it is to banish Ground-Elder.' There!

Words penned by EA Bowles – even as long ago as these, put down in 1915 – hit my ears with Gospel status. First, though, before you go shopping, you need to check that meddlesome desk-bound botanists haven't changed the plants' names in the intervening years. They've so far kept their hands off *speciosus*, but dear old easily-remembered and neatly descriptive *zonatus* now trips off the tongue as – lawks! – *Crocus kotschyanus* subsp. *kotschyanus*, after Theodor Kotschy, an Austrian explorer who 'found' it in Turkey in 1853 – useless info you'll thank me for at the next pub quiz.

Both are among a band of hardy autumn-flowering bulbs that contribute tear-jerking beauty to the September and October garden. *Crocus speciosus* has intricate veining on blue/mauve petals that surround a bright orange stigma, while *kotschyanus* is paler. Each sports a white variety. Plant them in July or August to flower now, flourishing in light shade, increasing steadily once settled in.

Colchicums (aka naked ladies, because the leaves come later, in the following spring) are often confused with autumn crocuses. With typical elan, Anna Pavord relates an intriguing story about them in her most recent book, *Bulb* (2009): 'The name comes from Colchis (an ancient kingdom – and home of all sorcery – set between the Caucasus to the north and Armenia to the south), where the first plants are said to have sprung from drops of the potion brewed by the enchantress Medea, daughter of the king of Colchis, to restore youth to the ageing Aeson.' They seem the ideal oldie plant for, as Ms Pavord continues, 'all parts yield the drug colchicine, a cure for gout...' Don't, however, set to with pestle and mortar and try to concoct your own homemade fix – colchicum bulbs are highly poisonous.

Cyclamen also begin to flower now and make companionable drifts with little effort on our part. Their flowering period is longer, keeping the show going up to and beyond snowdrop time. Unlike the grassy crocus foliage, many cyclamen leaves are highly decorative in themselves: marbled, smudged, dotted, enamelled and blotched in a myriad of silvery or pewtered patterns.

Other autumn flowerers to blaze among the season's dying, rusty hues are amaryllis (the Cape belladonna or Jersey lily, not to be confused with tender house or conservatory hippeastrums, sometimes sold as amaryllis). Plant them in a hot, south-facing border for best results. Pink-flowering nerines relish the same situation.

If your taste runs to strong yellow at this time of the year, to take over from, say, the range of canary-coloured crocosmias, then try sternbergias, crocus look-alikes as bright as March celandines. My small colony of *Sternbergia lutea* emanates from a few bulbs given to me by a former gardening editor of *Country Life* who, in turn, was given them by his friend, that great, long-lived artist/plantsman Sir Cedric Morris (1889–1982). Morris famously bred (and painted) irises at home in Suffolk, but dug these sternbergias in the days when such dark deeds were not frowned upon during his travels in the hills of southern Spain. I, for one, forgive him.

A revolutionary caterpillar
BLOG VALERIE GROVE, 2019

Ask any child: who ate one piece of chocolate cake, one ice-cream cone, one pickle, one slice of salami, one lollipop, one piece of cherry pie, one sausage, one cupcake and one slice of watermelon?

Any child will answer: *The Very Hungry Caterpillar.*

He arrived in 1969; the second book by Eric Carle, who is 90 years old today. Three or four generations of children – 146 million so far in 60 languages – have the story by heart and don't mind how many times they hear it. So, happy birthday, Eric Carle!

When I met him in 1984, the gentle and genial, bearded Carle was already able to live comfortably on the royalties from the caterpillar alone. But he has carried on ever since, in his house in the New England pinewoods, producing tales of *Very Busy Spiders*, *Bad Tempered Ladybirds* etc.

He couldn't really fathom the caterpillar's instant global success. Later, he said he thought it was because it introduced to children the idea that they could become something different. A caterpillar can become a beautiful butterfly.

But I think it's because children love following the caterpillar's omnivorous progress, making a hole in the book. It's a game. Carle pioneered the book as plaything. He felt so sorry for children, whisked from the security of home into the strangeness of primary school: from toys to books.

'*The Caterpillar* is half-toy, half-book. A book you can play with, a toy you can read.' The idea was much copied: fold-back flaps and cut-outs, pop-ups and peep-throughs and other paper-engineering feats have now become commonplace.

Carle was born in America but when he was six his parents were persuaded by his grandmother to return to their German homeland. 'Think of the shock for me. I had just started at a bright, sunny, open American school... The teachers were creative and fun. And suddenly I was in a German school in Hitler's Germany, 1935. My parents regretted it from the moment they arrived and I longed to get back to America.' He was 22 when he returned, and first worked in advertising. He asked a literary agent, 'Is it possible to make money from children's books?' and she told him, 'You will.'

Still with us

Edward Mirzoeff talks to Denis Forman, the 93-year-old Granada Television grandee about what went wrong with British broadcasting

You either got killed, or you got wounded. For an infantry officer, there was no other option.' Denis Forman was lucky. He lost his lower leg at Monte Cassino in 1944, but he lived. (Marmaduke Hussey, later chairman of the BBC, lost rather more of his leg in the same week and at much the same place.) Two thirds of a century later, this doyen of television grandees and last surviving giant of its golden age has just celebrated his 93rd birthday.

Sir Denis was one of the pioneers of Granada Television, which in his time produced *World In Action, Coronation Street, Brideshead Revisited, Disappearing World* and his favourite child, *The Jewel in the Crown.* He's still a busy and active man. A little less mobile nowadays, he is nevertheless off to Goa for five months at the end of the week. He can spare me an hour at his Belsize Park flat.

The first impression is of a big, untidy man, rather dashing in striped shirt and capacious tweed trousers held high by bright red braces. His manner is engaging and entertaining. He tells me that he learned 'to become a showman and a show-off' telling jokes in the downstairs hall at Craigielands, Dumfriesshire, where he was brought up. 'The servants were my loyal supporters, they never told tales.'

It's just a day or two after the government has announced its finance plans for the BBC and Forman is eager to discuss them. 'I think the licence fee should be abolished. It's not fair that people who never watch the BBC at all should be made to pay for it. There should be a direct grant from government. It would make an honest woman of the BBC.' But the grant should be for a period of years, and not annual, he says, otherwise planning becomes impossible.

'The BBC was wrong and foolish in the extravagant way it paid its top executives. It's rubbish to say that if you don't pay more, you'll lose the best people. Granada always paid 10 per cent less than the other companies, but it had the first

Top: Forman at home, 2010
Above: Geraldine James and Charles Dance in *The Jewel in the Crown* (1984)

choice of all the biggest names. The important thing for people is not what they're paid, but what they do.'

Forman was hired by Cecil Bernstein on Christmas Eve 1954, with Granada just a few days old. 'I had no designation, and no contract. There were just four of us then.' In the back-stabbing world of television, their mutual admiration was very striking, and the young Denis finished up chairman and managing

director. 'The Bernsteins knew how to make a good show, to get the public on their side, make 'em suffer, make 'em laugh' – all within a tight financial discipline and staff structure. 'Only one committee, no market research, no marketing nonsense. Just a top echelon of a few creative people, recruited in our own image and out to make programmes of quality.'

Programmes are what really matter to Forman. '*Jewel in the Crown* was entirely mine, and it's the one I'm proudest of. It took just five minutes to get the Programme Committee to agree it. I said I'd read the *Raj Quartet*, and how good they were, and that was that.' Forman took Paul Scott's complex books apart, wrote down each scene in chronological order on a chopped up roll of wallpaper, and pinned the sheets around the office. From that he wrote the outline, helped to assemble 'the most dazzling cast ever to play in a major television series' (led by Dame Peggy Ashcroft), and persuaded Mobil to underwrite it. It was just a minor setback when the studio in Manchester burned to the ground with all the costumes, props and scenery. In a week they were replaced and ready for filming (all except Tim Pigott-Smith's artificial arm, which took a few days longer).

He's generous to his rivals' programmes, too, picking out BBC comedy and period drama for special praise. '*The Barchester Chronicles* was the most elegant series ever made. Perfect casting, director, costume, sets, camerawork. The BBC could come good in every department sometimes.'

But not so often nowadays, and for this he blames one of Granada's own trainees, John Birt. 'He's so clever at planning and organising, not an ounce of creativity. He made the BBC a mechanical business, mundane. It should work like a club, not like a bank. Its quality was its club-like atmosphere, like-minded people, cultured, enthusiastic, devoted to the medium. David Attenborough, the greatest broadcaster of our age, Huw Wheldon, Paul Fox. Where are their like today? The BBC lost its identity under John Birt. It's never recovered from his idea that it's all a business, and it has a horrible fear that it can't be left out of anything. It should be looking after its listeners and viewers by making good programmes.' As for ITV, he believes it is no longer a channel with any pretensions to quality television. Open commercialism has been allowed to take its course.

> ### 'It's rubbish to say that if you don't pay more you'll lose the best people. Granada paid less but had first choice of all the biggest names'

Actually Forman is far from a grumpy old man, and his sense of fun and mischief is never far away. Suddenly he remembers an incident with the Oxford historian Hugh Trevor-Roper. 'He was so rude. But I got my own back – arranged for his shoes to disappear from the dressing room just before the broadcast. Gave them back afterwards, saying they'd just been found...'

Forman has enjoyed a spectacularly wide-ranging career. After the war he joined the Central Office of Information, where his first film was the temptingly titled *Low Sugar-Content Jam Making*. He married his boss at the COI ('I saw at once that here was the most beautiful and intelligent woman I had ever met'), and then took over her job. (Forman's second wife, Moni, is the widow of the great journalist James Cameron.) He was chairman of the British Film Institute, and deputy chairman at the Royal Opera House for many years. But when I ask him to name his most important achievement, I'm surprised by his answer. It is one of his books. Not one of his three highly regarded and sensitively written memoirs, but a volume on the Mozart piano concertos, a revolutionary analysis of the structure of the first movements. He gets up to find it for me. I see that it is a work of love and scholarship.

And then he's off to the kitchen – it's time for him to make lunch.

Sir Denis Forman died in 2013

MIND THE ᴬᴳᴱ GAP

'Tell her to take her swimming things,' my mother says, when I tell her my daughter is going to Cornwall with friends in December. 'It's always so hot in their house.'

By this she means they have central heating and they use it, a practice she regards as a shameful waste of money and resources. My parents have central heating, but they rarely use it, except perhaps in extreme weather for half an hour 'to warm the place up'. It doesn't. Half an hour with the thermostat on six degrees is never going to warm up a detached house on a hill in the middle of the countryside.

If my parents were to advise George Osborne on where to save money I am sure they would tell him to get rid of the cold weather payments. 'Snow,' my father insists, 'insulates.' 'Yes, it keeps in the warmth,' my mother agrees, opening a window onto a blizzard to let some of this supposed warmth out.

'What warmth?' we slightly younger people mutter, wondering just how many layers of thermal underwear it is possible to wear at any one time.

'Aren't you hot?' my mother asks. Apparently simply sitting on the sofa doing the crossword is enough to make her sweat, or perhaps it is reading about the latest mandate from Europe, which has made her blood boil. Either way she will never need to follow Edwina Currie's advice to wrap up warm in winter.

'I'm a bit cold,' I venture, pulling my coat tighter around me. I am fairly certain it's warmer outside than it is in their sitting-room. 'The trouble with you lot,' my father tries to warm us up by spouting hot air, 'is that you're too soft.'

My parents cannot get their heads round the idea that central heating is not just for special occasions. Their generation was brought up on fresh air and the occasional coal fire. If you wanted to warm up you had to put on more coal, or more layers, or run around a bit. They cannot abide the fact that we just turn the thermostat up.

I know the planet is warming and the fossil fuels are running out, but I also enjoy not having had a single chilblain, since I left home, and being able to concentrate on whatever I am doing rather than thinking 'I am cold.'

'Why don't you put another jumper on?' my mother suggests. Has she seen me? Could I get another jumper on over the three I am already wearing? Then she relents a little. 'I'll put the potatoes on to boil. That will warm the kitchen up.' 'Not if you open the window to let the steam out,' I protest, but she doesn't hear me.

Staying the night at my parents' house is like camping on the north face of the Eiger. At home I like to have a bath before going to bed. We have constant hot water so the bath can be hot and deep. My parents prefer to switch their immersion heater on for half an hour so that you can have an inch of bath water before going to sleep with all the windows wide open.

'It gets so stuffy with them closed,' my mother insists, even though their windows are old and warped and it's like Wuthering Heights with them closed.

Christmas is a difficult time of year for my parents – all those log fires and warm ovens, plus of course the terrible business of having to shop. 'I was going to get you an iTunes voucher,' my mother tells my daughter, handing her instead a £20 note. 'But when I went into the shop it was so hot, I had to come straight out again.' I make a mental note in future only to ask for things which can be bought at outdoor markets, preferably in Siberia.

The last time we visited my parents, my husband bought me a curious thing called a thermal kidney belt from our local Lidl. It's like a padded corset, which you put in the microwave before wrapping it round your midriff. I put it on before setting off for Wuthering Heights, and was able to take my coat off and sit on the sofa feeling pleasantly toasty. But my mother was aware that something was up. 'You look as if you've put on weight,' she said accusingly, looking closely at the bulge under my sweater. 'It must be making you hot. I'll open the window.'

Lizzie Enfield

In the spring of 1961, Edith Evans arrived in Stratford-on-Avon to begin rehearsing the role of Queen Margaret in William Gaskill's production of *Richard III*. She was accompanied by her old friend Esme Church, who had directed her as Rosalind in *As You Like It* in 1937 – a performance people still talked about decades after seeing it. When she arrived at the first rehearsal she discovered that her fellow actors weren't speaking Shakespeare's words but those of their own devising. It was Gaskill's great idea that the cast should improvise before committing themselves to the text, and what she heard that morning was distinctly – or in some cases, indistinctly – unShakespearean. She refused to get involved in a scheme she considered nonsensical, reminding Gaskill of her advanced age and the difficulty she had learning lines. She wasn't present when Christopher Plummer, playing Richard, reduced the wooing scene with Lady Anne, played by Jill Dixon, to a single pithy sentence: 'Lady Anne, I wanna screw you.'

Edith Evans always rehearsed with complete dedication to the play, as she had been taught by her mentor William Poel. After shaming us all with her ability to assume another person's character, she would return to her lodgings to watch her favourite American television programmes. She was particularly fond of *Sergeant Bilko* and admired Phil Silvers for his exemplary timing. But *Rawhide* pleased her most, and cowboy films were a lifelong passion. 'I've arranged for the theme tune of *Rawhide* to be played at my funeral,' she announced during a coffee break. 'I want to go out in a blaze of excitement.'

It was a miracle that *Richard III* ever opened. Ian Bannen, who had been contracted to play Buckingham, decided he couldn't do it after his Hamlet had received justifiably terrible reviews. His place was taken by Eric Porter, who put a very quick end to the improvising. He noticed that the improvisers were standing in straight lines, because Gaskill had insisted that they invent their own moves as well as their own dialogue. Eric brought order to what might have been chaos.

The next production that year was *As You Like It,* starring Vanessa Redgrave and the now-recovered Ian Bannen, directed by Michael Elliott. Edith Evans's Orlando in 1937 had been Michael

Grande Dame

Oldie theatre critic
Paul Bailey
remembers
Edith Evans, who at
her best was, he says,
the finest British
actress of the
20th century

Redgrave, Vanessa's father. One afternoon when Edith and Esme were sitting in the green room, listening to the play on the tannoy, the magical wooing scene began. There was no sound from the packed audience. I was sitting at the next table when Edith remarked in that incomparable voice, 'Esme, do you remember when I played this scene with Michael?' Esme, bang on cue, replied: 'How could I ever forget, Edith?' There

Cowboy films were a
lifelong passion and
she arranged for the
theme tune of
Rawhide to be
played at her funeral

was a pause as they listened to some more. 'Esme, when I spoke those lines, did people laugh? I seem to think they did.' Esme responded by saying that they laughed immoderately, thanks to her friend's gift for comedy. They paused again. 'No one's laughing today, Esme. I wonder why.' She knew exactly why: Vanessa Redgrave was employing her brand of dogged radiance rather than savouring the delicious wit with which Shakespeare imbues Rosalind.

Edith Evans had begun rehearsing for her last appearance as the Nurse in *Romeo and Juliet*. The director, Peter Hall, was using a revolving stage to speed up the action. Edith refused to act on it. She was well into her seventies, she told Hall, and didn't want to die courtesy of a revolve. Peter Hall agreed to her playing all her scenes at the front of the stage. She and Max Adrian, as Friar Lawrence, were the only radiant things in an otherwise lacklustre affair.

Edith Evans had earned a reputation as a grande dame because of her impersonation of Lady Bracknell, but watching her as the Nurse convinced me that she had the common touch at her command when needed: she relished the smutty asides. Thank God she was persuaded to appear in films in the second half of her life, not just as Lady Bracknell, but as the simple villager in Emlyn Williams's *The Last Days of Dolwyn* and the autocratic old Countess in Thorold Dickinson's adaptation of Pushkin's story *The Queen of Spades*, in which she dies on screen. No one has ever played a corpse so convincingly or so memorably.

I was a schoolboy, crazy about the theatre, when I first saw Edith Evans act, in a now-forgotten piece by James Bridie called *Daphne Laureola*. The setting was a London restaurant in wartime and part of the stage was sealed off to indicate where a bomb had fallen. Evans, playing a woman far gone in drink, had to make her unsteady way around it in order to reach the table where Peter Finch was sitting. She indulged in a small sherry at Christmas, so the brilliance of her interpretation had much to do with her powers of observation. I have lived with that vision of her for 60 years. I am privileged to have seen her at her best, a best surpassing that of any other British actress in the 20th century.

And the theme music to *Rawhide* was indeed played at her funeral.

"Whosoever plants a tree"

Why *Felix Dennis* has dedicated his personal fortune to the creation of a native forest in the heart of England

Recent headlines deploring the proposals to sell off English forests should not be allowed to obscure another dark truth: within our green and pleasant land we have a far lower percentage of native 'high tree cover' (as the jargon has it) than almost any country in Europe.

Nor is this news. In the preface to *Sylva, or a Discourse of Forest-Trees, and the Propagation of Timber*, published in 1664 for the Royal Society, John Evelyn warned Charles II that 'our Forests, the greatest Magazines of the Wealth and Glory of this Nation' were in peril. Unless remedial action was taken, insufficient oaks of the right size and age would be available to supply the wooden walls of the Navy.

And what was done? Precious little. Nor has much been done in the ensuing 350 years. Governments and politicians have always been better at promising than planting.

There has been plenty of official talk and promises made. Horrible alien trees like Sitka spruces have been planted under various government schemes and now disfigure swathes of Scotland and Wales. But British native trees? Statistics covering the reforestation of Britain by native tree species are often buried in the back of imposing official reports; they don't make for happy reading.

Why does it matter? It's simple. Our wildlife loathes foreign softwoods, having had insufficient time to adapt to them. By wildlife, I do not just mean mammals and birds, but insects, invertebrates, fungi and lichen, without which many birds and mammals cannot survive. A 200-year-old oak offers home and sustenance to hundreds of native species. A Sitka spruce might accommodate half a dozen.

Then there is the environment, in the old-fashioned sense of the word. Anyone who has trudged through a Sitka spruce plantation for mile after dispiriting mile knows this. They are barren, gloomy places, a testament to the arrogant idiocy of successive governments, planted because bureaucrats believed we might run out of pit props for coal mines, or wood needed for trenches in the next war.

Government ministers and agencies claim that England now has between 8 and 11 per cent of forest cover. France has 27 per cent – and far more of our tree cover consists of those useless alien softwoods that bureaucrats are so fond of. I estimate that we have less than 5 or 6 per cent of the total number of native trees you'll find in France, Germany or Italy.

That's a shocking statistic, and not one much talked about in all the self-congratulatory propaganda. Even New Labour's modestly named 'National Forest' initiative, while worthy in the sense of acreage and native trees planted, contained a fatal flaw: most of the National Forest is planted on privately owned land. What guarantees can there be that those trees will still be in the ground in 50 or 100 years?

We are a small, crowded nation. Trees

Our wildlife loathes foreign softwoods – a 200-year-old oak offers home and sustenance to hundreds of native species. A Sitka spruce might accommodate half a dozen

are desperately needed, not only for the obvious environmental reasons – carbon capture, preventing soil erosion, creating habitats for other plants and wildlife, flood prevention and filtering the air – but simply because we *are* so crowded. Walking in the woods brings joy and tranquillity and beauty into our harried modern lives. We owe it to ourselves, and not just to the environment, to reforest Britain with native broadleaf trees.

We need to stop talking and start planting. There are many wonderful organisations out there, from the Woodland Trust to the Tree Council,

Facing page: The Heart of England Forest Project, Warwickshire

from the Royal Forestry Society to small local groups who dedicate themselves to preserving a single wood, copse or community orchard. Charities and family trusts have a far better record than government in caring for our native woodland.

Many would say that the elephant in the room is the Forestry Commission. Weren't they responsible for all those disastrous alien softwood plantations? Yes and no. Times change and organisations can change with them. The Commission is government-funded but a body that many of us viewed as the Darth Vader of British woodland has transformed itself into a different organism, concerned far more with native habitat than with timber production.

Fifteen years ago I dedicated my fortune to the creation of a large – say 15,000 acres – native forest open to the public in the heart of England. Slowly – agonisingly slowly for an impatient chap like me – we have begun to made progress. With the help of volunteers and organisations – and the encouragement of the Forestry Commission – we have made a real start.

We now plant around 300 acres each year. By the end of this coming planting season, the Heart of England Forest Project will have planted 1,800 acres with some 800,000 native saplings of oak, ash, field maple, hazel, lime, yew, rowan, holly, beech, hornbeam and other native species. The project is funded through the Forest of Dennis Registered Charity.

It is a vast endeavour, what with the purchasing of land in the South Midlands, planning and consultation, the sourcing of local seed and nursery work, the creation of woodland pasture, coppice plantations, woodland rides and walks, wetland and pond areas. And yet it is less a labour than a joyous privilege. Last week I found a family of hares scampering about a clearing in one of my new woods – and I thought my heart would burst.

Whiteboard jungle

The shining eyes that make it all worthwhile, says *Kate Sawyer*

So here we have it. September. I'm not teaching. A term's sabbatical stretches ahead of me, and it feels very odd indeed. I worked like stink at the end of last term, writing lessons on how not to be homophobic, how not to be a teenage mother, how not to be racist. And one on *Animal Farm* for good measure, which was wonderful as I could think about writing. I swept and sorted out my cupboard. I cleared my desk for the new incumbent. Exhausted as we all were and pouring with slate-grey rain as it was, I managed a spring in my step as I worked towards these few months of … of what? Freedom, undoubtedly. But with the freedom from the school comes a new kind of tie. Without the discipline of the students to control me I must rediscover my own discipline. And with that comes the fear … now that I have time to think, will I still be able to?

There is another fear, too. At the beginning of every term, but particularly the autumn term, I always have nightmares about school. I lose my pupils, or worse I find them and have no control. I have no idea what I am supposed to be teaching, and then it's suddenly science instead of Shakespeare. All very obvious. I've been having those dreams for the past few weeks, even though I'm not going back until January. So how terrible will they be when I really am about to go back? Will I actually be able to go back? I'm contractually bound to, but will the stage fright finally take over and my courage fail?

So for now, while I make lists and plan a timetable to give myself the kind of structure I've been longing to leave behind but now find I need, I'm concentrating on the good in teaching, and on what I will miss. I have been with my tutor group for two years. They're just reaching the stage when we begin to enjoy spending time together. There are a few who I feel especially need and trust me, and I worry that there'll be no one to fight their corner in the next few months. Of course my cover is organised and professional and has been briefed about the children. But still … I wouldn't leave my own children for five months, would I?

My year 10 (now year 11) group is the only one carried forward from last year. They're a cheerful lot of girls, quite bright, but they need a careful mixture of wheedling, encouraging and threatening to keep them on their toes. Will my cover manage it? Of course she will. But what about the girl who told me that I'd changed her view of English and made it all possible? When I told them at the end of last term that I was taking time out, her eyes filled with tears and she said that as a result she'd fail her GCSE. Of course she won't … but I still feel very guilty.

And then I remember what another girl said to me when we were revising Owen's *Exposure* and I read it aloud to them. After I finished, there was a silence and I looked up, feeling the tears in my eyes, and almost begged them, 'Do you see? Do you see how beautiful that poem is?' The silence was prolonged until one of the girls put up her hand. 'No, miss, I don't. But I see that you see it, and you make me want to see it for myself.'

That is it. It is moments like that which ensure I will be back in January. The naughty boy who handed in his essay on *Henry V* (early) saying, 'I got it, miss. You made me get it and I loved it.' Another boy who wrote me a letter at the end of year 11 saying 'You taught me in year 9 and you made me love English. I'm doing A-level English next year and I want to thank you.' The young man who wrote saying he had just got a First in English and I had started it all. The girl who came with shining eyes thanking me for recommending a book which she loved. The girl who nearly gave up school but stuck it out and thought I had some part in helping her do that.

It is the old teaching cliché – but like all clichés it is fundamentally true. We make a difference. Not always, but often enough.

> It is the old teaching cliché – but like all clichés is fundamentally true. We make a difference. Not always, but often enough

I was a Hackney looter

Raiding Woollies and thieving from market stalls – *Derek Jameson*
and his fellow waifs and strays in Ma Wren's Thirties slum
knew all the tricks to make a quick bob

Harden your hearts. That cuddly toddler with the jet-black eyes plaintively demanding a handout is probably raking in a hundred grand a year for the folks back home in Bucharest. (Europe's gypsies long ago discovered there's money to be had on our streets for those bold enough to ask. The British have always been a soft touch.)

Perhaps that explains why the Scouting Association is reviving bob-a-job week in May next year, though this time around the campaign will be based on community projects rather than individual scouts knocking on doors offering to wash the car and mow the lawn. The service was suspended after 40 years in 1992 because of concerns about child protection (paedophiles, in

other words). Paedophiles certainly didn't worry us lot growing up at Ma Wren's. A few choice words and they would be off like frightened mice, though their tougher brethren manning barges down the road on the River Lea did feel entitled to a tanner's worth of our service – if they could catch us.

We operated our own help-thy-neighbour scheme at Ma Wren's gloomy Victorian slum in the hungry Thirties. Between the wars she raised some 70 of us – waifs and strays growing up on the streets of Hackney. Ma was the prototype old woman who lived in a shoe. Her only income was her 10/6d (52½p) weekly widow's pension plus a few shillings now and again from the so-called fallen women whose misbegotten progeny had landed in her lap. So it was a case of beg,

borrow or steal, as she never failed to tell us, and that meant getting out there in search of money. I was a major contributor from the age of seven.

Our richest pickings came from theft. Something for nothing has always appealed to the poor, though there's a price to pay if caught, as today's rioters have discovered. We would grab and run with anything that moved and had a potential value, though we never robbed our own kind – the impoverished working class. A gang of us would raid Woollies – Woolworth's – or street markets and create mayhem, running like the clappers from yelling traders. Once I ran a mile clutching a twopenny comb with a salesgirl breathing down my neck.

Jewish immigrants escaping the

pogroms made up much of the local population in those days. Harold Pinter's family lived down the road at Clapton Pond and Alan Sugar in a block of council flats off the high road. His family shopped at Charlton's the greengrocer, where I would crawl under the stalls to steal apples. We were perpetually hungry.

Orthodox Jews were not allowed to light fires or handle money on their

The only Christmas presents I recall ever receiving were a tangerine and a second-hand copy of *Robinson Crusoe*

Sabbath, beginning at dusk on Fridays, so I was on hand as a *shabbos goy* (sabbath gentile) to run errands or light a match to get around their religious scruples – Jewish enterprise! My aim was to light the fire badly in the hope it would soon go out. Foster-brother Len would be in the street outside awaiting a summons to have another go. Another sixpence in the kitty – a good earner in those days.

Money didn't always come that easily. Those were the days when there were more horses than cars at work in

the streets. I would go around with an old bucket and shovel collecting horse manure. Next thing was to find a house with a decent-looking garden and hammer at the front door.

'Her y'are Madam. Fresh today, lovely horse dung. Just right for your roses. Tanner a bucket.'

Most garden-lovers were only too pleased. A few would turn nasty. 'Git aht of it, you little guttersnipe, messing up my front step.' That was a good cue. Soon as they disappeared indoors, tip a load over the stoop.

Keep an eye open for repairs to tramlines on the main roads. Loads of wooden blocks covered in tar lying about – wonderful firewood at tuppence a bundle. Careful, though, the night watchmen striking out with their heavy boots could leave you covered in bruises for weeks.

Uncle Sid was a good earner. Ma Wren's middle-aged son, he was totally demented. She reckoned that when he was young, hooligans buried him up to the neck at the seaside and it turned his brain. Sid collected empty milk bottles for Dick, a sympathetic United Dairies milkman, at a tanner a day. Trouble was, Sid had an obsession that kind souls trying to help him were stealing his money, and the day came when he hit Dick over the head with an empty milk bottle. The kindly milkman let it go, as did the local Congregational minister. Sid earned a few coppers on Sundays pumping the church organ – until he stormed out of the organ loft and clouted the vicar mid-sermon, demanding his money.

Rough, tough times. But we needed the money. Electricity was replacing gas in those days, but we often couldn't afford a penny for the meter. Frequently our only light was a halfpenny candle flickering in a cocoa tin as we sat in the gloom around the kitchen table, supping tea out of empty jam jars. The adults claimed the only china cups.

Christmas was a Dickensian nightmare and 75 years later fairy lights and other festive baubles still bring on the vapours. The only presents I recall ever receiving were a tangerine and a second-hand *Robinson Crusoe*. To this day it remains my favourite book.

Happy days? Of course. We never stopped laughing.

RANT

How (and why) did the suffix 'ee' worm its way into the English language? It has long bugged and baffled me – why are people who escape from jail often called 'escapees' (they're not: they are 'escapers'); why are those who go to meetings habitually labelled 'attendees' (they're not: they are 'attenders').

I have fulminated for years against this replacement of the active with the (extremely ugly) passive, but was finally jolted into putting pen to paper by a notice near the driver (why not 'drivee'?) of a local bus which read '24 standees only'. I had been lucky enough to get a seat, so I suppose that I had become – in the eyes of the bus company – a 'sittee'.

In the United States the word 'retiree' is used continuously. The 'ee' ending is only accurate when applied to people who have had something done to them: 'amputee', 'parolee' are two (just) acceptable such uses.

Of course, some retired people have been booted out, but others – as *Oldie* readers know – have decided of their own volition to lay down their burdens and pick up their pensions. They are the 'retired', not 'retirees' with its implication that they have one foot in the grave and have become useless passengers on what remains of life's journey. How long until pensioners become 'pensionees' and diners 'dinees'?

The 'ee' appendage is far more linguistically offensive than the notorious greengrocer's apostrophe. It is added like salt sprayed thoughtlessly over every dish by people (like bus company officials) who should know better.

ROBERT CHESSHYRE

Human fascination with the owl stretches as far back as it is possible to go – they were beautifully portrayed by Palaeolithic artists on the wall of the Chauvet cave in Southern France 30,000 years ago. The image incised in the yellow ochre rock with a sharpened stick is instantly recognisable, with its large rounded head from which protrude two upright ear tufts. Its plumage is evoked – with an economy worthy of that great owl fancier Picasso – by a dozen tapering vertical lines.

That fascination derives most obviously from the inescapable sense of a supernatural affinity with ourselves – for good or ill. For the Athenians, the owl's physical appearance (particularly those forward-looking eyes), its contemplativeness and its stillness, symbolised the wisdom of their protective goddess Athena. Yet for many societies it is a portent of evil and death – not surprisingly, perhaps, being a creature of the night whose eerie cries the Scottish-American ornithologist Alexander Wilson compared to the 'half-suppressed scream of a person being throttled'. This is also a recurring Shakespearean theme: for Lady Macbeth, the shrieking owl becomes the 'fatal bellman which gives the stern'st goodnight', while for Puck it 'puts the wretch that lies in woe in remembrance of a shroud'.

These contrasting interpretations of the significance of the owl in human affairs are of course related: its seemingly human appearance and attributes being inextricably linked to the challenges of its way of life as a nocturnal predator – so much more so than for those birds of prey that hunt by day.

Silence is essential lest, hovering low over the hedgerows, it alerts its prey. This is made possible by its uniquely designed feathers, described by naturalist Desmond Morris as 'being delicately fringed with serrated edges and a soft velvety surface that dampens the swishing sound of its wings'.

And then there are those disproportionately large forward-facing eyes, so like our own. Not being placed, as in most birds, on either side of its head, they confer the inestimable benefit

The owl on the wall of the Chauvet cave

All of a piece

Profitable Wonders by *James Le Fanu*

at dusk of the most acute stereoscopic vision of any avian species. The presence of such large eyes in a relatively small skull would leave insufficient space for the brain were it not for their distinctive structure (fixed and tubular rather than circular and mobile). Unable to turn its eyes, the owl must rotate its head instead, which it is able to do up to an astonishing 270 degrees. This in turn is facilitated by an additional seven vertebrae in its neck (twice the usual number) permitting it to look almost backwards over its shoulder – as indeed it is portrayed in the Chauvet cave painting.

When its prey, whether fieldmouse or vole, is invisible in the impenetrable darkness of the night, the owl must rely on the exceptional acuity and directionality of its hearing to detect rustling in the undergrowth – the acuity facilitated by a concave ruff of feathers at

the entrance to the ear that acts like a satellite receiving dish. As for directionality, owls deploy the technique known as amplitude monopulse (reinvented for human use by radar engineers in World War II), where the asymmetric positioning of its ears on either side of the head permits it to detect the direction and position of its prey by the minuscule time difference (as little as 30 millionths of a second) it takes for the sound waves to reach either ear. When they coincide precisely the owl is looking directly at its potential victim.

Come the moment of the strike the owl relies not on its beak – short and downward-curved so as not to obscure its field of vision or hearing – but swings forward its four immensely powerful talons to grasp and crush its prey. This in turn is facilitated by two further unique adaptations – a fully mobile front outer toe that can switch to face backwards so as to strengthen the grip, and rough adherent tissue – like Velcro – on the under-surface of its feet.

The impressive aspect of each of these unique adaptations for nocturnal hunting is not just that they confer on the owl what might seem almost unearthly powers, but that they are all 'of a piece' to achieve its intended purpose. In this, the owl exemplifies, to a remarkable degree, the 'laws of correlation' originally proposed by the great 19th-century natural historian Georges Cuvier – where every species 'forms a distinctive whole, a unique and perfect system whose parts mutually correspond and concur to the same definitive end'.

House Husbandry

Giles Wood has mixed feelings about his daughter's lack of life-skills

Since going to university Girl P has lost five phones, a wallet, two railcards, a driving licence, a passport ... Her uni is cashing in on this generation of flakeheads, charging £66 for replacement keys to the halls of residence

Looking at polaroids of Mary as a teenager in a miniskirt, one hand hitching a lift at the start of a Northern Irish dual carriageway, a half-drunk bottle of red wine in the other, I wonder that her mother was not a nervous wreck.

But those were the days before mobiles, and her mother had no idea what she was up to. In any case, Mary gained little experience of vice as, apparently, most Irish motorists were too drunk, or too busy reciting limericks, to make passes at silly girls. Danger beckoned, however, when she came across a copy of the London *Tatler* which had found its way into her GP father's waiting-room. It seemed to Mary to show more glamorous people than she was meeting in the Province – although you can bet the English *craic* was never half so good as its Irish counterpart.

In London, Mary moved into a basement in Earl's Court. Most of the other residents of the dodgy lodging-house were petty criminals, but her mother remained in blissful ignorance because the telephone was not then a chat room but a medium through which messages were conveyed in a terse manner recalling morse code, and there was no time for descriptions of a picaresque nature.

Mary's conduct has, of course, been irreproachable for many years but, given the racketiness of her early life, you would think she would grant generous leeway to her own teenage daughter. On the contrary, Girl P was kept on an extra-short leash until the last possible moment – the day she left school – when she popped out of her parents' life with all the force of a champagne cork, leaving Mary quaking like an aspen ever since.

She says the world is a much darker place than it was when she was a girl when – realistically – the chief trauma she was likely to encounter might be meeting someone with BO. By contrast, she believes, our daughter lives in a world of proper bogeymen all waiting to slip Rohypnol into her drink while she distractedly fumbles in her bag for a phone with which to take pictures of her friends pulling silly faces.

Her school seemed to be more interested in teaching her Holocaust Studies than Domestic Science, or even just Common Sense. She never learned anything so mundane as how to prepare for a journey, keep her room tidy or clear up a Weetabix spillage. And why is her whole generation obsessed by the *Made in Chelsea* 'constructed reality' TV series, whose witless cast never seem to work, fill in forms, or clean a lavatory?

No surprise therefore, that since going to university, Girl P has lost five phones, one wallet, two railcards, one provisional driving licence and now her passport (estimated worth on black market: £1,400). Meanwhile the uni is cashing in on this generation of flakeheads, charging £66 a time for replacement keys to the halls of residence.

Is she on drugs? Apparently not, because she has a reputation for being the benevolent guide for unfortunate friends who, in a bid to achieve an out-of-body experience, accidentally enter 'K-holes'. I gather these are mental states of extreme disorientation due to ingestion of ketamine (a horse tranquilliser), the problem being that, for humans, a safe dose is a hit-and-miss affair.

Secretly, however, there is nothing I like more than driving to her uni, one hour away, to bring her something she has forgotten. I am wondering whether my sister, a family counsellor, would mention the words 'co-dependency', 'empty nest syndrome' or 'helicopter parenting' in her preliminary report on our plight. Could it be that we do not want Girl P to become independent because each crisis is a chance to interact with her?

I've always been there for Mary. And now I am here, there and everywhere for my daughter. It's lucky for Mary that I have been able to put my own career on hold to facilitate this new lifestyle option as a courier.

Modern life

What is...
the Ordinariate?

It was the Pope's idea and he kicked it off without telling many people, least of all the Archbishop of Canterbury, who felt quite miffed. The idea was something like a Bishopric of the Forces, only instead of servicemen, the people in it would be Anglicans who wanted to become Roman Catholics without losing their religious 'patrimony'. What this 'patrimony' meant was not clear. Certainly not churches, since they were not the property of the congregations jumping ship. The language of the 1611 Bible and the Book of Common Prayer might be more like it, along with an intangible attitude. Only time would tell.

That was in 2009, when Benedict XVI issued a document called a *motu proprio*, off his own bat. It was greeted with some suspicion by many Anglicans, who wondered whom it was meant to attract, since a lot of very High bells-and-smells clergymen didn't use traditional Church of England resources such as the Book of Common Prayer in any case, but some version of the Roman Missal translated into English. Since 1970 that had meant the English version of the so-called *Missa Normativa*, which British Roman Catholics used.

The clever money said it could never happen here in Britain, but might appeal to breakaway Anglicans in Australia. The United States already had traditional Anglicans who had been taken into the Catholic Church en bloc in 1980, and used a prayerbook called the Book of Divine Worship (published in 2003). Those Americans used bits from the Anglican Prayer Book, but not quite the Cranmer edition of 1662, rather an Episcopalian version of the kind used in Scotland by the 'Piskies'.

These things can be complicated, which delights the anoraks of the ecclesiastical margins. But a plain surprise came in January 2011 when the first Ordinariate as envisaged by the Pope suddenly sprang up, not in Perth, Western Australia, but in Westminster, England. It was called The Personal Ordinariate of Our Lady of Walsingham.

By 'Personal' was meant that it had jurisdiction not over a territory, like a diocese, but over people, in this case laity, clergy and members of religious orders nurtured in the Anglican tradition. About 1,000 joined at Easter 2011, and there are 56 groups, from Plymouth to Stornoway. Only ex-Anglicans need apply, but anyone in the Catholic Church is allowed to take part in their services and receive Communion.

It might have been expected that a bishop would run the Ordinariate. The problem was that the two leading Church of England bishops who joined it were both married. They were ordained priests once they became Catholics, but canon law forbade them from being consecrated as bishops. So the 'Ordinary' of the Ordinariate is Keith Newton, the former Bishop of Richborough. As a 'flying bishop' he had had the pastoral care in the Church of England of people who could not recognise the validity of women's ordination. He is now known as the Rt Rev Monsignor Keith Newton.

In 2012 the Ordinariate published its own prayer book, called the Customary.

Remarkably enough, it contains the translation of the Psalms made by the Protestant reformer Miles Coverdale in 1535, as printed in the Book of Common Prayer. Perhaps even more remarkably, it includes for liturgical use a passage from the works of TS Eliot (for the feast of Thomas Becket).

Quite a problem is that the Ordinariate hasn't got any money

Quite a problem is that the Ordinariate hasn't got any money, and £1 million given by an Anglican charity has lain untouched while lawyers work out whether it can be accepted.

At the beginning of the year, half the Anglican convent of St Mary the Virgin, Wantage, joined the Ordinariate. Equally excitingly, the pretty church of Our Lady of the Assumption, Warwick Street, on the respectable side of Soho, was given over to its use. It is a building connected with Roman Catholic worship in the penal days before Emancipation in 1829. The flavour of Ordinariate worship remains, not more Catholic than the Pope, but more ceremonial than most English Roman Catholics enjoy in their often ugly modern churches.

CHRISTOPHER HOWSE

Moron crossword

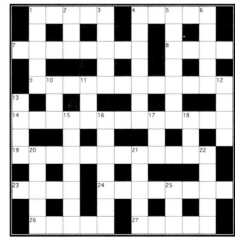

Solution on page 99

Across
1 Of a former South American empire (5)
4 Creature of Scandinavian folklore (5)
7 Intermittent (8)
8 Light green colour (4)
9 Perhaps (3,5,4)
14 Constancy (13)
19 Not for publication (3,3,6)
23 Molten rock (4)
24 Combat (8)
26 Paper size (5)
27 Ideal (5)

Down
1 Suggest (5)
2 Motor vehicle (3)
3 Gentle push (5)
4 Passes (7)
5 Waterproof garment (7)
6 Uncertain state (5)
10 Be obliged to pay (3)
11 Gesture of assent (3)
12 Sensible (4)
13 Capital of Norway (4)
15 Insurance risk assessor (7)
16 Anxious (7)
17 Persistent behavioural trait (3)
18 Be incorrect (3)
20 Talent (5)
21 Bordered (5)
22 Twilled cotton fabric (5)
25 Fasten (3)

The last judgement

Angry at his enforced retirement as a magistrate, *Trevor Grove* says this waste of his rich experience will be a blow for justice, too

In January I shall be 70 and no one will ever again address me as Your Worship. It was ludicrous but nice. Lawyers will not rise to their feet when I make an entrance or bow to me as they leave. I shall no longer have the chance to engage a confused, fatherless, gang-haunted teenage phone-mugger in the hope of stopping him from becoming a repeat offender. At three score years and ten, magistrates must call it a day and retire from the retiring room.

It makes me pretty furious. No one would have dared tell Lord Emsworth or Sir Gregory Parsloe-Parsloe they were too old to be Justices of the Peace. I bet Sir Francis Drake and Charles Darwin, who were both JPs in their day, decided for themselves when to step down. Yet here we are – hard-working, experienced, better-trained and, I dare say, more fair-minded than Drake or Darwin – given the heave-ho at the very peak of our judiciousness.

On my 70th birthday I will no longer be one of the 23,000 unpaid, volunteer lay magistrates who deal with over 95 per cent of all criminal cases in England and Wales. My local knowledge of drug-dealing at Turnpike Lane and kerb-crawling on the Seven Sisters Road will be of no further use. And I shall be sorry to have been ejected from one of the best examples of the Big Society in action.

For the past 15 years I have been putting on a suit at least once a week to sit at a magistrates' court in north London. It is always with a sense of anticipation. I never know what the day will bring or even with which two colleagues I'll be sitting. Our bench includes teachers, civil servants, nurses, businessmen and housewives. We have a taxi driver, a Tube driver, a priest, a World Service broadcaster and a Glyndebourne clarinettist. We are of all faiths and none. We have a deaf, lip-reading woman JP who used to come to court with her listening labrador, but who now manages without, since the dog died.

We are far more representative of society than the professional judiciary. At least half the magistracy is female. The age profile is another matter. A couple of years ago there was a 20-year-old on the Barnsley bench, but JPs under 40 are a rarity: employers no longer feel an obligation to let staff have time off to do their civic duty, as they did 50 years ago.

By 9.45am on court days we would form into threes to be briefed on the day's work by the legal advisers. If we're in a remand court, where most matters are being heard for the first time, there will be a long list to get through. Most will plead guilty and must be sentenced there and then or will have to be interviewed by probation for a pre-sentence report. For those pleading not guilty we must decide whether or not to grant bail while they're awaiting trial.

Bail can be tricky. The Crown may want someone kept in custody simply because he is of no fixed abode. But is that fair when you know he won't be sentenced to prison even if found guilty? At one of her first sittings, a woman who trained with me reluctantly agreed to give bail to a young man accused of robbery. A week later her own son was terrified by two knife-wielding boys who marched him to a cash machine. One of them, she discovered, was the lad she had freed on bail.

If we're doing trials that day, the legal adviser will explain the background and

'-and our pamphlet "101 things to do while waiting for your new knee"'

prepare us for glitches such as missing witnesses or delayed forensics. We will be warned about applications to adjourn from an overstretched, sometimes ill-prepared Crown Prosecution Service or a defence lawyer playing for time. Magistrates are under pressure not to adjourn except in the interests of justice. Turning round the adjournment culture which certainly prevailed when I started in 1999 has been an achievement.

Another has been learning to give reasons for our trial verdicts, like judges in the Crown Court. This not only makes deliberations more rational but also helps demonstrate that magistrates are not the prejudiced old buffers of popular demonology. No, we are not finding you guilty because you're covered in tattoos or have a stud through your tongue or wear your jeans too low. It's because we are sure you did it and here's why. Another consequence is that police officers now hear in open court why their evidence may not have been believed. These days they are more cautious about assuming they will always be taken at their word.

Sentencing is a hard part of the job. One wants the punishment to fit the crime, but also the criminal to stop offending. Fines clobber those who are already poor and make them poorer. The maximum prison sentence available to the lower courts is six months, of which the offender will serve three – too short a time for rehabilitation but long enough to make it hard for him to find or keep a job when he's released. Community sentences with unpaid work or a drug rehab requirement have a positive purpose; but the breach rate is pretty high and the public's confidence in them pretty low.

What I shall miss is the high and low drama of the magistrates' court: the bewildered young Pole who got so drunk one Friday night he murdered his best friend; the swaggering fraudster who fainted clean away when we sentenced him to jail, crashing to the floor as if he had been shot; the professional heavyweight boxer who pushed his way out of the dock and ranged around the courtroom waving his fists, terrifying us all until he suddenly calmed down and sheepishly locked himself in again.

Defendants come up with amazing excuses. A baby-faced 12-year-old, already on a youth rehabilitation order for setting fire to a petrol station, was stopped for driving a car in Crouch End. His cheery explanation was that he'd wanted to be on time for his meeting with the Youth Offending Service.

A dazed Irishman charged with driving while disqualified said: 'I'm sorry, Your Honour, but you see I was too drunk to remember I was disqualified.' The parents of a Chinese boy who had been repeatedly raping his little sister begged for him to be given bail so that he could stay at home: 'For us, family life is very important.' Last week we had a sad little wino who pleaded guilty, as he had hundreds of times before, to shoplifting. 'You see, sir,' he mumbled, 'I have nowhere to live and nothing to eat. Please, sir, will you send me to prison?'

Less disturbing was the very large African lady who arrived looking like a tribal queen. She wore a leopard-skin hat and a great cloak of what looked like zebra hide. She gave her evidence, in French, as though granting an audience to some pipsqueak colonial governor. When we said she could pay off her motoring fines in instalments, she waved a hand regally and gave the bench her blessing. '*Dieu vous bénisse*,' she said.

What I shall not miss are the long, dispiriting days of sentencing no-show fare-dodgers and road tax defaulters. I am especially relieved I shall no longer be an unpaid debt-collector for the BBC, an equally tedious undertaking.

People ask: why do you want to sit in judgement on your fellow citizens? Well, as Mrs Christian Annersley told Ronald Blythe in *Akenfield*, remembering the tiny bench she chaired in rural Suffolk in the Fifties: 'It is simply endlessly interesting. How people live, how people behave, how they think — and all at this vulnerable, naked moment in their existence... Good people in a muddle, bad people and just poor low people who never have an earthly.'

Trevor Grove is the author of 'The Magistrate's Tale' and 'The Juryman's Tale', both published by Bloomsbury and available as e-books.

Dangerous liaison

LEWIS JONES

The Children Act

by Ian McEwan

Jonathan Cape

Ian McEwan is a master who delights in celebrating the mastery of others, which he researches so thoroughly and describes with such inspired detail that it illuminates and echoes his own mastery. In his latest it is the law. *The Children Act* is billed as his 14th novel, though *The Daydreamer* (1994) was written for children and six of his 'novels', including this one, are actually novellas.

Fiona Maye is a High Court judge in the Family Division, whom the author establishes, in an opening paragraph of customary brilliance and concision, on a summer evening in her spacious Gray's Inn flat, with its fireplace ('not lit in a year'), bookcases, Renoir lithograph of doubtful authenticity, baby grand piano and so forth, as she lies 'supine on a chaise longue' – a pleasingly old-fashioned turn of phrase, and not the last; we subsequently learn of someone who has fallen 'victim to drink, of which she died' – with the draft of a judgement to hand on the floor beside her.

Aged 59 and regretfully childless, Fiona has been married for 30 years. Her husband, a classics professor, sets things in motion by asking her permission to begin an affair with a younger woman, pointing out by way of justification that it has been seven weeks and a day since he and Fiona last had sex together.

Would any husband make such a request? By McEwan's standards, such unlikeliness is negligible. In his

hyper-realistic world, everything is believable apart from the sex lives of his characters, which are reliably and catastrophically bizarre, but which we are compelled none the less to credit by his psychological acuity and hallucinatorily limpid prose.

This dichotomy – true to life, in its exaggerated way – has driven his fiction from the start. In the short stories which made his reputation, the reader was forced into imaginative engagement with child abuse and bestiality. The erotic behaviours have since grown less extreme, but thanks to their author's increasing mastery their impact is if anything more devastating.

I will not spoil the story here, but Fiona becomes involved in a liaison hardly more credible, but somehow more shocking, than the one in an early story, *Dead as They Come*, between a rich man and a shop-window mannequin, who cuckolds him with his chauffeur.

But if *The Children Act* is driven by strange sexual urges, its fabric is constructed from acute observation – of domestic routines, for example ('listening through closed eyes to the radio news') – and lovingly assimilated knowledge, principally but by no means exclusively legal. Fiona presides over her court 'with all the seriousness and obedience to process of a nuclear scientist'.

Other dramatic cases are recalled and referred to, but the one most important to her concerns Adam, a delightful 17-year-old who is dying of leukaemia but refuses the blood transfusion that would probably save his life because he is a Jehovah's Witness. Adam is a minor, and the hospital caring for him is seeking leave to treat him against his will. (These aspects of the case naturally entail further displays of expertise, both theological and medical.) How will Fiona rule, and what will be the consequences?

It's all very deft, urgent and morally plangent. One can't stop reading and wishes it were longer.

God
by *Sister Teresa*

A Carmelite Christmas is something that a few people envy us, but it would be a mistake to think it is a form of escape from activity. It entails a good deal of hard work, less sleep, longer hours in prayer and some stress. We miss out on Oxford Street, *Jingle Bells*, decorations being put up too early (they don't come out here till Christmas Eve) and the writing of duty thank-you letters for unwanted presents. What we gain is silence and the time to think about the enormity of what is being celebrated. This is the way we choose to spend our Christmases – it is not imposed on us, nor is it possible to take it away, for all of which we are truly grateful.

The Christmas season begins on the first Sunday of Advent: many of the Old Testament readings come from the very best of Isaiah, and there is a strong feeling of anticipation in the weeks leading up to the Nativity as the promise given in the Old Testament is about to be fulfilled in the New. The promise is the birth of Jesus Christ – the greatest present the world

has ever been given. The missing out on this greatness is one of the saddest features of modern times, with even the most important elements of Christian faith being neglected. But if one allows oneself to concentrate, then the opening words of Philipp Nicolai's hymn at Midnight Mass should stir the most faint-hearted:

Wake, O wake! With tidings thrilling
The watchmen all the air are filling,
Arise, Jerusalem, arise!

Childhood Christmases used to be blighted by the thought of Boxing Day and the prospect of being sat at a desk with writing paper and pen. If the present had been nice it was impossible to put one's gratitude into adequate words and this was shaming, and if nasty, then what was one supposed to say? Last Christmas

a very old friend sent me *The English Poems of George Herbert*, edited by Helen Wilcox and published by the Cambridge University Press. It is the result of a lifetime of scholarship and love of the subject and makes every single word of Herbert's poetry intelligible. It was the book I had been waiting for since my teens and thanking properly for it was an impossible task. What I did not want to produce instead of a thank-you letter was a dull A-level English essay, so by return of post I wrote 'Thank you for the lovely book, it was just what I wanted' (totally true for once), urged my friend to get a copy for himself and quoted the first and last verses of the poem 'Gratefulness':

Thou hast given so much to me,
Give one thing more: a grateful heart.
See how thy beggar works on thee by
    art...

Not thankful, when it pleaseth me;
As if thy blessings had spare days:
But such a heart, whose pulse may be
    Thy praise.

Mammon
by *Margaret Dibben*

Insurance companies can refine their premiums right down to your full postcode so you pay according to the precise risk that you, and a handful of your neighbours, pose. But an *Oldie* reader has uncovered one form of insurance, where the risk is negligible for everyone who buys it, yet premiums range from £12 to more than £250 based entirely on how much your house is worth. There is no logic to this pricing structure and insurance companies cannot defend it.

The sale of Josephine Williams's house was progressing smoothly until the buyers' solicitor demanded she pay for legal indemnity insurance. Josephine had replaced two Velux windows ten years ago but had no piece of paper to confirm that the work complied with building regulations. Windows, doors or roof lights replaced since 2002 must meet building regulations for improved energy efficiency. Homeowners need local authority approval unless they use a supplier registered with Fensa (Fenestration Self-Assessment Scheme) or a similar body.

Josephine had lost contact with the

window installer and her solicitor urged her to buy the insurance, costing £250. This virtually risk-free policy was expensive simply because her house is worth more than £1 million. Her solicitor could have suggested the buyers pay the premium if they were worried about the risk. There is no rule that sellers have to pay and sellers get nothing from it apart from appeasing the buyers. Some mortgage lenders insist on seeing certificates for building control consent but that again is the buyers' problem.

The vice-president of the Law Society, Jonathan Smithers, says it comes down to negotiation between the two sides. At the extreme, one party could threaten to delay the purchase or even walk away.

More sensibly, sellers can point out, perhaps, that they have already reduced the asking price or agreed to leave items behind. Buyers argue that the seller is at fault for not being able to produce a certificate.

Solicitors do not earn commission

from selling legal indemnity policies, although they can increase their bill to pay for their additional time. They prefer simply to recommend their clients pay up quickly, as to them £250 is peanuts when selling a £1 million house.

Usually with insurance you can shop around for a better price but not with legal indemnity policies. These are one-off policies insuring the property in perpetuity – far longer than any windows will last – so there is no repeat business and no competition. Few insurers produce them and sell them only through solicitors. A specialist insurance broker might quote but the premium would be the same.

Even for house-buyers, the policies are limited. They do not cover faulty goods or poor workmanship, only the consequences of the local authority serving an enforcement notice. Councils cannot do this 12 months after the work is completed yet policies do not come into effect until the first 12 months have passed, so the only risk is that the council, or someone else, takes out an injunction if they believe the work was dangerous.

If you have had windows replaced, check now that you have the necessary paperwork to avoid expensive insurance.

The happy jester

Craig Brown on Ken Dodd, our Oldie of the Year

About 15 years ago, I met the comedian Harry Enfield for lunch in a Chelsea restaurant. The first thing he said was: 'Ken Dodd ate here yesterday.'

'Did he?' I said.

'No – Doddy', he replied.

Since then, I've tried the same gag on any number of people, and it generally works pretty well, just so long as they don't reply, 'Oh, really?' Now aged 87, Ken Dodd has become part of the language, a byword even among those who don't know who he is. These days, 'Ken Dodd's dad's dog's dead' is a popular playground tongue-twister, and, after his 1989 trial for tax evasion, 'a Ken Dodd' became Cockney rhyming slang for a wad.

WH Auden wrote of Edward Lear, 'Children swarmed to him like settlers. He became a land.' The same might be said of Ken Dodd, though those who swarm to him – next month, he is performing in Dudley, Chesterfield and Bridlington – tend to be well into their seventies.

The first time I saw him on stage was at the Ipswich Regent. He opened the show by observing that though Ipswich isn't twinned with anywhere, it has a suicide pact with Grimsby. It was hardly the standard opening line of visiting royalty and politicians, but it went down a storm.

This was the opening salvo in a one-man show that began at 8pm and went on until well after 1am. Received wisdom has it that Ken Dodd's live act doesn't transfer well to television, yet no one ever offers the simple reason, which is that the standard television slot is five minutes and the standard Ken Dodd show is five hours.

'The sooner you laugh at the jokes, the sooner you can go home,' he says, after an hour or so. He aims to crack six jokes a minute, or roughly 360 an hour. He delivers them so fast that you are generally laughing at the last joke but three, or perhaps just generally laughing at the surrounding laughter. It is the speed and quantity of his jokes that matters rather than their quality. Some are entirely meaningless. 'Did you get your free sausage on the way in? Well, you will on the way out.' Professor Richard Wiseman has observed this curious phenomenon of laughter produced from nowhere. 'He gets a rhythm going with the audience and once you get into it (the rhythm is, I say something, you laugh), after a while it doesn't matter what he says. But you enjoy it and you keep going and it takes you over.'

After a while, the audience begins to suffer from a sort of collective Stockholm syndrome, howling with laughter as much at their inability to escape as at anything more obviously funny. And Doddy revels in his role as their captor. 'This isn't like television, missus,' he says, roughly three hours in. 'You can't switch me off!' To squeeze Ken Dodd into a guest spot on telly would be like trying to run through Wagner's *Ring Cycle* in a couple of minutes.

In 1965, Ken Dodd found his way into the Guinness Book of Records after telling 1,500 jokes in a 'Marathon Mirthquake' at the Palladium lasting three and a half hours. For some reason, the two-hour press conference that preceded it, packed with nearly as many jokes, went unmentioned.

'You think you can get away, but you can't,' he tells his audiences after four hours or so. 'I'll follow you home and I'll shout jokes through your letterbox.'

Just after midnight in Ipswich, he brought out a snack in a Thermos and a Tupperware box. 'You mean you didn't bring any?' he asked us. 'One thing about my show is that you always go home in the light. I've seen children grow out of their trousers while I've been on. Under your seat you'll find a will form.' An hour later, he was still at it. 'This is like antibiotics. You have to finish the course!'

Ken Dodd was born in the Knotty Ash district of Liverpool in 1927. His family was pretty well-to-do: his grandmother had been the first woman magistrate in Liverpool, and his father was a prosperous coal merchant. He still lives in the large former farmhouse in which he was born. Even more unusually, he keeps the table set just as his mother used to set it, with the HP sauce bottle always in its familiar place.

Unusually for a comedian, his childhood was very happy. His father lived for comedy, and nicknamed his son Professor Yaffle Chuckabutty. Even the young Doddy's one serious accident was somehow fortuitous: aged eight, he was trying to ride a bicycle with his eyes shut when he mounted the kerb and fell off onto the pavement. This resulted in his teeth sticking out at the same funny angle at which they have remained ever since. 'By Jove, missus,' he says. 'I'm the only one in our house who can kiss a girl and nibble her ear at the same time!'

Like many of the best comics, his routine is finely balanced on the borderline between sanity and madness, or, if you will, between craft and instinct. Offstage, he has made a lifelong study of comedy, accumulating a library of 10,000 books by psychologists and philosophers; onstage, there is no hint of the scholar – instead, he plays the giddy goat, or court jester, complete with tickling stick. In

Knotty Ash, he keeps what he calls a Giggle Map of Great Britain, which charts every single performance he has given, complete with time and date, first or second house, audience capacity and weather conditions, plus jokes that worked and jokes that failed to work. At each performance, his companion, Anne Jones, sits by the side of the stage with a clipboard, marking the jokes that get the most laughs. Those that get the least are ruthlessly discarded.

When not cracking jokes, he likes to analyse them. 'For 40 years, I have read every possible book on humour and the psychology of humour. I have formulated formulas for the creation of jokes and comedy and believe that I have cracked it. Some people say there are only seven original jokes. Well, I think there's 27 formulas.'

Yet at the same time, he acknowledges the ravine between theory and practice. When he appeared on *Celebrity Mastermind* before Christmas (coming a creditable second), John Humphrys attempted to ask him what makes a joke funny. 'Let me ask you what is probably an impossible question...' he began, before being cut off by the smiling Doddy, who said, 'I never lend money to a stranger.'

Victoria Wood has noted that Ken Dodd's uniqueness lies in his view of life as something worth celebrating. 'Whereas most comedians come on and say, "You know, I've had a terrible day," or "I'll tell you something awful that's happened," Ken comes on and says, "What a beautiful day..." I can't think of anyone else who starts in that way, who manages to get jokes out of something positive.'

Early in his career, he applied his brain to working out a suitable catchphrase. 'I wanted a catchphrase that would stand the test of time – that you could permutate. So I'd say, "How tickled I am," and then you could put another bit on to it – "How tickled I am under the circumstances. Have you ever been tickled under the circumstances, Missus?" '

In a just world, he would be Sir Ken, or Lord Dodd of Knotty Ash. Until that day comes, he can at least be tickled by his tattyfilarious new title of Oldie of the Year. After all, he richly deserved it. Did he? No – Doddy.

Alice Pitman: Home Front

My screen debut

There is a famous Charles Addams *New Yorker* cartoon depicting roaring caged lions about to be released on to the set of a Roman colosseum. Behind the scenes, a movie extra dressed as a Christian slave looks up from reading and enquires of his similarly attired colleagues, 'Holy smoke, have you guys seen this script?'

Those words came into my head when I read my son Fred's first short film screenplay (starring the Home Fronts). Fred had arrived back from university clutching a copy of Truffaut's book on Alfred Hitchcock and announcing he wanted to be a director. He pestered Mr Home Front to bring back a camera from work and they both disappeared to his bedroom for many hours. Eventually they emerged – looking a bit shifty – with a 10-page treatment. Fred bossily informed us that it would feature the whole family (including Lupin the dog) and that he would film and direct.

The synopsis of this modern gothic suburban horror is as follows: Man (played with disconcerting enthusiasm by Mr Home Front) comes home on Christmas Eve and murders his wife (me). The End. Fred smiled uncertainly as I read it, then said: 'So are you all right with that then, Mummy?'

The script directions were uncomfortably close to home (The Woman helps herself to another large glass of wine); the dialogue all too familiar (Woman to Man: You make me sick. I'm going to bed). So I decided to channel my inner Bette Davis to invest the role with an additional layer of pathos.

Fred turned out to be quite a formidable director, unafraid to confront both parents when he felt we were over-acting (which seemed to be the entire time). As Mr HF and I kept trying to outdo each other like a couple of spiteful old hams in rep, Fred would stop filming, cry 'Cut!'; then, after a devastating pause: 'You're telling him what you did with your day, not delivering the Gettysburg Address.'

Then there was the matter of the murder weapon. Mr Home Front favoured a hatchet. I pointed out that not only was

Wendy Hiller and Roger Livesey in *I Know Where I'm Going!*

this disturbing and extremely unpleasant, it was too unsubtle. People are sick of blood and gore, I told him. Stick to subtlety and suggestion. Besides, where were we going to get such a weapon from – the neighbours? ('Oh hello, Steve, have you got a hatchet I can borrow? I'm going to murder my wife and my son is going to film it.') The perfect murder weapon, I suggested, was the dog's slip lead. A seemingly innocuous object which works on the same principle as a hangman's noose. I also stipulated that there should be no depiction of Mr Home Front actually carrying out the deed (a faint possibility fiction and reality could become blurred). No, I said, the camera should merely pan in on Mr HF, alone in the hallway late at night, practising the strangulation on his wrist. Or even better, simply focus on the murderer's face as he stares thoughtfully at Lupin's lead hanging from the door.

Father and son conferred in lowered voices for some moments before reluctantly agreeing to change the hatchet to the dog's lead. We then wondered what music should be used for the soundtrack. The final decision rested with Fred, who opted for Peggy Lee's *Christmas Waltz*, to be played over shots of the neighbour's festive lights (we didn't have any).

When filming was over, I reflected how much nicer to have played Wendy Hiller's part in a remake of *I Know Where I'm Going!*, rather than *Woman (Victim)* in a five-minute horror film.

As for Mr HF, I am slightly concerned about his resemblance to Alfred Hitchcock. When I asked whether my screen death by dog's lead had given him ideas, he replied in his best Bermondsey accent, 'It's only a movie, Ingrid.' The film is currently being edited before its screen debut on YouTube. If this column fails to appear in the next issue can someone call the police?

The name game

Forgetting why you went upstairs is one thing but forgetting your best friend's name is a whole lot worse. *Mark Mason* on everyone's social nightmare

The late screenwriter Nora Ephron had a clever code she employed at parties. If someone was approaching whose name she had forgotten, Ephron would reach out and squeeze her husband's arm. This was their signal for: 'Quick, introduce yourself so that they have to respond in kind.' She was thereby saved from embarrassment and reminded of their name in one cunning move.

It is the worst trick a failing memory can play on you. Forget your pin number, or the reason you went upstairs, and the only person who knows it's happened is you. But the horror of a forgotten name exposes your failure to other people – and, worst of all, to the person whose name you've forgotten. They're left standing in the belief (however mistaken) that you don't value them enough to remember what they're called. Never mind that you've known them for years, have played tennis with them, gone on holiday with them ... still the name won't come.

We've all forgotten names in our time, but when someone forgets ours we don't think, 'Oh, the poor fellow, his memory's obviously let him down, it's a common occurrence.' We think, 'I knew it, he's never liked me, that's how insignificant I am, in fact I bet no one really likes me...' You, the forgetter, know what the forgettee will be thinking, so panic sets in as you try with increasing desperation to retrieve the information from your memory bank. But that only has the effect of closing down the bank even more securely, leaving you floundering and red-faced. It turns what should be an enjoyable social occasion into a terrifying minefield.

Ed Balls recently ended up in trouble despite the fact that his forgettee wasn't present. The shadow chancellor was on live television at the time, being challenged by *Newsnight*'s Emily Maitlis to list business people who supported Labour. Balls replied that he'd been at dinner with some of them that very evening. 'Who?' asked Maitlis. 'Well ... er ... Bill ... the former chief executive of EDF ...' 'What's his name?' probed the presenter. 'Well, to be honest his surname's just gone from my head,' admitted Balls, adding that this was 'annoying'. At least he got halfway there. Frank Skinner once completely forgot the name of a current player for his beloved West Bromwich Albion, a man he watched week in week out. Eventually, after hours of effort, Skinner got it. A couple of days later he told the story to a friend – and forgot the player again. 'I couldn't remember,' as Skinner put it, 'the name of the player I couldn't remember.'

How can we save ourselves from this horror? We could use mental images. Jeremy Lewis of this parish once had a 'shaming blank spot' about the then literary editor of the *Daily Express*, Maggie Pringle. 'I overcame it by thinking of one of those diamond-patterned V-necked jerseys made by Pringle – it always worked.' Or you could have an assistant permanently on hand. One of Damian McBride's tasks when he worked for Gordon Brown was to stand behind the Prime Minister at receptions, whispering reminders as people approached: 'Cheryl Cole, Girls Aloud, recovering from malaria, don't mention Ashley.' But even this could go wrong. Brown, informed several times that a journalist closing in on him was called Sumeet, still managed to boom 'Shambo!' Almost as baffling as the time Ronald Reagan introduced Princess Diana as 'Princess David'.

There's Henry Blofeld's tactic of calling everyone 'my dear old thing', stemming from the time Blowers completely forgot the name of Michael Melford, then cricket correspondent of the *Daily Telegraph*. The broadcaster Richard Coles has not one but two solutions. The first is to introduce the person using any old name. When they correct you, reply with a mystified 'Why, what did I say?', and blame it on a brainstorm. The other is to say 'And this is ... do you know, I've completely forgotten your name.' They'll say 'John', to which you reply 'No, of course I know it's John – it's your surname I've forgotten.'

But then Coles has a blackbelt in social adeptness. Were I to try either of these routines they'd backfire on me horribly. Even Nora Ephron came a cropper in the end. Eventually her husband's memory got as bad as hers, and he forgot what the squeeze on his arm meant.

'In response to public pressure we're cancelling your bonus'

From one myth to another

Rupert Brooke's centenary has fuelled assaults on his character with claims of sadism and misogyny. *Richard Davenport-Hines* scorns the detractors

There is nothing more giddying than to become a living legend in one's twenties. Among poets this was the fate of Byron, Swinburne, Wilde, Auden and Rupert Brooke – and it did each of them harm. They started playing up to their myth, making themselves notorious, and faking their feelings to their friends. 'One should always be a bit improbable,' said Brooke – quoting Wilde. He exploited his boyish beauty, exaggerated his impulsive rashness and posed as a pagan to foster his improbable myth.

The circumstances of Brooke's death in April 1915 – on a hospital ship in the Aegean, of blood poisoning from an insect bite on the lip – exacerbated the problem. He was going to fight in the Dardanelles, and Winston Churchill, the progenitor of the fatal Gallipoli campaign, wrote a militant and grandiose tribute in the *Times*. Posthumous myth-makers took over. Some reinvented Brooke as a 20th-century version of the gallant Elizabethan poet Sir Philip Sidney, who died of gangrene from a battle wound in 1586. Other soppy, battle-shy old bachelors depicted him as a neutered poetical Adonis.

Brooke's detractors made the most enduring myths. Ignoring the fact that he was a professed socialist, who wrote vehement articles for the *New Statesman*, progressives belaboured him as a purblind public school patriot for writing war sonnets ('there's some corner of a foreign field/That is for ever England'). At the centenary of his death, the denigration of him has not abated. In a priggish indictment, which appeared in the *Observer*, Robert McCrum attacked 'Brooke's near-reactionary conservatism', which he coupled with his 'repressed sexual identity'.

The idea seems to be that if only Brooke had enjoyed the 21st century's idea of a healthy sex life (with no secrets or guilt) he would have been as emotionally hygienic and politically righteous as any good, caring *Observer* reader. The possibility that this antiseptic paragon might also not have written a single memorable line is discounted.

Brooke's emotional experiments and free thinking also still seem threatening to the Right. A recent *Daily Mail* headline blared: 'Rupert Brooke was a vicious sadist who thought all women were "beasts".' The justification for this rant was an account of Edwardian

skinny-dipping in the river Cam in Lucy Beckett's newly published *The Second I Saw You: The True Love Story of Rupert Brooke and Phyllis Gardner*. Gardner recalled shy, tentative youngsters being daring and testing bounds by lying naked together on the river bank. Brooke pretended to strangle her, emptied the contents of his waterlogged boot over her glistening body, laid her flat, and leant over to kiss her. Gardner wrote of the sham throttling, 'I kept on smiling and patting him: I was in a sort of heaven, although once he made me choke.' Gardner's radiant, grateful memories continued with the two youngsters trudging back to Grantchester in damp clothes, eating supper and drinking stout before a roaring fire, and playing with an orange-coloured kitten.

As to the claim that Brooke was a vile misogynist who thought 'all women were beasts' (taken up by the *Daily Mail* and *Observer* in rare unison), Brooke's actual words to Gardner were, 'Don't gloom over my saying that all women are beasts. I've quite forgotten saying it, and apropos of what I said it. They mostly are ... So are most men. All men I think.' So much for the woman-hating strangler.

A huge amount of newsprint, police

time, public money and indignant frothing is being wasted at the moment on pursuing harmless old men because their courting techniques 40 years ago were a bit abrupt. This is just one expression of the moronic modern idea that young people's sex lives should be immunised from mistakes, regrets, frustration and sorrow. But sexual desire is inevitably mucky – not salubrious. Sexually inexperienced youngsters are bound to hurt, disappoint and vice versa. So, for that matter, are many of their elders.

It's silly to judge a man who died a hundred years ago by today's mores – and to assume that 2015 represents some proud high point of sexual etiquette. Most people over 50 reading *The Second I Saw You* will sympathise with Brooke's hesitant physical fumbling, his emotional wavering and his doubts of his own sincerity. As a Cambridge undergraduate, he changed his mind, tried new directions, and when thinking for himself anew, sometimes blundered or got overwrought. 'One hour I feel as if I could carry the whole world on my little finger,' he wrote. 'The next, as if I should shoot myself for misery.' His contradictory impulses and exasperated outbursts are no different from those of millions of civilised young men and women through the ages, but because Brooke died aged 27, just as he was settling his mature place in the world, purse-lipped critics now call him 'morally repellent' or 'intense and disturbed' for the brave, open contradictions that his contemporaries found exciting.

Discreet homosexuality was prevalent among Cambridge's male undergraduates of Brooke's generation. George Mallory, who became a national hero second only to Scott of the Antarctic when he perished near the summit of Everest, spent six months talking endlessly about sex with Brooke's friend James Strachey, and exchanging self-conscious caresses, before consummating their affair. By 1909 their friend Brooke was so embarrassed by his virginity at the age of 22 that he determined to shed it. This would be easier to arrange and less complicated afterwards with a boy than a girl, he realised, and fixed on an amenable youth called Denham Russell-Smith. 'I wanted to have some fun, &, still more, to see what it was like, and to do away with the shame ... of being a virgin,' he said.

By then he had also fallen for a schoolgirl called Noel Olivier. Further entanglements followed with several intelligent, artistic young women. He shared with them his avidity for country walks and nude bathing. He wrote to Phyllis Gardner in 1912: 'You are incredibly beautiful when you're naked, and your wonderful hair is blowing about you. Fire runs through me, to think of it.' McCrum jeers that Brooke 'was tactful, chivalrous – and boring' sexually,

Left: Phyllis Gardner in 1934. Above, Rupert Brooke in all his boyish beauty

because when she crept into his bedroom at night and lay in his arms, he told her not to be afraid: 'I wouldn't do anything you wouldn't like.' His affair with Gardner collapsed after he suggested that they use contraceptives and have full sex. What abuse would modern goody-goodies hurl if Brooke had forced moves in bed that she disliked or had not offered to use a condom?

Brooke shone with unpredictable and unfulfilled potential. The American poet Robert Frost had expected that he would develop into a latter-day metaphysical poet like John Donne. Virginia Woolf thought he would become prime minister 'because he had such a gift with people, and such sanity, and force'. His joy of life, his nonchalance about death, the excitement he aroused in his friends all remain inspiring. 'He was essentially hard: his hatred of slosh went deep,' said his friend EM Forster, and I think he would have scoffed – as we should – at the puritanical pieties being circulated against him.

The gentle lyricist

Valerie Grove remembers taking
Michael Flanders on a tour of Hampstead
Garden Suburb ten months before his
sudden death 40 years ago

Forty years ago I was writing an *Evening Standard* series called *Where I Was Young*. Each week I would take someone back to the London street where they grew up and we would walk around the area, reminiscing. They weren't all famous, but John Betjeman (Highgate) and Monica Dickens (Notting Hill) were among the first, and Kingsley Amis (suburban south London) was one of the two youngest, aged 53. The other 53-year-old was Michael Flanders, in his self-propelled wheelchair.

To everyone who grew up in the 1950s, the timeless comic songs of Flanders and Swann were indelibly engraved on our collective memory. Today whenever the railways come up on the news, the BBC still plays *Slow Train* and we are forever intoning 'It all makes work for the working man to do' or, when in the bath, 'In the bath!'

Flanders had grown up in Hampstead Garden Suburb, where we met on a punishingly hot day in early June. The Victorian philanthropist Henrietta Barnett had planned her garden suburb as an Arcadian enclave of substantial redbrick homes in culs-de-sac and closes, with Dutch gables, leaded windows, expansive lawns and cedars; and so it remained in 1974, the saplings of Flanders's childhood now vast. Nearby stood Lutyens's austere church, St Jude's, and, up the hill, the Old Bull and Bush. His family's detached house with its wooden veranda and honeysuckle hedges stood opposite the Wylde Wood of Hampstead Heath, and backed onto a tennis court. His parents (concert violinist mother, cinema manager father) had to take in lodgers, some of whom brought pianos. One was a painter: Flanders said he recognised his two sisters in the painter's semi-clothed nymphs and naiads. Next door in Heath Close had lived Sir Bernard Spilsbury, the

forensic expert, and on the other side a veteran of one of Scott's expeditions. The Flanders family had become 'honorary Jewish' when German refugees and East End Jews began to settle in 'The Suburb'; when the butcher said 'I haven't had your order for Passover yet, Mrs Flanders', she had to ask Mrs Lerner next door what she should ask for.

Accompanying us on that day in 1974 was Flanders's younger daughter, the now famous Stephanie, then aged five, who eagerly accepted (as did I) a home-made lemon ice lolly from a Heath Close resident.

From this house Flanders attended Westminster School, alongside Peter Ustinov and Tony Benn. And from there he went up to Christ Church, Oxford, to read history, a 6ft 4in tall, lanky, athletic youth who sprinted and rowed for his college. His stentorian voice made him the outstanding Ouds actor of his day. Then in 1943, commissioned with the RNVR as a sub-lieutenant, he contracted polio; after three years in hospital in an iron lung, he was destined to a wheelchair life – and his college

refused to take him back to complete his degree. Eventually, having done some BBC Schools broadcasting, he linked up with his old schoolfriend Donald Swann to write revues that were gently funny yet rebarbative and never politically correct: 'Examine the Irishman, Welshman or Scot/You'll find he's a stinker as likely as not!' They were a global hit. Flanders and Swann gave 2,000 performances in 11 years, and the recordings by George Martin still sell today.

After our day out in Hampstead Garden Suburb, Michael Flanders endeared himself to me for ever by sending a handwritten letter: 'The piece you wrote was so accurate I fear you may be drummed out of the NUJ.' Only ten months later, I had a call from his distraught wife, Claudia, the American daughter of the great radical journalist Claud Cockburn. Michael Flanders had died suddenly of an aneurysm, while on holiday in Wales. He was still only 53.

Six-year-old Stephanie later graduated from Balliol, became economics editor of the BBC, and is now chief European market strategist at J P Morgan. In 2007 she presented an excellent *Archive Hour* on Radio 4, belatedly discovering the father she had so briefly known and who had been so widely loved.

Father of us all

RORY KNIGHT BRUCE

Edward Thomas: From Adlestrop to Arras

by Jean Moorcroft Wilson

Bloomsbury

We all remember *Adlestrop* as for years it was taught in schools across the land, a short, accessible poem about a train stopping one summer day in Gloucestershire's Evenlode Vale. Its author, Edward Thomas, was on his way from Paddington to Dymock where he spent a lot of time with Robert Frost who convinced this misanthropic journalist and prodigious book reviewer that he should become a poet.

Jean Moorcroft Wilson, herself married to the nephew of Leonard Woolf and something of a hand at the 'Bloomsberries', likens this productive friendship, somewhat fancifully, to that of Wordsworth and Coleridge, and sees both as pioneers of modern poetry. 'He was the father of us all,' was Ted Hughes's verdict on Thomas.

Edward Thomas, of Welsh descent, was born into an ambitious lower-middle-class family in south London in 1878, and sent briefly to St Paul's. His father's scorn when he failed at sport marked him for life. Yet Thomas got into Oxford where, then as now, the impressionable, awkward undergraduate affected the dress and drinking manners of a gentleman or aristocrat. But it was earlier visits to Swindon and his paternal grandmother, where he met a local countryman, David Uzzell, that unleashed in Thomas a profound love of walking and the countryside. He called Uzzell 'Dad' and referred to him in the poem *Lob*: 'An old man's face, by life and weather cut/ And coloured, – rough, brown, sweet as any nut.'

Thomas became a devotee and biographer of Richard Jefferies, whose love of rural Wiltshire opened his eyes to botany, birds, plants, trees, seasons and 'apparently endless leisure'. But Thomas's life was to be anything but leisurely, churning out books and reviews,

Edward Thomas in about 1905

constantly poor and moving home with his long-suffering wife Helen, whom he married at 20, and three young children, whose intrusion he resented.

Both, however, believed in Jefferies's dictum: 'If you wish your children to think deep things – to know the holiest emotions – take them to the woods and the hills, and give them the freedom of the meadows.'

Thomas was frequently absent from home and, in London, met influential writers and editors like JC Squire and Lascelles Abercrombie. On three occasions he stayed with Joseph Conrad, admiring in particular *The Secret Sharer*, but was overawed by him.

The couple settled for a while in Hampshire and Helen began teaching at Bedales, where they managed to send their children. A regular visitor and supporter was the travel writer Norman Douglas, also on the lookout for Bedalian boys, who recalled in his memoirs *Looking Back* (1933): 'Often I told him that it was no use trying to be a gentleman if you are a professional writer.'

Thomas's own sex life is a conundrum. He contracted gonorrhoea at Oxford from using prostitutes and (like Eric Gill)

marked his diary with an 'x' whenever he had 'lovemaking'. He tried to leave Helen and then formed what some described as a ménage à trois with her and the plumply adoring Eleanor Farjeon, but there is no suggestion he and Farjeon got to the 'x' entry.

Like so many writers of his time, Thomas was happiest in male company, which may explain why, when in 1915 he enlisted to fight in France, he welcomed both the order and income that the army provided. It was, after all, his first proper 'office' job. The decision to enlist may also have been to assuage his father's stinging childhood accusation of cowardice. Robert Frost believed it stemmed from an ugly altercation with a gamekeeper (the very breed he had trusted on his Swindon childhood holidays) when he was caught trespassing on Lord Beauchamp's Madresfield estate.

Although he wrote poetry about the war, much of which does not stand the test of time, Thomas was not a 'War Poet' like Owen or Sassoon. The last thing he wrote in his 'field notebook' before his death at Arras aged 39 was perhaps his saddest. 'I never understood quite what was meant by God.' A child in a meadow in the woods and the hills could have told him the answer to that.

The tombstone revolution

For nearly 30 years, Harriet Frazer has campaigned for better memorials to the dead. *Harry Mount* assesses her achievement

Harriet Frazer's dedication to the art of letter-carving was borne out of tragedy. In 1985, her stepdaughter Sophie Behrens, a 26-year-old writer, took her own life. After her struggle to commission a suitable tombstone, Frazer found herself setting up Memorials by Artists, which creates beautifully lettered monuments to the dead.

'We asked a sculptor friend to come up with a design for Sophie,' says Frazer, 71, who steps down in May after 27 years running Memorials by Artists. 'We showed it to the vicar and he said no. It didn't pass the rules and regulations for the diocese. You were only allowed scripture or well-known hymnal words.

'I wouldn't have started the whole thing if we'd got what we wanted to begin with. But if you're angry, you start doing things.'

Fired by anger, Frazer persevered and ended up commissioning a heart-stopping tombstone from the sculptor Simon Verity for her stepdaughter. The stone is inscribed with a sculpted bird, flanked by bunches of grapes, echoing Sophie's love of wine and Italy. It stands today in the churchyard of St Peter and

St Paul, in Salle, north Norfolk.

From this acorn grew Memorials by Artists, which has now put 5,000 people in touch with artists to create unusual, stirring memorials for their loved ones. The company has expanded to encompass other letter-carved works for all occasions, including birthday presents, architectural inscriptions and house signs. It is now run by the Lettering and Commemorative Arts Trust, which encourages letter-carving through apprenticeships, books and workshops.

In 2013, the trust opened an office, shop and gallery devoted to letter-carving at Snape Maltings – the arts centre, famed for its concert hall, founded by Benjamin Britten. There are three shows a year. At present, there's a new show of the work of Michael Renton (1934–2001), a master of lettering in wood, stone and ink.

It was a strange career change in middle-age for Harriet Frazer, who had been working in a Suffolk job centre when letter-carving crashed into her life.

She claims to be no good at the actual carving side of it all. 'Although I did enjoy playing post offices as a child – stamping

things,' she says in her diffident way. But her lack of knowledge about the whole world of letters and tombstones was, in fact, a bonus.

'I'd never heard of the Crafts Council and Eric Gill,' she says, 'but it was useful to be ignorant. It meant I could see what people felt when they came to it all new.'

It also meant she could look upon traditional epitaphs with a fresh eye. 'I remember thinking, "In loving memory"...' she says, 'well, that's all right, isn't it? And then thinking, "No, not really".'

In fact, letters do run in her blood: her father was Heywood Hill, who founded the eponymous Mayfair bookshop in 1936. Whatever the reason, letter-carving struck a deep chord with her.

'It was unlike anything I could imagine myself doing,' she says. 'It was amazing. It suddenly seemed to make sense. I found I could really help people. I could help them negotiate the rules of memorials. I could match them up with the artists. And there was this extraordinary untapped demand. It began to take off.'

Britain has had an exceptional collection of tombstones since the Middle Ages. There are some delightful 18th-century epitaphs in twirly italics in Snape churchyard, next to two of Frazer's recent commissions; another commission is engraved into a church window at Snape. It was only after the First World War – and the melancholy flood of memorials it brought – that dioceses began to grow so prescriptive about tombstone design and lettering.

Memorials by Artists has revived the art of original tombstone design. Among the thousands of works commissioned is the film-maker Derek Jarman's simple slab of riven Welsh slate, inscribed with his signature. Another in Somerset, in Cornish slate, is to Auberon Waugh – 'of Combe Florey – writer and journalist' – with a cheering variety of letterforms, reflecting Waugh's mastery of the written word.

Never say 'font' to a lettercutter, by the way. I said the dreaded word to one, working in the Snape Maltings gallery. 'Not font,' he barked. 'Letterform.'

Portland stone, Purbeck stone, York stone ... Britain is blessed with such a rapidly changing geology that the available variety of colours and surfaces in a churchyard is near-infinite.

Not quite as infinite as the choice of inscriptions – one in the eye for that dreary Norfolk vicar who vetoed Sophie Behrens's initial tombstone. Recent Memorials by Artists inscriptions include a quote from Robert Louis Stevenson's own epitaph for himself: 'Here he lies where he long'd to be; Home is the sailor, home from sea, And the hunter home from the hill.'

Beautifully designed tombstones don't come cheap, ranging from £2,000 to £7,000. Given that a plain slab of unengraved, masoned slate starts at £1,000, that doesn't seem too much to pay for a near-permanent piece of art

that fulfils one of the most vital roles of all: remembering the dead.

Much of Frazer's work has involved discussing designs with the bereaved – in meetings held at her home near Snape, until the move to the Snape Maltings

> Portland stone, Purbeck stone, York stone ... Britain is blessed with such a rapidly changing geology that the available variety of colours and surfaces in a churchyard is near-infinite

office. 'It can be exhausting,' she says.

Most moving of all are the memorials to children. Frazer, with Hilary Meynell, has written a practical guide for the memorials to young people, children and babies. The inscriptions are nearly unbearable to read. 'Play, dance and blow bubbles for me' is the line to a 10-year-old girl, dotted around with little bubbles carved into the stone. To a 19-year-old girl, the simple inscription reads, 'We wish she could have stayed longer.'

A second memorial to Sophie Behrens hangs on the wall of Harriet Frazer's farmhouse. The black stone disc features a jug, bursting with flowers, surrounded by words from Sophie's last letter to her family: 'I have thought that life was rich and miraculous.'

How right, then, that past lives should be remembered so richly and miraculously.

The Lettering and Commemorative Arts Trust: www.letteringartstrust.org.uk

Mrs Thatcher, culture vulture

She was regarded as a philistine but this is wide of the mark, says *Miriam Gross*. In fact she loved poetry and was fanatical about opera

When I tell people that one of Margaret Thatcher's favourite composers was Bela Bartok, they are dumbfounded. Wasn't she, whatever else you might think about her, one of history's undisputed philistines?

No, as it turns out, she wasn't. When, in 1988, Bartok's remains were being transported for reburial from the US to his native Hungary, Mrs Thatcher took time out to travel to Southampton, where the ship had docked, to attend a memorial concert. And here she is, speaking at a 'Britain Salutes Hungary' reception in 1989: '… then of course I have always been wherever Sir George Solti has been doing Bartok … isn't it fantastic? I did not really fully appreciate the marvels of that particular music, but Sir George Solti was a pupil of Bartok and together they do absolute wonders.'

Mrs Thatcher, it appears, had a genuine love for music, and was impressively knowledgeable about it. I learned of her attachment to Bartok, along with many other astonishing facts about her cultural activities, while doing research for Volume II of Charles Moore's superb biography, *Everything She Wants*. Some of my findings appear in his book, but there were many interesting details for which he didn't have space.

For example, continuing for the moment with her musical life, Isaiah Berlin recalls that when he met Mrs Thatcher at the Royal Opera house during a performance of *Prince Igor* by Borodin, she informed him that while at Oxford (where she had sung in the Bach choir) she had taken part in the university's production of the opera.

Her choices for *Desert Island Discs* included Beethoven, Dvorak, Verdi, Mendelssohn, Mascagni and *Smoke Gets in Your Eyes*. 'Music', she told Roy Plomley, 'is what I go to when I want to take refuge … from the very logical life I've lived, and always been trained to live.' The highlight of her year, according to her long-term adviser and friend Charles Powell, was the Salzburg Music Festival; and she went to Glyndebourne at least once a year.

Various musical people I talked to – Claus Moser, Jeremy Isaacs, Robert Armstrong – who had accompanied her to opera productions said that she knew the works inside out, sometimes better than they did. James Lees-Milne recounts in his *Diaries* that when John Julius Norwich took her to *Tosca*, 'She knew everything about past performances, when and where and who sang them. When the performance was over, he asked her whether she had not thought it a splendid one. "Yes", she replied, "but the fichu should not have been scarlet but cerise".' (A fichu, Google informs me, is a small, triangular shawl.)

No doubt she was a swot and a bit of a show-off, and, yes, she enjoyed the musicals of Andrew Lloyd Webber. But was she, as Mary (Baroness) Warnock – Mistress of Girton College Cambridge at the time – put it, 'just a Muzak person who liked stuff that was pumped out and absolutely tasteless'? Warnock was being interviewed by the journalist Graham Turner, who kindly lent me the transcript of his interviews. His article – 'Why Britain's Eggheads look down on Mrs Thatcher' – appeared in the *Sunday Telegraph* in 1988. Most of the eggheads he talked to agreed that Mrs Thatcher lacked any glimmerings of artistic sensibility.

Anthony Burgess (who lived in Monaco) went so far as to claim that 'She is never to be seen at concerts, plays or operas'. The author Robert McCrum, writing in the *Guardian* the day after she died, judged that 'Margaret Thatcher was the most philistine PM in decades'.

These detractors presumably didn't realise that Mrs Thatcher was a fan of TS Eliot and Philip Larkin. Or that she was a lifelong reader of poetry, her favourite poets, according to Charles Powell, being Kipling, Walt Whitman and Longfellow, the last of whom she quoted in various speeches in the US. Or that she knew a great deal of poetry by heart, much of it – Wordsworth, Tennyson, the words of numerous English hymns – learned as a girl at her grammar school.

Researching into her reading habits brings out just as many surprises as her musical life. When she was leader of the opposition, a Methodist minister and friend of her father asked her to name her eight 'desert island' books for an article in his church magazine. She chose: a collection of sermons by John Wesley; Churchill's *History of the English Speaking Peoples*; Elizabeth Longford's biography of Wellington; Robert Blake's *Disraeli*, Pepys's Diary; Kenneth Clark's *Civilization*; a dictionary of quotations; and *The Albatross Book of Living Verse*, a volume compiled by the Marxist American poet and critic Louis Untermeyer.

She had also been much influenced by Arthur Koestler's anti-Communist novel *Darkness at Noon*; and she referred in several speeches to the impact on her thinking of *A Time for Greatness* by the American historian Herbert Agar.

At the same time, as she herself made clear, she 'lapped up' detective stories of any sort 'to read late at night'. And she was, as Nigel Lawson wrote, 'an avid reader of the works of Frederick Forsyth'. So, as in the case of music, her tastes were not always entirely highbrow.

But she was a passionate self-improver. The philosopher Bryan Magee recounts that, in the Seventies, when he was a Labour MP and she not yet leader of the opposition, they had been introduced while queuing in the Members' Dining Room. 'Not *the* Bryan Magee', she had enthused, 'the author of *Karl Popper*! I liked the book so much I read it twice.' They subsequently often sat together enjoying philosophical conversations.

The visual arts, on the other hand, were not Mrs Thatcher's strong point. Richard (Lord) Luce, who was arts minister at the time, told me that, to counter her ignorance, she would ask various museum directors to take her

GARY SMITH

round 'incognito' to point out and explain paintings of interest. She learned a lot, he says, but more about the technical than the aesthetic aspects of painting. Even so, hers was not the behaviour of a confirmed philistine.

Another surprise: even though she didn't care for tax payer funding of the arts (and she did much to encourage private sponsorship), government spending in total actually went up, not down, during her time in office. But some

in the arts world did better than others. Theatre people in particular felt hard done by and it's true that contemporary theatre was not Mrs Thatcher's favourite art form. She only once attended a performance at the National Theatre, Peter Shaffer's *Amadeus*, and was scandalised and incredulous at the depiction of Mozart as a foul-mouthed buffoon.

Peter Hall, director of the National Theatre during her premiership, has this

to say in his memoirs: 'I saw the Thatcher government dismantle the performing arts, spoil our education system and partially destroy our great tradition of public service broadcasting.'

What??

Mrs Thatcher's bourgeois gentility seems to have driven Left-leaning arts people completely over the top. But, for all their contempt, there is more than enough evidence to show that she was certainly no philistine.

Nature as a mirror for Me

The 'new nature writing' is a riot of egotism in which city-dwellers discover themselves in the Hindu Kush of the Norfolk Broads. It is a far cry from Dorothy Wordsworth, says *Frances Wilson*

In one of his most pugnacious essays, 'On Going Out for a Walk', Max Beerbohm noted that dread moment when, following lunch on a country house weekend, the suggestion is made – in a 'sharp imperative tone' that the speaker would otherwise not dream of employing – of taking a wander. Why, wondered Beerbohm, would anyone leave a warm dry room for a cold damp field? And why is walking considered an essentially 'noble' and 'virtuous' activity? His final point is the most penetrating: how is it that people who, leaning on the mantelpiece, are epigrammatic and witty become such crashing bores when they

are striding through the grass with a stick, observing their surroundings?

I was raised in a clan where marching over the Lake District in stiff green garments that squeaked at the joints and glowed in the rain was seen as a measure of moral courage, and preferring to sit in an armchair and read – as I did – was regarded as indolent. To raise my stature among my siblings, I read books about walking. Nature was always better in books. Writers like Dorothy Wordsworth made the business of being outside sound mystical rather than worthy. When Dorothy heard the call of a raven, 'the dome of the sky seemed to echo the

sound … it called again and again as it flew onwards, and the mountains gave back the sound, seeming as if from their centre; a musical bell-like answering to the bird's hoarse voice'. When Dorothy saw sheep, it was the 'glittering silver line on the ridges' of their backs that she noted, 'which made them look beautiful but with something of a strangeness, like animals of another kind – as if belonging to a more splendid world'. Dorothy Wordsworth's observations were recorded in her Grasmere journal, which was never meant for publication. What I have always loved about her was that she wrote without ego – nature was, for

TOBY MORISON

Dorothy, an out-of-body experience. Oscar Wilde put it perfectly. Egotism, wrote Wilde, 'is entirely the result of indoor life. Out of doors one becomes abstract and impersonal.' In an ideal world, that is.

Beerbohm and Wilde were of course dandies, and the dandy sensibility, drawn to all things man-made, has always been metropolitan. For the dandy, the city is the home of self-consciousness and the country is the place in which we are exposed as unaccommodated animals, poor and bare-forked. Not any more however! Take a look in your local bookshop. Gone are the Alfred Wainwrights, bad-tempered eccentrics who wrote guidebooks for like-minded misanthropes. Were I given the choice today between going out for a walk or staying behind to read the latest book about walking, I would grab my Hunters and break down the door in desperation to get out.

The millennium has ushered in a ghastly new literary brand called 'new nature writing' which, like the new men who participate in it, is as wild as Wilde himself and as artificial as Oscar's green carnation. This new nature writing, practised by the likes of Robert Macfarlane, is a marriage of self-consciousness and superiority, a riot of egotism in which city dwellers discover themselves in the Hindu Kush of the Norfolk Broads or the Sussex Downs, and explore their specialness in acres of nimble and airless sentences. 'All elsewhere is milk,' muses Macfarlane in Holloway. 'A void.' Ah, I see. Macfarlane's prose is as calcifyingly earnest as that of Rebecca Solnit, doyenne of American nature writing.

In Solnit's latest book, *The Faraway Nearby*, she ponders the significance of Iceland and a box of apricots: 'What size is representation?' she asks. 'The whiteness of the page before it is written on and after it is erased is and is not the same white', she explains further on. (Edmund De Waal, who has applied new nature writing techniques to porcelain, similarly worries, in *The White Road*, about the 'sound of white'.) 'Writing', continues Solnit, reflecting with fascination on her own procedures, 'is saying to no one and to everyone the things that it is not possible to say to someone.'

The most irritating recent addition to the genre must be Simon Armitage's *Walking Home: Travels with a Troubadour on the Pennine Way*, a work of comedic arrogance and condescension in which the author pursues his pointless journey with no money in his pocket, bestowing daily poetry readings on the locals in order to earn his keep.

The new nature writing is about Me and Nature, with nature as a mirror for exploring the wonders of Me. 'I now understand it to be certainly the case',

> Were I given the choice today between going out for a walk or staying behind to read the latest book about walking, I would grab my Hunters and break down the door in desperation to get out

proclaims Macfarlane, his focus as ever firmly on himself, 'though I have long imagined it to be true, that stretches of a path might carry memories of a person just as a person might of a path.' Perusing such a path, Macfarlane notes how his 'shadow falls undistorted by my side'. Dorothy Wordsworth had no interest in whether Lake Grasmere remembered her, or how poetic her shadow looked as she made her way home. She had no interest in herself at all, which is precisely why she is interesting.

I am far from alone in my allergy to the breed. It seems that, despite the sales figures, everybody hates them. Bashing the new nature writers, an act of transgression which raises a fearful snigger in us all, has become known as Mac-stabbing and you can't throw a clod of earth without hitting a Mac-stabbing journalist. Each attack on the Macs is followed by page after sweating page of vituperative rage from the likes of Richard Mabey, defending the tribe without any sense of why they are so irritating.

Reviewing Macfarlane's *The Wild Places* in the *London Review of Books*, the Scottish poet Kathleen Jamie created an unforgettable image of the new nature writer at work:

'What's that coming over the hill? A white, middle-class Englishman! A Lone Enraptured Male! From Cambridge! Here to boldly go, "discovering", then quelling our harsh and lovely and sometimes difficult land with his civilised lyrical words.'

The response from the new-crew? It was as if Jamie had swung off the Cenotaph. Eileen Battersby, in the *Irish Times*, bravely described the 'fey eccentricity' of Helen Macdonald's tone in *H is for Hawk* as 'quite maddening'. The book, observed Battersby, was 'one of those trendy personal memoirs masquerading as nature writing'. RIP, Eileen Battersby!

It seems that Oscar was right all along. In 'Pen, Pencil and Poison', his essay on that other Wainewright, the artist murderer Thomas Griffiths, Wilde observed that 'Like most artificial people, he had a love of nature'.

'So, what's for dinner?'

Taking a walk

The Quantocks by moonlight

ADAM NICOLSON

It is the time of year to go for a night walk. Pick a full moon and by far the best place I have ever had a moon walk is in the Quantocks in Somerset. Coleridge and Wordsworth and Mrs Coleridge and Wordsworth's sister Dorothy lived there from the middle of 1797 until the following summer. They weren't all in the same house but a few convenient walking miles apart, the Coleridges crammed into a damp and horrible hovel in Nether Stowey (now super done up and belonging to the National Trust) and the Wordsworths (with servants) in a country house three miles away in its own park at Alfoxden.

Walking was what they did, as a way of feeling close to nature, and as a democratic gesture: no grandee vision of the country from the back of a horse, but down there with it, intimately connected, feeling the wind in their faces and the mud on their boots. People tend to think of Coleridge as a drug-wreck and Wordsworth as a stuffed-up Victorian monument, but the great poets of this Quantocks year were young, in their 20s, energetic, anxiously alert to what they could write and be.

The first of Dorothy's journals was written at Alfoxden. The first inklings of the poem that became *The Prelude* were stirring in Wordsworth's mind in the spring of 1798. Coleridge was writing *The Ancient Mariner* and *Christabel* and *Frost at Midnight* and probably *Kubla Khan* (although that would not see the light of day for many years). It was the high point of Coleridge's tragic life, and the beginning of Wordsworth's greatness.

They usually worked in the morning, reading and writing, and would set off for a walk only as the light began to fade from the sky. If you want to follow the way they often took, park in the little village of Holford (or at the very nice Combe House Hotel) and set off through the woods and open grasslands of Alfoxden park (the Wordsworths liked to think of it as 'all the foxes' den' but nowadays it is boringly called Alfoxton and is in a sorry state, half abandoned, half redeveloped). Beyond it, though, you can climb up the old stony road on to the great ridge of the Quantocks, looking out over the Bristol Channel to the north, and west into the folds of Devon.

It was a walk they took nearly every day, up from the enclosing trees of the woods around Holford to the big open air of the moory heights, a kind of daily transcendence. At first the moonlight vies with the dropping light of the sun, so that a sheen lies across the colours of the fading day. But go slowly, and the moonlight will soon make for magic. The big Alfoxden beeches throw shadows across the old lane, deep blue within the blue, looking like early photographs, silvered and half real, a Coleridgean world of reduced stimulus and heightened awareness.

You hardly need to go to Tahiti. It is all here in Somerset, earth translated into another language. Theatricality lies all around you. The moon lights up the damp mist down in the Levels to the east, so white it is like a fall of snow. The clouds below the moon are rimmed silver in a blue-black sky, as if they were islands on which a cartographer had somehow illuminated the leading edge. The trees make a shadow lattice on the path in front of you as you come back down through the wooded combes to the village. The lane itself turns to a burnished lead, spotted with pools of lightlessness. Venus goes yellow as it sets, the owls start their hesitant hooting and dogs bark. Unforgettable: no gap between now and 1798.

Map: OS Explorer 140 Quantock Hills and Bridgwater. About 3 miles

Pedal plus power

Don't imagine an e-bike will do all the work for you – you still have to make quite a bit of effort. That suited *Deborah Maby*

On the day of my first e-biking experience, I made my partner, Christian, get up at 7am to play tennis before we left because I was afraid we wouldn't get enough exercise, such was my ambivalence about the idea of a motor-powered bicycle.

I had imagined that riding an e-bike entailed nothing more than pressing a button, and off you went. This may be true of some models, but the ones we were on were far superior, I was assured by their owner, Tim Hudson, who, along with his wife, Louise, and an engaging young Italian called Matteo Baffi, runs Inspired Italy, which has just ventured into e-biking tours.

We met the couple because Christian part-owns a house near them in Umbria. There is a large expat community here, but Tim and Louise are rather different from the rest: they are younger, for a start, and are still working – very hard. Every winter they decamp with their four dogs to a rented flat in the Dolomites, from where they organise so-called ski safaris, taking punters on five-day tours around the area. These have proved so successful that they have now decided to adapt the same principle to e-biking tours in Umbria in the summer months.

We had no intention of doing the whole tour but were persuaded by Tim to try out a sample day, with him as guide. As keen and fit cyclists, we had always made it clear we thought e-biking rather more suited to real oldies or people who were extremely lazy or unfit. Tim was determined to prove us wrong.

E-bikers in front of the Roman theatre below Gubbio, built in the first century BC

We picked the bikes up at their showroom in Lisciano Niccone, which is full of e-bikes, panniers, water bottles and maps. I was pleasantly surprised by the bikes' appearance – they were not at all the frumpy old-lady contraptions I'd imagined. (They are made by Raleigh, sadly not in Nottingham but China, and powered by Bosch.) They are fitted with thick canvas panniers but if you do a tour, your serious luggage is taken to each hotel by car.

Tim explained the different settings on the bikes. You always have to pedal, and the harder you pedal the more power the bike gives you back – a bit like paying into a workplace pension scheme. There are five settings: the lowest simply neutralises things, so the weight of the bike is offset by the power, making it the same as riding a standard push-bike. Then comes Eco, which gives you a bit of extra oomph, Tour, Sport and finally Turbo for really steep hills or when you're late for dinner. 'I use Turbo all the time,' said Tim cheerfully, 'because I'm a fat lazy bastard' (not true).

Christian and I spent the first half-hour boringly discussing which mode we were in. He claimed to be in Off a lot of the time, which I didn't believe, while I was very happy in Eco, with occasional spurts in Tour, and Sport for hills. I am only an averagely fit cyclist but I am rather good on hills, so it was annoying to know that people would simply assume I had just whacked my e-bike into Turbo.

Tim had planned a 65km round trip, which included a castle, a lunch stop, a stretch on a traffic-free track alongside Lake Trasimeno, and a visit to the site of the Battle of Trasimeno in 217 BC. All of these are included on one or more days of the week-long tour.

We set off and climbed up to Castello di Pierle, a medieval castle that stands guard above the Niccone Valley to protect Cortona from the enemies of Perugia. It is ruined, but still commanding. Our next stop was the Castello di Sorbello, an extraordinary, partly ruined fortress, still lived in for some of the year by the Marquis Ranieri Bourbon del Monte, whose name suggests he is the sire of several dynasties, and his wife and sister, who allowed us to look into their dungeons. He was sitting outside, two dogs at his feet, a book on his lap, baggy corduroy trousers held up with string, looking like something out of a Molly Keane novel about faded Anglo-Irish aristocracy.

On we cycled towards the wonderful hilltop town of Preggio, location for several music festivals in the summer, but turned off before the road rose steeply and spent the next half-hour or so on a completely deserted route running through a lush valley. Umbria manages to be both green and rugged and wild, and is to my mind infinitely preferable to the manicured beauty of Tuscany. Then we whacked the bikes into Sport mode and up we climbed to the Pian de Marte for lunch in a beautiful country house hotel, and to charge up the batteries – the modern equivalent of watering the horses. After lunch, up, up and up we

went to Castel Rigone, with its stunning views of Lake Trasimeno. This was where the bikes really came into their own, as we felt we were pushing ourselves, but didn't arrive at the top completely wiped out.

The descent and a long ride along the lake were rewarded with an ice cream in the town of Passignano and the return to Lisciano Niccone was via the site, near Tuoro, of the slaughter by Hannibal of 15,000 Roman legionaries in 217 BC.

Out of interest, Christian and I rode our ordinary bikes up to Castel Rigone a few days later. The difference was astonishing: I felt the hill would never end. This makes me wary of e-bikes, as you could so easily get spoilt and seduced by the ease of it all. I'm not quite ready for an e-biking holiday myself yet, but I can certainly see the attraction. You can cover so much more ground for one thing and, because you're not so intent on the physical effort required, you are free to enjoy the scenery much more. I can certainly imagine myself on one very happily in a few years' time.

'You've burned off 1,700 calories,' Tim informed me, consulting some app on his phone. 'That's only 792 fewer than you would have done on a push bike.' I really needn't have bothered with the tennis that morning.

Inspired Italy offers a seven-night, six-day Electric Bike Safari through Tuscany and Umbria, following roads and routes once favoured by St Francis of Assisi and Hannibal. Full details at www.inspireditaly.com

The neglected face of English art

'Look at art with an open mind, an open eye and an open heart. Then you might enjoy it.' *Andrew Lambirth* on the pleasures of collecting pictures that deserve a bigger audience

It worries me when art critics don't surround themselves with art – it's like coming across a music critic who doesn't listen to music at home. As if work could possibly be separated from leisure when it comes to the arts. The half-hearted are the dangerous ones, those who fancy themselves as cultural commentators or historians of ideas and constantly quote Barthes and Bachelard, not to mention Guy Debord or Georges Bataille. Art-less art critics produce in me the same sense of deep unease as writers who speak of 'the paper-less office'. Where's their grip on reality? My writing room may be crowded out with books and files and pictures, but at least I can check my references in books people have taken a great deal of trouble to produce, rather than the hastily loaded data of a computer screen.

Art is of course much more than a matter of facts, it is about intelligent connecting, and the primary experience for the viewer of the visual arts is just that – viewing. Standing in front of the work of art and receiving the impulses and sensations that come off it. It's like looking at an old building or a beautiful landscape, except that a lot of people seem unable to do it without blinding themselves first with prejudice. The best way to look at art has always been with an open mind, an open eye and an open heart. If you can avoid preconceptions, you're in with a chance of actually experiencing some of the joy and beauty (or horror and disquiet) that the artist is attempting to convey.

As a collector, you have the choice of what to surround yourself with and what to learn from. As I have collected pictures over the years, always unfortunately with a limited budget, certain categories of interest have emerged. I love landscapes, yes, but paintings of trees in particular; then there's 1950s abstraction and self-portraits.

I was inspired to collect artists' self-portraits by the example of Ruth Borchard (1910–2000), who began her own collection of 100 of them in the late 1950s. She wrote to artists offering to buy a self-portrait for anything between seven and 21 guineas, and was remarkably successful in her efforts, eliciting work from the likes of Roger Hilton, Keith Vaughan and Cecil Collins. The Borchard Collection offers a kind of chronicle of the period through the varied styles of some of its artists, and is endlessly rewarding for its inclusions and juxtapositions.

The exhibition I have selected for Gainsborough's House focuses on some 60 portraits and self-portraits from my collection and spreads the net a bit wider. I have bought pictures by artists I never met, but long admired, like Augustus John and Walter Sickert, David Jones, John Nash and Wyndham Lewis. Then there are works by artists I've known and written about: Eileen Agar, whose autobiography I helped to write back in the 1980s; John Bratby, whose biography I started but abandoned when I realised I was not cut out to be a biographer.

A long-standing interest of mine has been to re-direct public attention to artists who, for one reason or another, have been unfairly neglected. Jacob Kramer (1892–1962) is one of these, a Leeds artist of originality and power, who was tangentially involved with the Vorticist movement (his brother-in-law was the artist William Roberts), but is better known as a distinctive realist painter of impressive range. He is represented in this show by a large self-portrait ink drawing and two pastel and chalk portrait drawings; all repay close attention. Then there's William Dring (1904–90), largely forgotten these days, though once a stalwart of the Royal Academy. I have several of his landscape and flower studies, and show here a remarkable oil from his student period of the young artist in the act of painting an old man with silvery locks. Youth and age incarnate.

Among contemporaries who have not received their due are Michael Carlo and Mike Harvey, both inventive artists doing new things within the tradition of realism. Even some of the older statesmen of British art such as Jeffery Camp, Anthony Eyton and Keith Grant, although well loved and respected among their peers, are not as widely known as they deserve to be. To balance the equation we have the justly celebrated Leon Kossoff and Maggi Hambling, Allen Jones and David Inshaw. And some mid-career artists, including Arturo Di Stefano, Robert Dukes, Sam Marshall, Martha Parsey, Mark Shields and Jo Welsh: all of them offering valid and beguiling interpretations of the human countenance.

I first went to Gainsborough's House, the country town house in Sudbury, in Suffolk, where the painter Thomas Gainsborough (1727–88) was born and which is now a museum to his art and life, back in the 1980s in the company of Jeffery Camp. It gives me great pleasure to return there now in Jeffery's company once again (he is represented by a self-portrait and a portrait of his wife, Laetitia Yhap), and with other artist friends, living and dead. I have learned more from artists and their works than from any book, however enlightening. And their companionship has made it easier both to endure this world and to enjoy it.

'Face to Face: Portraits from the Andrew Lambirth Collection' was at Gainsborough's House in October 2016.

Clockwise from above: portrait of Rodney Thomas by Eileen Agar, 1927; self-portrait by Jacob Kramer, c 1949; Thomas Hennell by Mike Harvey, charcoal on paper, 1995; Eileen Agar as a student by Leon Underwood, 1921

On the Wiggins way

James Pembroke is surrounded by Lycra-clad bottoms in Mallorca following Sir Bradley's tracks, but delights in the island's quieter side

My grandparents fell in love with Mallorca in the late Fifties, and were followed there by my young aunt. She promptly married Juan Bestard, who at 5ft 10in was the tallest man on the island. Their son, Carlos, returned there 12 years ago, and devoted all of his considerable charm to his estate agency with the reassuring strapline 'not all estate agents are Bestards'. Until the Sixties, the Mallorquins had stayed away from the coastal areas, leaving any beachside land to their daughters, who then cleaned up by building piles of holiday apartments around Palma. Mercifully, the rest of the island was saved due to its poor roads.

I last visited as a small child in the late Sixties, and had no positive preconceptions of the island, apart from vague ones of Robert Graves and Deia. We had been drawn there by Carlos and the promise of good walking, so I bought the brilliant *Mallorca Car Tours and Walks* by Valerie Crespi-Green, on AbeBooks. I was still wondering whether they had any Watney's Red Barrel left over from the Seventies when we boarded the plane, which started to fill up with men clutching cycle helmets and the Richmond Women's rugby team. They talked noisily of the Serra de Tramuntana, Bradley Wiggins's favourite training ground for the Tour de France, which runs along the length of the northern coast.

Our intention was to walk as much of the Dry Stone Route (GR221), which has been recently opened and stretches 65 miles across this enormous natural wall from Port d'Andratx to Pollenca. The Consell de Mallorca has sensibly divided it up into eight stages, ranging from three to eight hours, so it's entirely achievable in a week. And, although we walked for only three days, none of the climbs was anything like as arduous as fell-walking.

Rising to 4,686ft, this dramatically

IAN SHAW/ALAMY

**Opposite: Cyclists hit the heights on Mallorca, which has become a training ground for the Tour de France.
Left: A tram links the town of Soller to the seafront at Port de Soller**

hewn mountain range shields the flat plains behind. Bradley has certainly started something. Carlos told me that from mid-January to the middle of May, the island's roads are filled with the Lycra-clad. Who can blame them? Where else in Europe can one find such magnificent views and such perilous descents? And that wonderful feeling of knowing one has circumnavigated and conquered an island?

We had booked a hire car at Palma airport. Although we are only licensed to drive automatics, car hire companies refuse to believe this. So, inevitably, the nice man at Europcar continued this automotive discrimination, and tried to foist a manual car on us, when I had ordered the cheapest automatic, some sort of Nissan, which the manufacturers couldn't offload to the most bankrupt of banana republics. 'But I can only drive automatics. Are there none left?' I wailed to him and the now growing queue of macho cyclists and Magaluf blokes. 'No. All gone, sir.'

'Give 'im a bloody automatic,' bellowed the large Brit behind me, whose paw was permanently fixed in a beer can grip. It's amazing the effect an obese tattooed Brit can have on a diminutive man in a Terylene green uniform. 'Good news. A Mercedes C-Class has just been dropped off. Yours for the same rate, sir.'

There are men all over the world for whom such an astonishing upgrade to a two-door sports car would be the zenith of their motoring lives. I am not that man. I am car blind. I have never driven such an amazing car. Or, rather, I have

We realised this James Bond car was incompatible with a walking holiday

never been driven by such an amazing car. My contribution was a few turns of the wheel; the car even put my seat belt on for me, and did most of the parking with a special camera in the boot.

It wasn't until the next morning when we donned our shorts, walking sandals and sun hats that we realised just how incompatible this James Bond car was with a walking holiday. Pedestrians turned and glared at us, as we slid into Deia, which I had imagined to be a large village of narrow streets. Instead, it's a collection of yellowing terracotta houses spread wide over a steep hillside, overlooking the sea. It barely has a centre: just a bus stop, a shop and a few cafés, none of which is named after its most famous inhabitant. Robert Graves's house is now a wonderful museum to the man, but Deia has avoided the very British affliction of overplaying the connection.

After following groups of shiny-black-bottomed cyclists up the hill to Deia, it was a relief to have such peace on the three-hour walk to Soller. Only the birds matched the cyclists in quantity. The island boasts more than 200 species, including falcons, vultures and eagles, but also the tawny pipit, the hero of Bernard Miles's patriotic 1944 film of the

same name. Just before we arrived at the Soller Basin, a golden bowl of citrus orchards, we stopped at Son Mico, a large restored farmhouse whose hosts offered cakes and quiches and 20 varieties of tea. They also have four bedrooms from €100 a night. The views from their terrace alone make it the ideal base, but the GR221 also has plenty of *refugis*, some of which offer double rooms.

The town of Soller was a delightful surprise but properly busy on May Day. Most of the crowds eschewed the Modernist museum, packed with works by Miró, Cézanne, Klimt and Gauguin, in favour of the tram, which took an age to chortle two miles to the lively Port de Soller. The main square is dramatically shadowed by the 16th-century church of St Bartholomew which was restored by Joan Rubió, a disciple of Gaudí, in 1904; its candelabra façade can be seen from all over the valley.

However, our favourite place was the old station whose two waiting rooms have been given over to semi-permanent exhibitions of Picasso and Miró, whose grandfather was born in Soller. The Picasso room has more than 50 ceramics from 1948 to 1971.

We were based near Pollenca, the prettiest town we saw, with its cafés and main square, where it is only too easy to get distracted from scaling the nearby Cap de Formentor. Indeed, we found ourselves losing an afternoon at Ca'n Cuarassa, a beachside restaurant along the coast between Port de Pollenca and Alcudia, which has a perfect view of the villain's castle in *The Night Manager*.

We got to the airport in plenty of time. As we entered the car return area, my wife remarked how this was the first time that we hadn't scraped a hire car, so, to celebrate, we ran into a concrete bollard.

www.birdinginspain.com
www.gr221.info
Son Mico, Soller (tel: 00 34 618 232 674); inescollcapelle@hotmail.com

'Allowed to roam free? This chicken's had a better life than me!'

'Remember, lads, next week: staff appraisals'

'Can you say why she crossed the road?'

'Come on, Dad. You should make an effort to understand the new technology'

'They've developed a very sophisticated form of communication'

'I preferred his earlier work'

Too close for comfort

Michael Barber on the fall-out that can ensue when writers borrow real people for their novels

When the banker Sir Jeremy Morse died last year, his obituaries mentioned that Colin Dexter, in a tribute to Sir Jeremy's skill as a solver and setter of crosswords, had named Inspector Morse after him. More recently it was noted of the late Lord Prior that he inspired the character of Peter Morrison MP in *Alms for Oblivion*, the gamy *roman fleuve* by his old schoolmate Simon Raven. All Sir Jeremy and Inspector Morse had in common was their name, but how much of Jim Prior was there in Peter Morrison, of whom it was said that he could 'touch pitch yet remain undefiled'? Or, to invoke *Alms for Oblivion* again, of William Rees-Mogg in Somerset Lloyd-James, the devious editor whose machinations run like a thread through the whole sequence?

Raven, who knew just how far to go too far, admitted that to begin with he had drawn from life, but that quite soon his characters started to diverge and acquire a momentum of their own. Luckily for him, everyone he depicted was too busy 'getting on' to recognise themselves while they still resembled themselves, and by the time they became more self-important the resemblance had passed.

A character whose antecedents still invite speculation is Anthony Powell's Widmerpool, the 'château-bottled shit' with whom Iris Murdoch said she was falling in love. 'Now I know how Frankenstein felt,' Powell is supposed to have groaned after yet another fan buttonholed him about his monster. Powell's brother-in-law Lord Longford insisted that he was the model for Widmerpool. But he also said he was the model for another character in *The Music of Time*, prompting Powell to protest: 'Come off it, Frank. How many characters do you want to be – the whole bloody lot?'

While agreeing that he and his narrator, Nick Jenkins, had a great deal in common, Powell used to say, 'He's like me, but he isn't me.' He thought human beings needed to be licked into shape before appearing in a novel. But according to Kingsley Amis, even intelligent readers overestimated the degree of identification between the author and his hero, particularly a hero as disorderly as 'Lucky' Jim Dixon. Shortly after *Lucky Jim* appeared, Amis was introduced to the writer Marghanita Laski in the *Spectator*'s local pub. 'She looked at me in something not far from panic. What was I going to do? Leap on her? Pour my beer over her? Start swearing?'

Another deliberate connection that many readers may have missed involved Ernö Goldfinger, the modernist architect, and Auric Goldfinger, one of James Bond's nastiest antagonists. The choice of the villain's name by Ian Fleming was not a coincidence. In fact it was what the fictional Goldfinger would have called 'enemy action'. Fleming disliked the architect's buildings and loathed his Marxist beliefs. On learning that Erno intended to sue, Fleming threatened to insert an erratum slip, changing the name to Goldprick and giving the reason why. But his publisher took fright, paid Erno's costs and made clear in future editions that all the characters were fictitious.

Ian Fleming's wife, Anne, could be malicious, which may explain why, after reading *Officers and Gentlemen*, she mischievously identified the 'caddish' Ivor Claire as Bob Laycock, Evelyn Waugh's legendary CO in Crete, to whom the book is dedicated. Waugh gave notice on their 'beautiful friendship' should she ever mention this again: 'For Christ's sake lay off the idea of Bob = Claire ... Just shut up about Laycock, Fuck You, E. Waugh.' But perhaps Mrs Fleming had hit a nerve. In his diary, Waugh wrote that he had forbidden her to breathe a word of this 'cruel fact'.

KITCHEN GARDEN
SIMON COURTAULD
BROCCOLI

During his election campaign in the US in the 1980s, the former president George Bush Snr was questioned about his vegetable likes and dislikes. Broccoli, he said, was his least favourite and promptly had to apologise to the large number of American broccoli growers and those who import the vegetable from Mexico. Bush was referring to what is more correctly called calabrese, with a bunched green head and thick stalk.

I know that broccoli contains all sorts of vitamins and is meant to lower your cholesterol, but it is not my favourite vegetable. It is not growing broccoli that presents any particular problems, provided that your soil is not too acid, in which case add lime, and that no brassicas have been grown in the soil in the previous year. But I find it difficult to boil or steam the vegetable without either over-cooking the head or undercooking the stem.

Once the main head has been cut from the plant, it will produce thinner, tastier and more easily cooked side-shoots. Which leads me on to purple- and white-sprouting broccoli, hardier than calabrese and an altogether more satisfying vegetable.

I have had only limited success in growing sprouting broccoli because, like all brassicas, they are at risk from two persistent predators: pigeons and cabbage caterpillars. Netting is essential, but when, a couple of years ago, the net blew off in a gale, the birds got there before I did. Last season I decided to try growing the romanesco broccoli, that slightly odd-looking vegetable with little pointed pale green heads. Everything was going well until the end of August when I went away for a fortnight and returned to find the leaves stripped by caterpillars. Having got rid of the little creatures, the leaves did regrow but the plants had been weakened and it was too late for the hearts to form. So we have been enjoying the leaves steamed and added to winter soups.

Keep your hair on? If only...

Many bald men will tell you losing your hair is no big deal. Don't believe a word of it, says *William Cook*

'There are worse things than being bald,' said my wife, as I stared morosely at the stranger in the bathroom mirror. After several years trying (and failing) to thicken my thinning mane with a vast array of expensive potions, I'd finally admitted defeat and had been to the barbers for a number-one crop. 'It looks much better like that,' said my wife, in the sort of reassuring tone she usually reserved for telling our young son that one of his pet goldfish had gone to heaven. 'Much better than your old comb-over.' 'I don't have a comb-over!' I replied. 'Of course you don't, dear,' she said. 'At least, not anymore.'

That was 15 years ago, in my mid-thirties and, looking back, I realise she was quite right. There are worse things than being bald, it did look better cut short, and I did indeed have a (sort of) comb-over: not a full-blown Bobby Charlton or a Robert Robinson but a comb-over nonetheless. Since that fateful day, I've been out and proud about my shiny pate, and I find my baldness has come to define me. Many bald men will tell you losing your hair is no big deal. Don't believe them. There isn't one of us who wouldn't have his hair back tomorrow, given half a chance.

Naturally, compared with genuine ailments, male pattern baldness is an utterly trivial affair. Nevertheless, it was still a tremendous shock. Unlike a lot of baldies, I never thought I'd lose my hair. My father never went bald, and neither did either of my grandfathers. Having started out with a thick head of hair, I suddenly went completely bald, in the space of a few years. I'm embarrassed to admit it but, when my barber first revealed the ghastly truth, I actually fainted in the his chair.

Why was I so upset? As any bald man can confirm, it may be a harmless affliction, but few physical changes are quite so stark. Once I'd given up the ghost and shaved off what was left of my rapidly retreating thatch, my appearance changed so dramatically that some old acquaintances didn't recognise me. Ever since I went bald, in my mid-thirties, I've felt like a hairless ghost of my old self.

Being bald is a complete pain in the arse. Unless you wear a hat, your head gets terribly cold in winter and horribly sunburnt in summer. I'm still searching for a way to cover up without making myself look like a total prat. As William Hague learned to his cost, any bald man over 30 looks ridiculous in a baseball cap – and most other hats aren't much better. My experiments with flat caps, trilbys and fedoras have all been abject failures – making me look like one of those strange middle-aged men you see loitering in the

When my barber first revealed the ghastly truth, I actually fainted

background on the *Antiques Roadshow*. Since we now live in a hatless age, you're bound to look the odd one out.

Most women swear that baldness is attractive, but hard evidence doesn't bear this out. Would Beatlemania have ever happened if the four moptops had been the four slapheads? Would a bald Elvis have been so big? Elton John flew the flag for bald pop stars for a while but, having come out of the baldy closet, he acquired a miraculous new head of hair and promptly went back in again. It's the same story on the screen. Sean Connery is the sexy bald actor par excellence, but he wore a toupée throughout his time as James Bond and there's never been a bald Bond since. Most bald actors are character actors. Bruce Willis is an exception, but even he looks better with a rug.

You'd think politics, show business for ugly people, would give us baldies a better chance but the verdict at the ballot box is even worse. The last bald man to be elected president of the United States, Dwight D Eisenhower, had to win a world war to get elected. Every US president since Ike has been heroically hirsute. Donald Trump is living proof that we're instinctively biased against baldies. Do you really think he'd have won the election without that synthetic ferret on his head?

Here in Britain, we haven't elected a bald prime minister since Clement Atlee, a man who governed before the television age, when hats were still de rigueur. Iain Duncan Smith would have been unelectable even with a full head of hair, but Hague was a fine candidate – until that baseball cap debacle. Neil Kinnock (bald *and* ginger) never stood a chance.

So what are the upsides of being bald? It's a pretty short list, but there are a few minor compensations. Going bald forced me to get fit. I'd always been a bit chubby but, like Kenneth Clarke, my hair helped to conceal it. The prospect of being fat *and* bald was too hideous to contemplate (imagine Ken Clarke with a chrome dome). For the first time since I left school, I started exercising again, and I've never really stopped. In a broader sense, going bald made me get my act together. You'll never get a clearer signal that your youth is well and truly over, and that any headway you make from now on will be due to the stuff you do, rather than the way you look.

Although I'm eaten up with envy for any man over 40 with a bouffant barnet, I sometimes think a hairy head can hold a good man back. Look at Melvyn Bragg. His *South Bank Show* was brilliant to begin with, but it eventually became a running joke, thanks to cutaways of Melvyn preening his luscious locks. On the radio, where every broadcaster is a bald man (or a plain woman), his performances are masterful. On television, Melvyn is the thinking woman's crumpet – on the wireless, he's one of the great thinkers of our age. If only he'd gone bald when he was 35, like me, just think what he might have amounted to.

Back to the future

Lucy Lethbridge on publishing's new big idea: the retro look

In the world of publishing, ever alert to the New Thing, looking back is the way forward. Retro is where it's at. In your local bookshop, the area round the till is a riot of brand-new, old-fashioned covers. A reassuring familiarity prevails. Those little Ladybird volumes, for example, showing manly men with briefcases and womanly women washing up; or what about Mary Gernat's evocative cover illustrations for books by Enid Blyton, showing small boys in shorts having adventures unrestricted by health and safety regulations? And next to them there are the decoratively packaged Edwardian books of etiquette or corsetry; and then again there are the wartime rationing diet books, or yet another volume in the 'Keep Calm and Carry On' franchise – a veritable magic porridge pot of commercial possibilities.

A closer look shows that retro books can be roughly divided into three categories: spoofs, facsimiles and common-sense guides to practical problems – inspired by our ancestors' wholesome and crafty skills.

The spoofs are the newest contenders in the retro line-up. Not quite qualifying as nostalgic, they take images of the cosy certainties of a 20th-century childhood and use them to satirise the less-cosy certainties of now. Ladybird has been the leader in this field with the rip-roaring success of the 2015 series for grown-ups. Plundering Ladybird's enormous archive of images (going back a century: it was started in 1915) they covered pressing contemporary phenomena such as the hipster, the mid-life crisis, mindfulness and dating.

So successful was the first series – selling two million copies in a year – that a second quickly followed, tackling the sickie, the zombie apocalypse and red tape. Quite what Ladybird's original creators, the printers Wills & Hepworth, whose aim was 'pure and healthy' literature for children, would have made of it is difficult to imagine.

Now adult Ladybirds have in turn been hotly pursued into the bestseller lists by the Famous Five spoofs by Bruno Vincent.

The idea is the same: to send up middle-class modern England and middle-class 1950s England at the same time. 'Oh don't be so cis-gender,' says girly Ann to head prefect Julian. Vincent, writing in the *Daily Telegraph*, said that he absolutely was not sending up Enid Blyton. Perish the thought! 'These books aren't mocking Blyton's prose style or her values – they're making fun of modern life and the trials of adulthood.' *Five Go to Brexit Island* still languishes near the top of the Amazon bestsellers, as does *Five Go on a Strategy Away Day*. Soon to come is *Five Help Gran Go Viral*.

The retro facsimile goes back further than the spoof. That 1970s bestseller *The Diary of an Edwardian Lady* is a key text in the genre. If a found-in-the-attic volume of watercolours, cartoons, recipes, beauty tips or a *vade mecum* for the generally perplexed hits bestseller gold, then tea-towels, notelets and fridge magnets will follow.

Books like this take very little work and sit comfortably in the loo library. Just find your text and reproduce it beautifully in hardback with perhaps a ribbon marker – it becomes a perfect present for an awkward relative. Illustrations are a must – old advertisements, watercolours or perhaps funny contemporary cartoons. British Library Publications is particularly prolific. Among the books it has reprinted is a Regency cookbook, Thomas Gowing's *The Philosophy of Beards* (for the hipster

in your life) and *Lady Cycling: What to Wear and How to Ride*.

Other books simply reproduce images without comment – especially using the 1970s – now, style-wise, both far away and familiar: orange plastic kitchen gadgets, chicken bricks, family games of Ker-Plunk – we can't have enough of them. Source material is boundless: knitting-pattern catalogues, advertisements, magazines, provincial postcards and family snaps are only the half of it. James Innes-Smith's popular *Bad Hair* book with its pictures of terrible mullets, quiffs and sideburns was in the tradition of the photographer Martin Parr's collection of *Boring Postcards*, published very seriously by Phaidon.

In the third category are the commonsense guides etc. These have been around since the *Edwardian Lady* hit the shelves. Richard Mabey's *Food For Free* has been in print since 1972, and I can't be alone in experiencing a dismal summer of foraging for wild horseradish and elderberries so that my mother could experiment with disgusting ancient rural recipes. The shelves now groan with tomes inspired by wartime propaganda on rationing and make do and mend, or guides to cleaning with vinegar and bicarb. Anything with Mrs Beeton in the title goes down well – ditto 'grandma', 'vintage', 'gentleman' or 'lore'. Chris Martin's *A Gentleman's Guide to Beard and Moustache Management* has been an Amazon bestseller since its publication in 2011 (hipsters again).

There is often an overlap with greenery – as grandma's tips so often involve yummy natural ingredients such as cucumbers and yoghurt. In 2012, Nicola Burnett founded an imprint called Pretty Nostalgic that catered exactly for this trend through a membership society, the Nostalgianeers. Said Burnett: 'It celebrates simple, sustainable living and unites creative individuals who share a passion for the past.' Three years later, Pretty Nostalgic were partnered with the History Press.

They were on to a winner.

How I love to hate

There is nothing more blissful than falling out with one's friends, writes expert feuder *Damian Thompson*

The words are scorched into my memory. 'If she knew how much I hated her, she wouldn't leave the house.' The speaker was a pink-cheeked, elderly lady on the top deck of the bus, talking to a friend. Her tone of voice – chatty and companionable – implied a gentler message: 'Dorothy does bake a lovely, moist sponge,' that sort of thing. My heart warmed to her immediately. I recognised a fellow feuder.

The conversation drifted on to other matters; so I never discovered why this woman hated the third party, but I had no doubt that she hated her very much indeed. On the other hand, I suspect she'd be disappointed if her enemy really cowered indoors on account of the hatred. Because, if she did that, then the pink-cheeked antagonist would have been deprived of the opportunity to snub her. Natural-born feuders – and, as I say, I'm one – are theatrical creatures. When it comes to put-downs, we are endlessly inventive. But this is performance art, and feuds cry out for a stage and an audience. Deprive us of the appropriate setting, and we sulk.

A friend of mine tells the story of encountering me at a party given by a Catholic organisation at the supremely comfortable Brown's Hotel in Albemarle Street, in the heart of smart London. 'Why are you looking so gloomy?' my friend asked. 'It's a lovely party.' 'It's terrible,' I apparently said, 'There's only one person here I hate.'

When my friend told me this story, I had to run through my telephone directory of historic feuds to remember who that person was. I think I've worked it out; I didn't exactly hate him, I just objected to his presence. He's a saturnine figure in the Catholic sect Opus Dei. He materialises at smart Catholic parties, falling into conversation with bright young men who would be prime catches for Opus. So, if possible, I disrupt things on the spot, by warning his targets of the dangers of signing up to the outfit. Failing that, I give my foe the evil eye as he slithers round the room.

That's a very low-level feud by my standards. But it amuses me if people notice. Feuding is a spectator sport, and we participants have an endless repertoire of tricks.

Cutting someone dead, for example. It sounds crude – but, executed skilfully, it can be a thrilling pas de deux, a real treat for nosey parkers.

Polly Toynbee is a prima ballerina of the public snub. I know this because my friend and *Oldie* contributor Mary Kenny once gloriously re-enacted being cut dead by the grande dame of the *Guardian*. Pressed up against Mary at a soirée, Polly had to resort to limb-threatening contortions in order to avoid meeting her gaze.

I don't know whether the two women had once been friends, in Mary's long-distant, Lefty past. But it's likely.

In my experience, if two people are ostentatiously not on speaking terms, it's a safe bet that they were once the best of pals. I speak from experience. All my most flavoursome feuds have been with ex-friends. I would love to name them, but I mustn't. It wouldn't be fair because, more often than not, I was the guilty party.

More importantly, I'm too much of a coward. Most of my friends, and therefore my ex-friends, are journalists. They have platforms on which to give their own version of events. And it works both ways. It's called mutually assured destruction. Much safer to stick to death stares across the vols-au-vent.

Never have I seen such a display of theatrical snubs and turned backs

So you'll understand why I don't name the miserable, treacherous enemy, a friend for 25 years, whom I had to avoid at a bash before Christmas. Nor can I give the reasons for our falling-out. But it's a pretty intense feud. I didn't shoot him a death stare: I didn't trust myself to go near him. But, as I watched him boasting pathetically to the grandest people in the room, I visualised myself as *American Psycho*'s Patrick Bateman. I could feel my heart thumping as I walked away from the party. But then I asked myself if I'd enjoyed myself any less because the treacherous enemy had been there. And the answer was that, on the contrary, I felt refreshed by my white-hot rage.

A feud isn't fun, exactly, but it does make life more interesting. For the feuder, anyway. But it's also a dangerous habit. Nurturing grudges is as addictive as self-pity – and as unattractive. Lots of people enjoy watching a 'scene', some melodramatic 'unpleasantness' they can chew over on the drive home. But feuders can easily turn into bores. As I say, we're talking about addiction: for some of us, rehearsing grievances is so delicious that we keep banging on, despite the chorus of 'Is that the time?' from fellow guests.

What makes it addictive? The broken friendships are a clue. It's a less extreme version of rejected love: there's the same urge to scratch a wound until it bleeds. A married friend of mine has a theory that homosexual men are instinctive feuders. 'My gay mates won't let go of a grievance,' he says. I didn't take offence, because I remember being at parties in the 1990s given by a rich, gay businessman. Everyone seemed to have a bitter enemy lurking across the room. The guests were almost exclusively older men, 'not of the marrying kind' (though, these days, they may well have Latin American husbands young enough to be their grandsons). Never have I seen such a display of theatrical snubs, 'old-fashioned looks' and suddenly-turned backs. Everywhere I looked, nattily-dressed gentlemen were weaving and ducking to avoid former friends who were now dead to them. The choreography was worthy of Balanchine.

Alas, I haven't been to one of those parties for years. Perhaps they are dying out naturally. Then again, now I come to think of it, my former host and I aren't currently on speakers.

Wilfred De'Ath
My week on church floors

Seven Cambridge churches and one synagogue have joined forces to offer floor space to men who would otherwise be sleeping rough during the winter. The scheme is staffed by nearly 400 volunteers. They provide a sleeping bag, a blanket and a pillow and give you a good meal before lights out at 9pm.

Returning from France without accommodation, I had no alternative but to apply. My first port of call was Christ Church, a conservative, evangelical church on the Newmarket Road. They took pity on me in view of my age (80 in July) and arranged for bed and breakfast four miles away, somewhere out by the Cambridge airport. It felt lonely out there; so I decided I would put up with the hard church floor from now on.

Next evening, we were at Little St Mary's, a very 'high' Anglican church in the town centre. The floor was extremely hard, as one might expect, and it was freezing cold in there; so they gave us an extra blanket. Presiding over everything was a saintly girl named Lucy McKitterick, whose idea the CCHP (Cambridge Church Homelessness Project) was. (I once asked Lucy to marry me, but she wisely turned me down.)

Next night, we were with the Methodists on Castle Hill. They are ultra-efficient. After laying out the sleeping bags at 7pm, they stand by the 'beds' like soldiers on parade. The food is good, too.

Thursdays alternate between Great St Mary's, the main church of Cambridge,

and Beth Shalom, a modern synagogue on the Newmarket Road (I have never been to a synagogue before). One girl seemed to take a fancy to me and asked if she could see me again. She wasn't pretty but, given my age, I was flattered to be asked.

Friday we were at OLEM (Our Lady and the English Martyrs), the great Roman Catholic 'cathedral' on the Hills Road – this is my own church. The volunteers were exceptionally nice, even kinder than usual, and the food really excellent. One elderly volunteer said to me, 'This is the Roman Catholic Church at its best.' He was quite right, since the church is a strange mixture of trial and error but that is the bit they do well.

Saturday: St Philip's, miles down the Mill Road. You are really 'knackered' by the time you arrive there, particularly if you are carrying heavy bags like me; so you sleep like a log on the floor. Good food, too.

Sunday: St Paul's, back in the centre of town. There were three girls named Clare among the many volunteers and I was rather smitten by one of them.

Monday – back to Christ Church. This time I slept on the floor along with my 15 or so fellow guests, including a number of Poles, who never stop talking. The scheme is an excellent one and I only wish they did it all year round. One gets into a rhythm after a while and I have to say I began to enjoy it. Monks have a saying that their way of life is 'a hard bed to lie on but a soft bed to die on'. I hope I shall die soon – and happily.

Palach's Prague remembered

BLOG BY KENNETH CRANHAM 2019

Fifty years ago, on 19 January 1969, Jan Palach, a student of history and political economy at Charles University in Prague, had burnt himself to death in protest after the end of the Prague Spring, resulting from the 1968 invasion.

A few months later, I toured Europe with the English Stage Company with two Edward Bond plays. I was cast as Len, the main character in *Saved*. A play set in Japan, *Narrow Road to the Deep North*, was the second production. I played Kiro, the young monk at the centre of the narrative.

Prague, one stop on our tour, was both exhilarating and fearful; it was occupied by Soviet troops.

Our play about British imperialism and the Japanese became a play about Prague and the Soviet occupation. One of the cast, Nigel Hawthorne, had a line that went unnoticed in London: 'Politicians are so stupid.' It got a huge reaction.

In the Japanese play, my character escapes a palace revolution with Shoqo, the head of the city, who is captured by soldiers and killed. My character's response is to take his own life. He kneels facing the audience. I had a knife with a retractable wooden blade. I also had a sort of money belt with a pouch that contained a Strepsils tin with around ten reels of scarlet ribbons in it. After I'd sunk the blade into my left side, I pulled the scarlet ribbons out, catching the light; then I pitched and turned onto my back, my upper torso hanging over the edge of the stage. Hara-kiri meets *Blue Peter*.

At the time, I was unaware of Palach's recent death. And my stage suicide caused the entire audience to audibly weep. The sobbing and wailing reached the stage from the far corners of the building.

STEVE WAY

Travel

"....book a holiday with us today"

info@andersenboats.com / (+44)(0)1606 833668

www.andersenboats.com

CERTIFICATE of EXCELLENCE 2015 Winner
VisitEngland tripadvisor

MARITIME BREAK IN HAMPSHIRE

Experience Maritime history on this two night stay

Portsmouth Historic Dockyard home of Nelson's HMS Victory, HMS Warrior the first Iron clad warship, Tudor Flagship the Mary Rose, National Museum of the Royal Navy, Harbour Tours, Royal Navy Submarine Museum plus many more.

Your Dockyard Pass can be used on more than one day until all the attractions have been seen. The number 700 Stagecoach bus stops directly outside the hotel to take you to the Historic Dockyard gates, so no need to take the car and worry about parking

YOUR TWO NIGHT BREAK INCLUDES:

❖ Ensuite accommodation ❖ Two course dinner ❖ Full English Breakfast ❖ Tickets for Portsmouth Historic Dockyard
Entry to the Mary Rose is not included in the Dockyard pass, but can be purchased at the exhibition.
Overnight parking at the Hotel is subject to availability at £5.00 per car per night

£329.00 based on two sharing

The Brookfield Hotel, Havant Road, Emsworth, Hampshire PO10 7LF
T: (01243) 373363   www.brookfieldhotel.co.uk   bookings@brookfieldhotel.co.uk

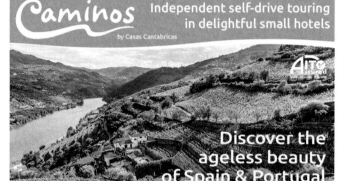

Caminos
by Casas Cantabricas

Independent self-drive touring in delightful small hotels

AITO assured

Discover the ageless beauty of Spain & Portugal

Casas Cantabricas   01223 328721 • www.caminos.co.uk

Education

"OH JAMES! IT'S SUCH A SHAME."

YES, IT'S A CRYING SHAME...

...that she left it too late to apply for Hurtwood House, because it's simply the best for acting, dancing, singing, film-making – "A utopia for creative minds" – as the Good Schools Guide says.

And crucially, this exciting school is equally successful academically. In fact, it's statistically one of the top co-ed boarding schools in the UK.

So, if you're looking for a really exciting and rewarding change of school at 16 – don't leave it too late.

Contact Cosmo Jackson or visit our website for more information.

HURTWOOD HOUSE

T: 01483 279000 E: info@hurtwood.net
hurtwoodhouse.com

The PeNN CLUB

The Penn Club is a Members Club with a strong Quaker ethos, open to non-members for B&B. We are located just off Russell Square, close to the British Museum, the British Library, several buildings of the University of London and other attractions and places of interest.

"Home from Home"

PENNCLUB.CO.UK
020 7636 4718
office@pennclub.co.uk

NARROWBOAT HOLIDAYS WALES

Cruise the Monmouth and Brecon Canal, through the Brecon Beacons National Park.

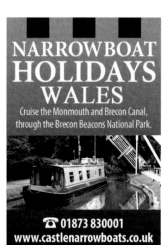

☎ 01873 830001
www.castlenarrowboats.co.uk

Entertainment

ROYAL ALBERT HALL EXCLUSIVE BOX HIRE

8 seat box available.
Superb position.
Tickets sold by owner.

Please call
01494 683907

Video

precious moments...

cinefilm, slides & video to dvd

CARROLLmedia

01903 725217

www.carrollmedia.co.uk

Genealogy

YOUR ANCESTORS FOUND

Retired school inspector, Cambridge history graduate, genealogist for 40 years, researches and writes your family's history. No task too big or small.

Phone 01730 812232 for brochure, sample report and free estimate.

Books & Publishing

Health

Making reading a pleasure again.

Amazing new technology Lamps that give you the clarity you only get when reading in direct sunlight

If you struggle to see print then this what you need.
New technology Ultra High Definition reading lamps brought to you by by the Craftlight Company Ltd and designed in the UK.
Raising the contrast to make black appear blacker and the background whiter as well as more vibrant colour with better seperation. Giving the user a more quality experience when reading.

With prices starting at £59.95 for floor lamps, they make a good investment for your reading pleasure.

Most of the floor lamps can be made down into table lamps, they give off very little heat and consume only 6watt of electricity.
They are all metal construction.

The Reader Floorlamp 1.5 mtr on offer at £69.95 inc p+p

The Craftlight Company
www.craftlights.co.uk

Better By Design.

To order.

Go to **www.craftlights.co.uk** and look under heading newspaper and magazine offers to get the discounted prices. Or call 01502 587598 for help and advice.

DRY MOUTH?

STOP dry mouth disturbing your sleep with XyliMelts® long-lasting adhering discs.

- Stimulates saliva production
- Moisturises and coats for hours
- Reduces plaque and tooth decay
- Freshens breath
- All natural

www.xylimelts.co.uk   0800 612 8806

HAPPY TUMMY
Natural Charcoal
capsules for

Acidity

Gas   **IBH**

Indigestion

Most tummy problems

0800 612 7496
www.finefettlefeed.com

What's in a bar of soap?

Each bar: 125gr.

onevillage.com

Most soap is made from a cocktail of chemicals in a cheap fat heavily scented with synthetic fragrances.

Ours is not at all like that. The substance of our soap is expensive active vegetable oils – such as neem oil from neem seeds, known for centuries for its amazing healing properties for skin and wellbeing.

No *sodium lauryl sulfate*, no *triclosan*, no *antibacterial chemicals*, no *ammonium*, no *artificial scents*, no *animal fats*. Our **sandalwood** is authentic powder and oil from the tree – a natural energizer and antiseptic.

Neem or sandalwood soap. *True wholesome soap like no other.*

Here's your opportunity to try it. For only £16 you can order 4 bars, including free UK p&p. Order at Onevillage.com

One Village
Charlbury
OX7 3SQ
✆ 01608 811811

Books & Publishing

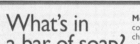

Your Book Is Written To Be Read

Books published - novels to academic History, Biography, Autobiography

Submission to:
Janus Publishing Company Limited

The Studio, High Green,
Great Shelford, Cambridge, CB22 5EG
Email: publisher@januspublishing.co.uk
www.januspublishing.co.uk 020 7486 6633

Arelle

CONTINENCE CARE

Arelle provides high quality products for men and women

For more information and your discreet mail order brochure call Arelle FREE on 0800 389 3597 or visit: www.arelle.com

- BED PROTECTION • PADS
- BRIEFS • ACCESSORIES

FREEPOST SWB11095, Bridgwater, Somerset, TA5 1ZA

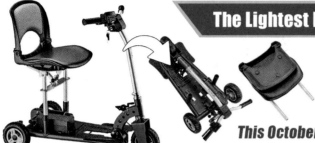